Policies to Reduce Microplastics Pollution in Water

FOCUS ON TEXTILES AND TYRES

OECD
BETTER POLICIES FOR BETTER LIVES

Please cite this publication as:
OECD (2021), *Policies to Reduce Microplastics Pollution in Water: Focus on Textiles and Tyres*, OECD Publishing, Paris, *https://doi.org/10.1787/7ec7e5ef-en*.

ISBN 978-92-64-96102-9 (print)
ISBN 978-92-64-55939-4 (pdf)

Photo credits: Cover © design by Chantal Rivière/grafiklab.fr based on images © smirart, LeManna/Shutterstock.com.

Corrigenda to publications may be found on line at: *www.oecd.org/about/publishing/corrigenda.htm*.

Preface

The widespread presence of microplastics in the environment, including in remote and pristine areas such as mountains and the Arctic, is a source of concern for ecosystems and human health. Due to their small size, microplastics can be easily ingested or inhaled by organisms, potentially leading to adverse health impacts on wildlife and humans. The potential for long-term and irreversible risks to ecosystems and human health calls for mitigation measures to halt the accumulation of plastics and microplastics in the environment.

Plastics pollution captures the attention of scientists, the public, governments and businesses around the world. Although plastic materials bring several benefits to society, growing plastics production, use and disposal are creating ever-greater environmental pressures, among which the accumulation of plastics in natural habitats is arguably the most evident. At current trends in plastics production and waste generation, the problem of plastic pollution will continue to exacerbate. Once plastics enter the environment, they do not easily biodegrade and may continue to pollute natural habitats for centuries. Furthermore, plastics in the environment may fragment into microplastics, smaller plastic particles that may enter the food chain.

OECD countries substantially contribute to microplastics leakage into the environment and have an important role to play in mitigating this type of pollution. Indeed, many governments are now actively working to reduce risks associated with plastics and microplastics pollution, for instance via the regulation of single-use plastics, bans on microbeads intentionally added to products, and improvements in solid waste collection and management.

Microplastics emitted unintentionally during the use phase of products remain largely outside of the scope of policy frameworks existing in OECD countries. This report ambitions to bridge that gap, by focusing on the complex challenges posed by microplastics released from tyres and garments. The report brings together the most recent science and knowledge on the pervasiveness of such particles, their route into the environment, and the potential consequences on environmental and human health. It identifies best practices and technologies that could help mitigate the environmental pressures, and potential policy interventions to mandate or encourage their larger uptake. In line with previous work on contaminants of emerging concern in water, the report highlights opportunities for future policy intervention that builds on new knowledge and new technical capacities and that cuts across sectors and policy areas.

Policies to reduce microplastics pollution in water: Focus on textiles and tyres has been developed jointly by the Environmental Policy Committee's Working Party on Biodiversity, Water and Ecosystems and the Working Party on Resource Productivity and Waste. This timely report brings together expertise on waste, resource efficiency and water quality to support government efforts to reduce risks associated with microplastics pollution, and protect the environment and human health.

Rodolfo Lacy,
OECD Environment Director

Acknowledgements

This report is a joint output of the OECD Environmental Policy Committee's Working Party on Resource Productivity and Waste (WPRPW) and the Working Party on Biodiversity, Water and Ecosystems (WPBWE). The report was developed under the overall responsibility of Shardul Agrawala, Head of the Environment and Economy Integration Division, and Simon Buckle, Head of the Environment, Transitions and Resilience Division.

Elena Buzzi was the lead author, with guidance from Peter Börkey and Xavier Leflaive of the OECD Environment Directorate and Elisabetta Cornago (Centre for European Reform, previously OECD Environment Directorate). Hannah Leckie (New Zealand Ministry of Foreign Affairs and Trade, previously OECD Environment Directorate) also played a pivotal role in the conceptualisation and development of this report and the related expert meetings. Francesca De Falco (University of Plymouth, previously Italian National Research Council), Josiane Nikiema (International Water Management Institute) and Stephan Wagner (Hof University of Applied Sciences, previously Helmholtz-Centre for Environmental Research - UFZ) co-authored Chapter 3 and provided valuable feedback on selected parts of the report. The work also benefited from substantive contributions from Marit Hjort (UN Development Programme, previously OECD Environment Directorate) on the relevance of Best Available Techniques for microplastics pollution mitigation.

The OECD Secretariat acknowledges the contributions of the delegates of the Working Party on Resource Productivity and Waste (WPRPW) and the Working Party on Biodiversity, Water and Ecosystems (WPBWE). The report benefited from the insightful discussions of the OECD Workshop on "Microplastics from Synthetic Textiles in the Environment: Knowledge, Mitigation and Policy" held on 11 February 2020 in Paris and of the OECD Workshop on "Microplastics from Tyre Wear: Knowledge, Mitigation Measures, and Policy Options" held virtually on 18-20 May 2020. The Secretariat would like to thank all participants for their valuable contribution.

The authors are thankful to the several experts and colleagues who provided valuable comments and suggestions throughout a number of iterations, in particular: Aimée Aguilar Jaber, Andrew Brown, Katherine Farrow, Frithjof Laubinger (OECD Environment Directorate), Julia Del Valle and Dorothy Lovell (OECD Centre for Responsible Business Conduct), Greet De Gueldre and Oliver Loebel (EurEau), Alejandro Navazas (European Recycling Industries' Confederation), Bettina Heller (UN Environment Programme), Farhan Khan (University of Oslo), and Francis Peters (Business at the OECD) and colleagues from the World Business Council of Sustainable Development. The authors would also like to thank Roland Geyer (UC Santa Barbara) for providing data on plastic production.

Seamless administrative support was provided by Ines Reale, Aziza Perriere, and Jack McNeil. Chantal Rivière (Grafiklab) created the graphic design of communication material for the report.

The Secretariat is grateful to the Government of Sweden and the World Business Council for Sustainable Development for their generous financial support in developing this report.

Table of contents

FIGURES

TABLES

Abbreviations and acronyms

B2B	Business-to-business
B2C	Business-to-consumer
BAF	Biological aerated filter
BAT	Best available techniques
BOD	Biochemical oxygen demand
CIS	Commonwealth of Independent States
CSO	Combined sewer overflow
CSS	Combined Sewer System
CWs	Constructed wetlands
DW	Dry weight
EPDM	ethylene propylene diene monomer (rubber)
EPR	Extended producer responsibility
ETRMA	European Tyre and Rubber Manufacturers Association
EU	European Union
FWs	Floating treatment wetlands
Gt	Giga tonnes
MBR	Membrane bioreactor
MP	Microplastics
Mt	Million tonnes
PAH	polycyclic aromatic hydrocarbons
PCB	polychlorinated biphenyl
PCCPs	Personal care and cosmetic products
PM	Particulate matter
POP	Persistent organic pollutants
SSS	Separate Sewer System
TPE	Thermoplastic elastomers
TRWP	Tyre and Road Wear Particles

UK	United Kingdom
US	United States of America
WHO	World Health Organisation
WW	Wet weight
WWT	Wastewater treatment
WWTP	Wastewater treatment plant
ZDHC	Zero discharge of hazardous chemicals

Executive summary

Microplastics pollution is one of the most pervasive emerging environmental issues. Tiny plastic fragments, particles and fibres now widely contaminate oceans, freshwaters, soils and air. Once in the environment, microplastics may continue to fragment into smaller particles and persist for a long time. Aquatic species, from plankton to large mammals, as well as humans are commonly exposed to microplastics via ingestion or inhalation.

A myriad of emission sources contribute to microplastics pollution. Examples are accidental industrial spillages, the discharge of microplastics intentionally added to products (e.g. rinse-off cosmetics and detergents) and the wear and tear of synthetic products (e.g. synthetic textiles, vehicle tyres) occurring during their use. Up to 3 Mt of microplastics enter the environment every year. Additionally, the degradation of plastic waste discarded into the environment further contributes to microplastics pollution.

Microplastics pollution is a reason of concern for water quality, potentially affecting ecosystems and human health. Laboratory experiments have shown that microplastics ingestion can induce adverse health effects in aquatic biota, although large uncertainties persist with regards to the thresholds at which risks may occur. Concerns are mainly driven by the presence in plastics of toxic chemicals and known or suspected endocrine disrupting additives, as well as by the potential for microplastics to sorb persisting organic pollutants from the environment. Although data gaps hinder reliable risk assessments, the persistence of plastics and the projected fast and continued increases in pollution levels call for policy measures to mitigate current and future risks to ecosystems and human health.

In recent years, microplastics pollution prevention has gained increasing policy attention in OECD countries. Attaining resource productivity, managing plastics in a sustainable way, preventing leakage to the environment and preserving water quality are key elements of environmental policy objectives in OECD countries, as also reflected in Sustainable Development Goal targets 6, 12 and 14.1. The OECD Council Recommendation on Water calls for Adherents to prevent, reduce and manage water pollution from all sources, while paying attention to pollutants of emerging concern, such as microplastics.

Recent policy action – notably restrictions on single-use plastics and microbeads in rinse-off cosmetics, and improved waste management practices – may contribute to reducing some plastic uses and mitigating leakage to the environment. However, the emission of microplastics from the wear and tear of products is a complex issue that remains largely untargeted by current policy frameworks, despite accounting for a substantial share of releases. Furthermore, while the leakage of plastic waste mainly occurs in emerging economies, OECD countries contribute substantially to the emission of microplastics. North America, Western Europe and Japan alone account for almost a third of direct microplastics releases, of which the abrasion of tyres and synthetic clothing account for 62%. In this context, several OECD countries are increasingly looking for solutions to better control these emissions.

This report develops policy insights on how to minimise microplastics emitted unintentionally from products and their potential impacts on human health and ecosystems. It assesses the feasibility and relevance of available mitigation measures for microplastics pollution of marine and freshwater environments, with a focus on textile products and vehicle tyres, which contribute to between one-half and two-thirds of microplastics releases into the environment (excluding the degradation of leaked plastics).

Microplastics emissions occur and are influenced by several stages of the lifecycle of textiles and tyres. As such, a broad range of entry points exist for the implementation of mitigation measures, including via:

- *Source-directed approaches*, such as the sustainable design and manufacturing of textiles, tyres, and complementary products (i.e. washing machines, laundry detergents, road surfaces and vehicles), to minimise the tendency of products to contribute to microplastics generation;
- *Use-oriented approaches*, such as the uptake of best use practices (e.g. laundering parameters, eco-driving) and mitigation technologies (e.g. microfibre filters), to reduce preventable releases;
- *End-of-life approaches*, such as improved waste management practices, to prevent waste leaking into the environment and potentially contributing to microplastics generation;
- *End-of-pipe approaches*, such as improved wastewater, stormwater, and road runoff management and treatment, to retain the emitted microplastics before these reach water bodies.

Policy insights: a lifecycle, holistic approach to close knowledge gaps and exploit synergies across different policy areas

Given the degree of persisting uncertainty and the potential for widespread ecosystem and human health impacts of microplastics, effective mitigation action is recommended. Mitigation action should be proportional, consistent with existing policy frameworks, based on adequate cost-benefit analysis considerations, and sufficiently flexible to encourage scientific research and innovation in mitigation solutions. Where microplastics pollution mitigation brings additional costs, attention will need to be paid to their fair allocation and to ensuring that responsibility for the implementation of mitigation measures is shared among stakeholders along the textile/apparel and tyre value chains.

The most cost-effective way to tackle the issue is likely the implementation of a mix of policy tools targeting several mitigation entry points along the lifecycle of products. Measures aimed at minimising the emission of microplastics at source are likely to have the largest mitigation potential. Especially for diffuse sources of pollution (e.g. tyre wear particles, airborne textile microfibres), prevention is often more cost-effective than treatment/restoration options downstream. At the same time, given the variety of entry pathways, measures upstream cannot entirely alleviate the risk of microplastics pollution of the water cycle. Thus, upstream intervention will need to be supplemented by effective end-of-pipe solutions.

The control and management of microplastics released from products is likely to require a strategic prioritisation among possible interventions as well as a consideration of their full impacts. Research has identified several mitigation practices and technologies implementable at different stages of the lifecycle of textiles and tyres, yet often further research and data is required to assess their cost-effectiveness, implementation feasibility, and potential for unintended consequences or trade-offs with other policy objectives. Policy options targeted to consumers (e.g. reduction in textile consumption, changes in driver behaviour) would benefit from further investigation of the likelihood of behaviour change occurring.

Although microplastics pollution alone is unlikely to drive costly investment decisions or to justify trade-offs with other relevant policy objectives, there are important gains to be made by exploiting or adapting existing measures in other policy areas. For instance, reductions in passenger vehicle use and shifts towards more sustainable transport modes, generally driven by a need to reduce GHG emissions and air pollution, can also contribute to mitigating microplastics emissions from road transport. Similarly, certain end-of-pipe mitigation options, such as improved wastewater treatment technologies or nature-based solutions, primarily designed to manage other risks (e.g. other pollutants, flooding), can generate significant co-benefits for microplastic mitigation.

Taking into consideration the points above, the following guidance emerges for policy action to manage textile- and tyre-based microplastics pollution:

- *Further research* is required in order to reduce data gaps as regards the toxicity of microplastics to wildlife and humans, perform more robust risk assessments for microplastics in different environmental media, and inform cost-benefit analyses for mitigation interventions. *International and interdisciplinary cooperation and information sharing* will be key to the advancement of research and to the *standardisation and harmonisation of test methods* (providing for variability of locations and research sites), such as test methods for the rate of microfibre shedding and tyre tread abrasion. Further, the development of common databases can reduce time and costs associated with documenting robust policy decisions at national and international levels.
- In the short term, significant progress in microfibre and tyre and road wear particle emission mitigation can be achieved by focusing on *"no-regrets" mitigation options*. These include good practices and technologies which have low implementation costs and low risk for potential unintended consequences (such as environmental burden shifting) and/or which generate *co-benefits* aligned with other environmental policy objectives, such as those addressing the environmental impacts of the textile and apparel sector and of road transport, climate change mitigation, air quality legislation, and improvements in water quality.
- When information on the effectiveness of mitigation measures has improved, *additional and more specific policy measures* will be needed to mandate, incentivise or encourage the uptake of mitigation technologies and best practices. Some of these policy measures, such as requirements to add microfibre filters to washing machines and consumer-awareness initiatives, are already being explored by governments.

1 The case for microplastics mitigation

This chapter sets out the motivation for the development of this report. It summarises current knowledge on the sources and flows of microplastics into the environment and on the adverse impacts on the health of humans and other living organisms. The chapter concludes by making the case for policy action on microplastics pollution and for further consideration of mitigation measures for two sources of microplastics: textile products and vehicle tyres.

1.1. Introduction

1.1.1. Growth in plastics use and environmental consequences

Since the invention of plastic materials, their production, use and disposal has continued to increase. Due to their numerous desirable properties (e.g. durability, resistance, lightness), versatility and low costs of production, plastics have gradually penetrated almost all sectors and substituted traditional materials such as concrete, glass and wood in countless industrial applications. From 0.5 Mt in 1950, global annual plastics production soared to 465 Mt in 2019, as presented in Figure 1.1. Trends indicate that demand for plastic materials will continue to increase in future years, mainly driven by increasing shares of plastics consumption in emerging economies (IEA, 2018[1]).

Figure 1.1. Global primary plastics production by sector, 1950 to 2019 (million tonnes)

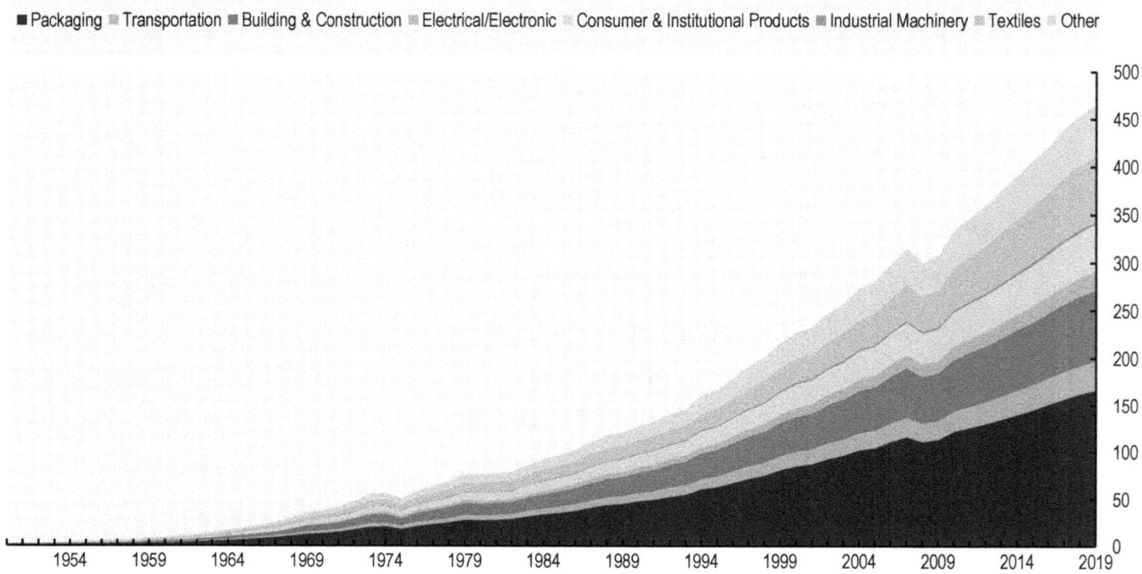

Source: Update by the authors of (Geyer, Jambeck and Law, 2017[2])

The large production and use of plastic materials comes with several negative consequences for the environment and climate. Plastics production is a fossil fuel-intensive activity, consuming 4-8% of global oil production (by mass) (World Economic Forum, 2016[3]). Approximately 400 Mt of CO_2 were released in the year 2012 during the production, transport and disposal of plastics (EU, 2018[4]). The large use of plastics, especially in products with short life spans (e.g. single-use plastics), also puts significant pressure on waste management systems (Geyer, Jambeck and Law, 2017[2]). In 2010, failure to channel waste to the adequate disposal systems resulted in the discharge into the oceans of 4.8-12.7 Mt of the 275 Mt of plastics waste generated on land (Jambeck et al., 2015[5]). Approximately 14 Mt of microplastics have accumulated on the ocean floor only (Barrett et al., 2020[6]).

Plastic materials are generally very resistant to degradation: they can last for prolonged periods of time if released into the environment, leading to several adverse consequences to our environment and economy (Geyer, Jambeck and Law, 2017[2]). Detrimental consequences on freshwater and marine ecosystems include ingestion by marine species and impediment of food acquisition, entanglement of wildlife in lost or discarded fishing nets and damage to coral reefs (Derraik, 2002[7]; Macfadyen, Huntington and Cappell, 2009[8]). Adverse economic consequences of plastics pollution may in particular affect coastal communities relying on tourism (e.g. due to the detrimental effects of marine and coastal litter on tourism, which also increase beach maintenance costs) and those affected by plastic pollution of internal water streams (e.g. as a consequence of the blockage of road drains).

1.1.2. Microplastics: framing the challenge

While the environmental consequences of plastic items dispersed in the environment have long been scrutinised by the scientific and media communities, concerns are now rising over microplastics (MP), plastic particles smaller than 5 mm (see Box 1.1).

Box 1.1. What are microplastics?

Microplastics are generally defined as solid synthetic polymer particulates with a size < 5 mm (Arthur, Baker and Bamford, 2009[9]; ECHA, 2019[10]; GESAMP, 2015[11]). Because the definition of microplastics has not yet been standardised, existing studies have been employing different definitions and cut-off sizes. The upper size limit is generally set at 5 mm (although a cut-off at 1 mm is also employed by some studies), while there is some discrepancy with regards to the lower cut-off sizes employed, which range between 1 and 100 nm (ECHA, 2019[10]; GESAMP, 2015[11]; California State Water Resources Control Board, 2020[12]). Usually, plastics with a size below this lower bound are referred to as nanoplastics (SAPEA, 2019[13]). In general, the lack of consensus over the definition of microplastics has been an issue as it renders results of microplastics surveys and toxicological studies difficult to compare and aggregate in order to draw general conclusions, respectively on occurrence and risks. Work is underway to standardise definitions for microplastics in the environment (see CEN prEN 17615 Plastics – Environmental Aspects - Vocabulary).

Microplastics can be considered an array of contaminants of diverse sizes, shapes, colours and physico-chemical composition (Rochman et al., 2019[14]). They are usually found in the environment as fragments, fibres, pellets, or beads. Plastic polymers commonly employed in the manufacture of plastic products (e.g. polypropylene, polyethylene, polyethylene terephthalate) account for a large share of microplastics, although particles from other synthetic polymers such as rubber (e.g. in vehicle tyres) are also considered microplastics (SAPEA, 2019[13]). Microplastics are also always found in the environment as a complex mixture or diverse suite of chemicals, either those which have added during manufacturing or which have been adsorbed from the environment (see Section 1.5).

Note: despite the commonly employed upper size limit for microplastics, microfibres with a diameter larger than 5 mm can also be considered microplastics. For instance, the ECHA restriction on the intentional use of microplastics sets limits as follows: i) for particles, all dimensions between 1 nm and 5 mm, and (ii) for fibres, a length between 3 nm and 15 mm and length to diameter ratio of >3 (ECHA, 2019[10]).

Microplastics are stock pollutants, i.e. pollutants with a long lifetime and for which the ecosystem has little or no absorptive capacity. Biodegradation is the process of complete destruction of the polymer chain and its conversion into small molecules such as carbon dioxide, water, or methane by the action of microorganisms (UNEP, 2015[15]). Full biodegradation of microplastics requires a set of conditions (e.g. the presence of microorganisms capable of breaking down plastic polymers, appropriate temperature, adequate pH and salinity in case of the aquatic media) which are not typically present in the natural environment (UNEP, 2015[15]; Wagner and Lambert, 2018[16]). Current evidence of microplastics biodegradation in the natural environment is limited and the majority of microplastics is believed to persist and accumulate in the environment, only slowly degrading into smaller microplastics and potentially nanoplastics.

1.1.3. Objectives of this report

The continuous use and disposal of plastic materials around the globe has led to the pollution of all types of marine and freshwater environments with microplastics (Andrady, 2011[17]; Thompson et al., 2004[18]). Given projected trends of plastics production, use and disposal, concentrations of microplastics are likely to continue to increase, raising concerns over the potential environmental and human health hazards posed.

This report assesses mitigation options for microplastics pollution of marine and freshwater environments, with a focus on microplastics originating from textile products and vehicle tyres. It presents mitigation solutions implementable throughout the lifecycle of products, from manufacturing processes to the use phase and the end-of-life stages of textiles and tyres. Besides OECD countries, this report also assesses the perspective of major textile and tyre manufacturing countries, in particular China and India.

The remainder of Chapter 1 provides a justification for the development of this report. Chapter 2 traces a typology for microplastics released from textile products and vehicle tyres and outlines entry points for mitigation action. Chapter 3 provides an assessment of the available mitigation best practices and technologies implementable at different stages of the lifecycle of products. Chapter 4 argues that policy action to tackle unintentional releases of microplastics is emerging but remains limited and discusses selected policy instruments which could be employed to mandate, incentivise, or encourage the uptake of mitigation best practices and technologies. Chapter 5 presents key messages to guide mitigation policy action on microplastics released from textiles and tyres.

1.2. Types, sources and pathways of microplastics

1.2.1. Types and sources of microplastics

Microplastics are typically categorised into primary and secondary. *Primary microplastics* are manufactured at the micro scale to be used in particular applications, while *secondary microplastics* stem from the fragmentation of larger plastics (GESAMP, 2016[19]; UNEP, 2018[20]).

Table 1.1 summarises the main types of microplastics and the relative sources and modes of emissions. Pre-production plastics are primary microplastics which may be unintentionally released into the environment, mainly due to accidental spills or run-off from processing facilities. Plastic pellets, the intermediary good between the polymers and plastic products, are known to regularly leak into the environment during production, transport and storage (GESAMP, 2015[11]). During use, numerous products may release microplastics intentionally-added during manufacturing. Microbeads used in personal care and cosmetic products (PCCPs) such as scrubs and toothpastes are examples of primary microplastics intentionally discharged into sewage waters or into the surrounding environment during the consumption stage.

Secondary microplastics can be further categorised into two groups. *Use-based* secondary microplastics are generated unintentionally due to abrasion occurring during the use of products containing synthetic polymers. Common examples are microfibres released from synthetic textiles during washing, tyre and road wear particles emitted during road transport activity, and paint flakes worn off from the surface of buildings, roads and ships. *Degradation-based* secondary microplastics are those originating from the fragmentation of larger plastic items discarded in the environment after their useful life, mainly as a consequence of exposure to solar UV radiation (GESAMP, 2015[11]).

Table 1.1. Main types and sources of microplastics

Type of microplastics	Examples of common sources	Mode of emission
	Primary microplastics	
Pre-production plastics	Accidental spills occurring during the transport and storage of plastic pellets Emissions and run-off of pre-production plastics and production scrap from processing facilities	Unintentional, occurring at the production and recycling stages
Microbeads and other MPs intentionally added to products	Rinse-off personal care and cosmetic products (PCCPs) with exfoliating properties (e.g. toothpaste, scrubs, soaps) Other rinse-off and leave-on PCCPs (e.g. make-up, hair and skin care products) Detergents and maintenance products containing microbeads (e.g. laundry detergents and fabric softeners, cleaning products) Industrial uses of microplastics (e.g. in offshore oil and gas exploration activities)	Intentional discharges occurring during the use of products.
	Use-based secondary microplastics	
Synthetic microfibres	Use, washing and drying of textile products (e.g. clothing, carpets, cloths)	Unintentional emissions occurring during the use phase, due to abrasion and wear of products containing synthetic materials.
Tyre wear particles	Use of vehicle tyres during road transport activity	
Paint flakes	Wear and loss of paint applied to ships, buildings and road surfaces	
Other land-based MPs	Losses of rubber granulate from artificial sports turfs Losses of Polymer Modified Bitumen (PMB) in asphalt pavement Wear and tear of utensils containing synthetic polymers (e.g. cooking utensils) Wear and tear of brake pads	
Marine-based secondary MPs	Routine wear and tear of fishing gears Wear and tear of aquaculture equipment	
	Degradation-based secondary microplastics	
Land-based mismanaged macro plastic waste	Littering, disposal of macro plastic waste in unregulated dumpsites; Loss of material during extreme weather events and natural disasters;	Fragmentation of macro plastics leaked into the environment due to waste mismanagement
Marine-based mismanaged plastic waste	Fishing gear and other plastic material lost or discarded from ships, recreational boats, fishing vessels, aquaculture facilities, or agricultural fields	

Note: There can be numerous overlaps across categories. For instance, some microplastics here categorised as "use-based secondary microplastics" could also be considered primary sources of microplastics. One example is rubber granulate, which is manufactured in the MP size and intentionally added as infill material to artificial sport turfs.
Source: (ECHA, 2019[10]; GESAMP, 2015[11]; Fraunhofer Umsicht, 2018[21])

1.2.2. Entry-pathways into the natural environment

Microplastics enter the natural environment via a number of pathways: i) direct discharge, ii) wastewater networks, iii) dry and wet deposition and surface run-off and iv) fragmentation of plastic waste that has leaked into the environment. These are summarised in Table 1.2 and further discussed in the following sections.

Transport via the municipal wastewater network (point-source microplastics)

Urban wastewater networks collect used water resources originating from households and/or industries. They receive microplastics originating from several sources, such as synthetic microfibers emitted during laundering (and manufacturing) and plastic microbeads contained in rinse-off consumer products. Additionally, the wastewater network may also collect diffuse-source microplastics contained in urban runoff, i.e. the flow of excess water occurring in urbanised areas containing a variety of pollutants washed off during precipitation events.[1]

Table 1.2. Selected microplastics sources classified by entry pathway into the environment

	Direct discharge	Transport via the wastewater network (point-source)	Transport via dry and wet deposition and surface run-off (diffuse)	Degradation and fragmentation of leaked plastic waste
Emission sources	• Plastic pellets spilled during transport and storage • Wear off of paint applied to ships	• Discharge of microbeads intentionally added to PCCPs, detergents, etc. • Industrial emissions of microplastics • Textile microfibres emitted during washing • Diffuse microplastics collected by the sewage system	• Textile microfibres emitted during wearing and drying • Tyre and road wear particles emitted during road transport activity • Wear off of paint flakes from buildings and road surfaces • Rubber granulate leaked from artificial sport turf • Unregulated incineration of solid waste	• Mismanagement of land-based macro plastic waste • Mismanagement of sea-based macro plastic waste
Environmental fate	Direct discharge into aquatic or terrestrial environments	Discharge into industrial or household sewage. • Capture by existing wastewater treatment infrastructure • Release via wastewater effluent or directly (e.g. during CSOs) • Land application of sewage sludge (terrestrial pollution).	Deposition on surfaces or suspension in air. • Direct dispersal in the environment • Transport into the environment via stormwater runoff • Collection by urban sewage systems	Rate of MP generation and environmental fate vary depending on type of plastics and environmental location

Note: The leakage of pre-production plastic pellets is a well-known issue which is being targeted by voluntary initiatives (PlasticsEurope, 2017[22]). Globally, 75 plastics organisations and allied organisations have signed voluntary signed the Declaration of the Global Plastics Associations for Solutions on Marine Litter, which includes commitments to steward the transport and distribution of plastic resin pellets from supplier to customer to prevent product loss (Marine Litter Solutions, 2011[23]).
Source: Author

Currently, urban wastewaters constitute a significant pathway for microplastics to enter aquatic environments. Over 80% of global used water resources are released into the environment without treatment, meaning that large amounts of microplastics and other pollutants are discharged directly into aquatic environments (WWAP, 2017[24]). The lack of wastewater treatment is an issue in several upper-middle and low-middle income countries (especially in Sub-Saharan Africa and in the Asia-Pacific region), where respectively only 38% and 28% of wastewaters are treated (Sato et al., 2013[25]; WWAP, 2017[24]). Overall, several non-OECD still lack the wastewater infrastructure required to guarantee adequate water supply and sanitation and to preserve water quality (OECD, 2015[26]).

In OECD countries, more than 80% of the population is connected to wastewater treatment facilities and the presence of at least secondary level treatment is prominent (OECD, 2015[26]). The treatment technologies already in place can significantly reduce microplastics concentrations of the wastewater influent (e.g. microplastics retention rates of up to 99% for wastewater treatment plants located in Finland) (Lares et al., 2018[27]; Talvitie et al., 2017[28]). However, the vast volumes of wastewaters treated imply that, in absolute terms, substantial amounts of microplastics are continuously being discharged from WWTPs into receiving water bodies.

The discharge of untreated wastewater from the waste water infrastructure can have a significant impact on the release of microplastics and on the overall water quality of surface waters. Discharge may occur due to technical faults at wastewater treatment plants (WWTPs) or sewer overflows occurring when the hydraulic capacity of the wastewater system is exceeded (Baresel and Olshammar, 2019[29]). Wastewater systems can either convey sewage only to the wastewater treatment plant (Separate Sewer Systems, SSSs) or sewage combined with storm water through a single pipe (Combined Sewer Systems, CSSs). Where CSSs are employed, periods of heavy rainfall may overload the sewer management system with storm water runoff, causing untreated domestic and industrial waste to be discharged directly into receiving waters in order to prevent flooding in the system. As discussed in Box 1.2, combined sewer overflows events are expected to become more frequent in future years due to climate change and continued urbanisation, unless infrastructure is adapted.

Furthermore, a share of microplastics retained by WWTPs can enter the environment via applications of wastewater sludge. Wastewater sludge is the waste by-product of wastewater treatment containing water pollutants removed from the influent. Sludge reuse for agricultural applications (via "landspreading", i.e. the application to agricultural soil or in fertiliser production) is encouraged in several countries, mainly due to the high nutrient content and its beneficial effects on crops, as well as to reduce the need for landfilling or incineration (WWAP, 2017[24]). Although common national and regional regulations require that sludge undergoes stabilising treatment prior to its disposal or safe reuse, these do not include restrictions on microplastic concentrations, which usually vary between 1 000 and 170 900 particles per kg of dry sludge (Iyare, Ouki and Bond, 2020[30]). Evidence indicates that large amounts of microplastics are likely being directly discharged onto terrestrial environments via sludge use in agriculture. An estimated 63 000–430 000 and 44 000–300 000 tonnes of microplastics are applied every year onto farmlands in Europe and North America respectively (Nizzetto, Futter and Langaas, 2016[31]). Sludge disposal practices vary widely by country, as presented for selected OECD countries in Figure 1.2.

Figure 1.2. Method of sewage sludge disposal in selected OECD countries (in 2017 or nearest year)

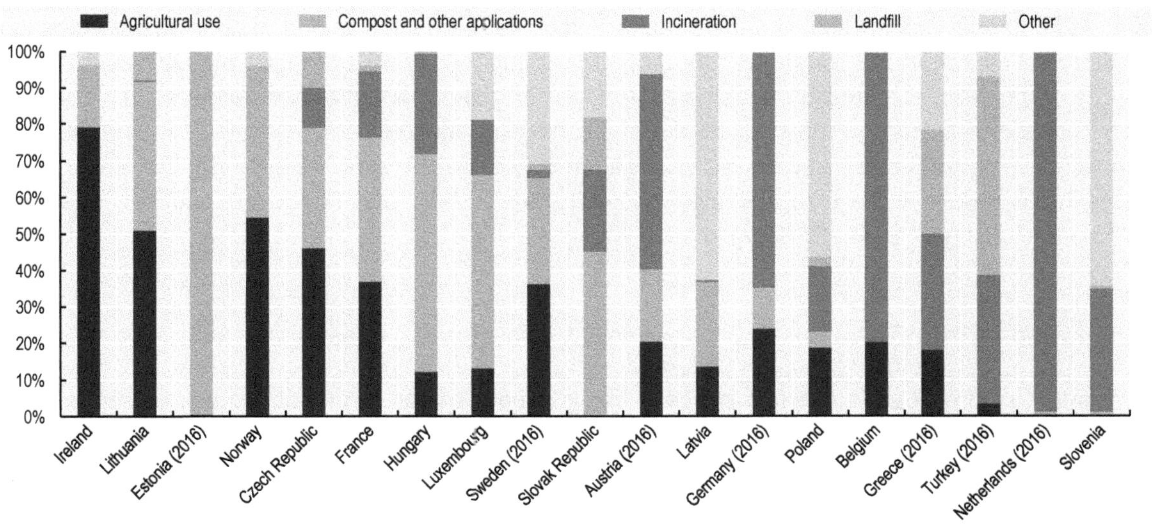

Note: data refers to 2017, or nearest year
Source: Eurostat Dataset, Sewage sludge production and disposal.

Transport via dry and wet deposition, stormwater and road runoff (diffuse entry)

The most significant entry pathway for diffuse-source microplastics is likely to be the action of rain events washing off particles and fibres suspended in air or deposited on outdoor surfaces (Dris et al., 2016[32]). Road runoff, i.e. the portion of precipitation which flows from road surfaces, is a known transport pathway for a variety of pollutants originating from diffuse sources (e.g. heavy metals, hydrocarbons, urban pesticides, litter), as well as for microplastics suspended in air or deposited on roads. Significant quantities of diffuse pollutants are washed off especially during the first minutes of intense rainfall.

Depending on the local context, road runoff can either be channelled into the wastewater network or be discharged directly into nearby surface waters or soil. In urban areas, runoff collected by drainage systems may be conveyed with sewage via CSSs to wastewater treatment plants to be treated. However, the majority of microplastics washed off by rain events likely end up directly in the environment (NIVA, 2018[33]). Especially in non-urban areas, road and stormwater runoff is commonly discharged directly into surrounding water streams, contributing to the deterioration of water quality. As outlined in Box 1.2, continued urbanisation and climate change are projected to magnify the incidence of diffuse pollution on the quality of surface waters, mainly as a consequence of the higher frequency of extreme precipitation patterns, increasing road traffic and sealing of surfaces, and the higher propensity for flooding and combined sewer overflows (OECD, 2017[34]).

Box 1.2. Impacts of climate change on water quality and microplastics pollution

Climate change puts increasing pressure on existing water quality challenges. Altered precipitation and flow regimes may result in higher volumes of runoff containing diffuse pollutants to water bodies, mainly due to a combination of increased pollutant loadings during heavy rainfall and an increased build-up of pollutants on catchment surface areas during long dry weather periods (OECD, 2017[34]). Furthermore, unless mitigation measures are taken, continued urbanisation and climate change are projected to worsen existing drainage problems and pose significant risks to the performance of sewer systems, potentially exacerbating the frequency and intensity of CSOs.

As climate change intensifies and extreme weather events become more frequent, this may also create higher pressures on aquatic plastic pollution. As indicated by recent studies, extreme weather events (such as heavy rainfall, flooding, droughts) discharge significant quantities of plastics and microplastics from land and river catchments into the oceans or river estuaries, either due to an effective flushing out of microplastics from rivers, or the transport of larger quantities of mismanaged plastic waste from land sources. For instance, a study conducted in Northern England found that flood events flush out 70% of the microplastics stored on the beds of rivers discharging into the Irish Sea (Hurley, Woodward and Rothwell, 2018[35]). Similar studies conducted in South Korea and India found that microplastics concentrations were three times greater following heavy rains and floods, respectively (Lee et al., 2013[36]; Veerasingam et al., 2016[37]).

Generation of secondary microplastics from macro plastic waste

The fragmentation of leaked macro plastics is likely to be a major contributor to microplastics pollution. Fragmentation into microplastics results from the degradation of ageing plastics, i.e. a change in the mechanical and chemical properties of materials (e.g. strength, colour, shape) causing the breakdown of plastic polymers.[2] This typically occurs via photo degradation under exposure to UV radiation, via thermo-oxidative degradation under the effect of oxygen exposure and moderate temperatures, via physical degradation caused by abrasive forces, or via a combination of these processes (GESAMP, 2015[11]; UNEP, 2015[15]; Fraunhofer Umsicht, 2018[21]).

The rate of generation of degradation-based microplastics is poorly understood and difficult to predict due to the complexity of factors which influence it, as well as the time variability in degradation patterns. In general, the rate of degradation is mainly influenced by:

- *Plastics composition and age*. Prodegradants are additives aimed at accelerating degradation processes and their utilisation (e.g. in oxo-degradable plastics) enhances the generation of microplastics (EC, 2018[38]). Conversely, the presence of additives aimed at preventing ageing and oxidation, such as UV stabilisers and anti-oxidants, generally slows down the degradation of plastics. While certain polymer structures may generate microplastics at a faster rate, this has not been extensively studied yet. In general, plastic polymers of items designed to last may be more resistant to weathering and degradation.

- *Environmental fate of plastics waste*. Since the degradation and fragmentation of plastic s is mainly driven by the exposure to certain environmental factors, the rate of generation of microplastics is highly dependent on the environmental fate of plastics. Table 1.3 presents estimated rates of degradation and fragmentation of plastics in different environmental media. In general, plastic degradation is assumed to occur slowly in aquatic environments. Temperatures are generally too low to prompt thermo-oxidative degradation processes and UV light may only reach plastics floating on the surface of water bodies. Also, the development of biofilms on the surface of floating plastics may shield away UV light or cause the plastics to sink, impeding degradation (Gregory and Andrady, 2003[39]; Fraunhofer Umsicht, 2018[21]). Fragmentation into microplastics may occur relatively quickly on beaches, due to exposure to moderate temperatures, UV light and oxygen, as well as the abrasive action of sand and sea waves on plastic debris (Cooper and Corcoran, 2010[40]; UNEP, 2016[41]).

Table 1.3. Degradation and fragmentation of plastics in aquatic environments

Environmental media	Presence of environmental conditions affecting the degradation and fragmentation of plastics	Degradation process	Rate of degradation and fragmentation
Beaches and coastal areas	UV radiation Oxygen available High/moderate temperatures	Photo degradation Thermal oxidation Mechanical abrasion	Fast/Moderate
Water surface	UV radiation Oxygen available Low temperatures	Photo degradation	Slow
Lower vertical compartments of oceans and sediments	UV radiation not available Low oxygen levels Very low temperatures	Negligible / Mineralisation	Very slow

Source: Adapted from (UNEP, 2016[41]; GESAMP, 2015[11]).

Modelling the environmental fate of marine plastic litter and its exposure to environmental conditions enhancing degradation remains a challenge due to the complex set of factors which may influence the horizontal and vertical transport of plastics in water, such as marine currents, the density of plastics compared to that of seawater and the creation of biofilms. Recent studies indicate that over 90% of mismanaged plastics entering the oceans end up in sediments and in the lower levels of the oceanic water column, where they may take a long time to degrade (Eunomia, 2016[42]; GESAMP, 2015[11]). The generation of microplastics may be relatively high on beaches and coastal areas, which receive approximately 5% of all plastic litter (mainly packaging and other single use-plastics) entering the oceans every year from land-based sources (Eunomia, 2016[42]).

The decomposition of landfilled plastic waste may also be contributing to microplastic pollution of the water cycle, through leachate from both active and closed landfills (He et al., 2019[43]; Praagh, Hartman and Brandmyr, 2019[44]). Landfill leachate is the liquid that has seeped through solid waste in a landfill and has been contaminated with pollutants originating from decomposing waste. It contains contaminants which are toxic for the environment and so it generally undergoes specialised treatment before being discharged. However, microplastics generated in sanitary landfills could leak into soil and groundwater where there are defects in landfill liners (He et al., 2019[43]). Further, it may also be the case that microplastics persist in leachate for a long time after the post-closure monitoring period (usually 30 years)[3] and that these are released directly into water streams. Overall, the occurrence of microplastics in leachate remains largely unknown and more research is required to estimate the contribution of landfilled waste to microplastics pollution of soils and water streams (Magnusson et al., 2016[45]).

1.3. Current trends in microplastics pollution

As illustrated in Figure 1.3, OECD and non-OECD countries tend to face different waste management and plastic pollution challenges. Even though the mismanagement of plastic waste is mainly an issue outside of the OECD area, microplastics leakage is an emerging reason of concern in most OECD countries. North America, Western Europe and Japan alone account for almost one third of global microplastics emissions and for 45% of total microplastics losses from tyre abrasion. This section discusses major trends in macro and micro plastics pollution in OECD countries and beyond.

Figure 1.3. Geographic distribution of losses of macro- and micro-plastics (million tonnes per year)

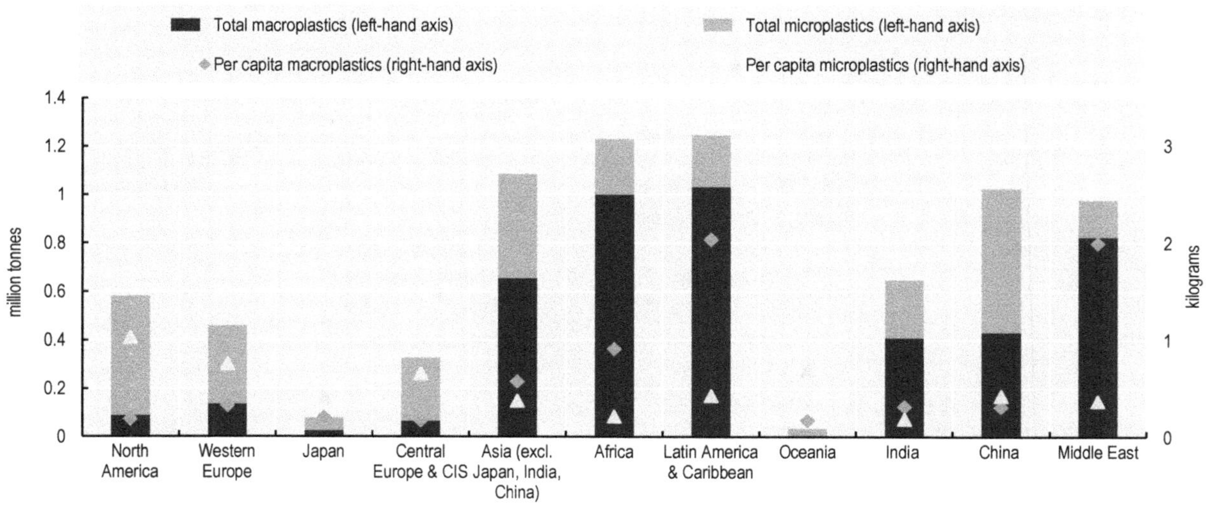

Note: CIS stands for Commonwealth of Independent States
Source: Elaboration of data from (UNEP, 2018[20]). World Bank (2017[46]) population data.

1.3.1. Flows of mismanaged macro plastic waste

Human activities on land contribute to approximately 80% of the pollution of aquatic environments with plastic debris (Li, Tse and Fok, 2016[47]). Plastic waste generated on land enters the environment mainly where collective waste management systems are lacking or unable to manage waste effectively. An estimated 2 billion people do not have access to solid waste collection and tend to resort to independent disposal practices such as open dumping, open burning and direct disposal in the environment (World Bank, 2018[48]). Dumped plastics as well as waste disposed of in uncontrolled landfills may easily disperse in the environment, for instance by the action of wind or currents in waterways (UNEP, 2016[49]).

Approximately 76 Mt of plastic waste are mismanaged every year in river catchment areas and may potentially enter rivers (Schmidt, Krauth and Wagner, 2017[50]). While rivers and river beds are important sinks of debris themselves, plastics with a lower density and higher propensity to float (e.g. bottle caps, plastic bags, plastic bottles filled with air) may be transported into marine waters by river currents and contribute to marine plastic pollution. Lebreton et al. (2017[51]) estimate that between 1.15 and 2.41 Mt of plastic waste enters the oceans every year from rivers. The top 20 polluting rivers, which account for 67% of plastic flows from the global riverine system into the oceans, are mostly located in the Asian continent (Lebreton et al., 2017[51]).

Proximity to the coast may result in large quantities of mismanaged plastic litter reaching the oceans. Assuming inputs into the sea are proportional to the amount of plastic waste that is mismanaged within 50 km of the coast, Jambeck et al. (2015[5]) estimated the amount of marine plastic debris generated in coastal countries at 4.8-12.7 Mt per year. Although the data employed does not allow for precise estimates, the study predicted that the majority of land-based emissions of plastic litter into the oceans occur in emerging economies in East and South Asia, mainly due to a combination of high intensity of human activities near the coast, high plastic waste generation and poor waste management. Especially in South Asian countries, waste collection rates are low and open dumping is common (World Bank, 2018[48]).

Oceans are also heavily polluted with plastic debris discharged directly from marine-based sources, such as commercial and fishing ships, recreational boats and offshore industrial sites. The incidence of marine-based leaked plastic litter may be particularly high in the open ocean. A recent study of plastics in the Great Pacific Garbage Patch found that marine-based sources contributed to at least 50% of all recovered plastics mass (Lebreton et al., 2018[52]). In particular, lost or discarded fishing gear has been identified as a significant source of marine pollution, including degradation-based microplastics (Macfadyen, Huntington and Cappell, 2009[8]).[4] The main factors causing the loss or abandonment of fishing gear are gear conflicts and overfishing (mainly caused by illegal, unregulated and unreported fishing), adverse weather conditions and the costs of gear retrieval (Macfadyen, Huntington and Cappell, 2009[8]; Richardson et al., 2018[53]).

1.3.2. Flows of microplastics and regional distribution

The main studies modelling the releases of primary and use-based secondary microplastics on a global (or macro-regional) level have been conducted by Eunomia (2016[42]; 2018[54]), the International Union for the Conservation of Nature (2017[55]) and UNEP (2018[20]). Table 1.4. presents a summary of available estimates of annual microplastics releases into the environment by source. Up to 3.01 Mt of primary and use-based secondary microplastics enter the environment annually (UNEP, 2018[20]). The wear of synthetic textiles and vehicle tyres alone accounts for between one-half and two-thirds of all microplastics releases (Eunomia, 2016[42]; IUCN, 2017[55]; UNEP, 2018[20]).

Table 1.4. Relative contribution to microplastics pollution by source

	(Eunomia, 2016[42])	(Eunomia, 2018[54])	(IUCN, 2017[55])	(UNEP, 2018[20])
Geographical scope	Global	EU	Global	Global
Environmental sinks considered	Marine environment	Aquatic environment	Marine environment	All
Synthetic textiles	20%	7%	35%	9%
Automotive tyre debris	28%	54%	28%	47%
Plastic pellets	24%	23%	0%	1%
City dust	-	-	24%	22%
Infill in artificial sport turfs	-	1%	-	-
Paint				
Buildings	14%	3%	-	-
Marine	2%	0.2%	4%	2%
Road	8%	8%	7%	20%
Personal care and cosmetic products	4%	-	2%	0%
Fishing gear	-	1%		
TOTAL (Mt)	0.95	0.2	0.8-2.5	3.01

Note: In the IUCN and UNEP reports, "city dust" includes losses from the abrasion of objects and infrastructure, the blasting of abrasives and intentional pouring (e.g. abrasion of synthetic footwear, utensils and building coatings, household and city dust, rubber granulate from artificial sports turfs).
Source: (Eunomia, 2016[42]; Eunomia, 2018[54]; IUCN, 2017[55]; UNEP, 2018[20])

There are significant differences in model estimates both in terms of total releases and in terms of the relative contribution of sources. Available models are largely based on national-level estimates of microplastics releases for a number of countries located in Northern and Western Europe, which may not be representative of emissions in other regions (Essel et al., 2015[56]; Lassen et al., 2016[57]; Magnusson et al., 2016[45]; MEPEX, 2014[58]). Further, differences in the methodologies employed, the environmental sinks considered and in the assumptions taken on the transport and fate of microplastics may also partially explain the divergences.[5] Overall, better and more representative geographical coverage of the source data as well as more industry-derived data (e.g. on fibre shedding from textiles, tyre abrasion, industrial emissions) are needed in order to improve the quality of estimates of the flows of microplastics from source to sink.

While all macro regions contribute to the release of microplastics, there are significant regional differences. Figure 1.4 presents microplastics losses to the environment by source and by macro region. In Western Europe, North America and Japan the primary sources of microplastics releases are the abrasion of tyres and road markings. For synthetic microfibres, the majority (72%) of losses occur in four macro regions: China, India, the rest of Asia and North America. Broadly, while in emerging economies microplastics releases tend to be high primarily due to the low rates of connectedness to wastewater treatment plants and large population sizes, in OECD countries diffuse sources of microplastics constitute the majority of emissions. With regards to synthetic microfibres, there are concerns that other stages of the use phase (wearing) as well as the production phase might also significantly contribute to microplastics pollution. While models so far have only considered the washing of textiles due to a lack of data and monitoring, the high volumes of microfibre emitted during washing in countries where the majority of global fibre and textile production takes place (e.g. China, India) suggests that microfibre releases into waterways from production could also be substantial. Further research is required in order to evaluate the contribution of industrial emissions to microplastics pollution.

Figure 1.4. Sources of microplastics releases to the environment by macro region (million tonnes per year)

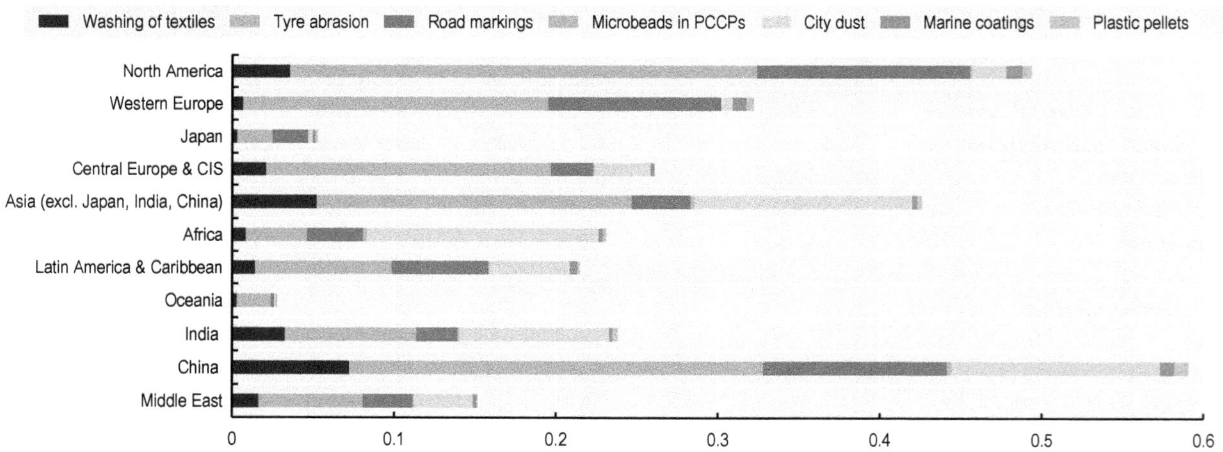

Note: PCCPs = Personal Care and Cosmetic Products. CIS stands for Commonwealth of Independent States.
Source: Elaboration of data from (UNEP, 2018[20])

1.4. Environmental sinks

1.4.1. Marine environments

The presence of microplastics has been documented in every habitat of the major ocean basins, including semi-enclosed seas, coastal environments and beaches and polar ice (Browne et al., 2011[59]; Desforges et al., 2014[60]; Eriksen et al., 2013[61]; Lusher et al., 2015[62]; Obbard et al., 2014[63]; Wessel et al., 2016[64]).

Microplastics are also present at all ocean depths, from the sea surface to the ocean floor (Barrett et al., 2020[6]; Browne et al., 2011[59]; Choy et al., 2019[65]).

Available surveys of marine microplastics are fairly recent and limited in number, but can provide a good knowledge base of the trends of accumulation of microplastics in marine waters. Coastal environments are particularly vulnerable to microplastics pollution, likely due to proximity to the point of emission (e.g. river and sewage effluents, coastal human activity) (Browne et al., 2011[59]; Cole et al., 2011[66]). A map of indicative microplastics abundance on the surface of coastal marine waters, based on data from Lebreton et al. (2012[67]), is presented in Figure 1.5. Concentrations of floating microplastic are especially high in semi-enclosed seas (e.g. the Mediterranean Sea) and eastern seas (GESAMP, 2015[11]). With regards to microplastics in the open ocean, hotspots of floating microplastics have been identified in gyres, i.e. areas where marine currents concentrate floating debris (Eriksen et al., 2013[61]; Cózar et al., 2014[68]; Van Sebille et al., 2015[69]).

Figure 1.5. Indicative risk of floating microplastics pollution in large marine ecosystems

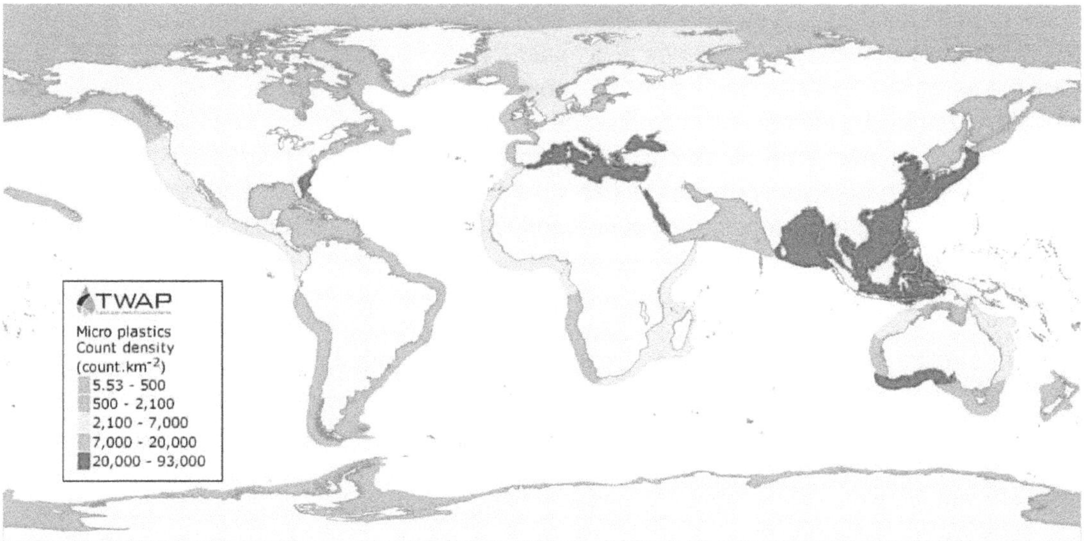

Source: Adapted from Large Marine Ecosystems Database, Estimated relative distribution of microplastic abundance in Large Marine Ecosystems, based on (Lebreton, Greer and Borrero, 2012[67]), http://bit.ly/2LK4ucM.

Significant knowledge and data gaps persist with regards to the quantities and distribution of microplastics in the oceans. Estimating microplastic concentrations in marine environments remains a challenge for several reasons:

- *High variability.* The distribution and transport of microplastics is highly variable and difficult to model, due to the complexity of factors influencing it (e.g. marine and wind currents, the density of the plastics compared to that of seawater, the creation of biofilms). Large differences in microplastics concentrations may exist across oceans areas as well as different depths (Cózar et al., 2014[68]; Claessens et al., 2011[70]; Eriksen et al., 2014[71]). High variability limits the representativeness of individual studies and poses limitations for the global scaling up of results (GESAMP, 2015[11]). Also, knowledge gaps persist with regards to the rate of degradation and fragmentation under different environmental conditions or due to interaction with living organisms.6
- *The lack of harmonised sampling and characterisation methodologies* for microplastics also poses challenges to the extrapolation of global-level results. Surveys of marine microplastics tend to employ a variety of sampling methods, cut-off sizes and metrics to present results, rendering findings difficult to compare and aggregate.

- *Limited geographical coverage of sampling*. In recent years, the use of manta trawls (i.e. net systems designed to collect microplastics from seawater over long distances) has allowed for the expansion of the geographical coverage of microplastics surveys (SAPEA, 2019[13]). Yet, sampling coverage remains largely limited to surface waters which are more accessible (such as the Mediterranean Sea) or which are already the focus of research on macro plastics pollution (such as subtropical gyres).
- *Methodological issues in sampling surface waters*. A significant drawback of the net system of mantra trawl methods employed to sample the ocean surface is that they cannot retain smaller microplastics (generally below 0.333 mm). Surveys of the ocean surface have consistently found lower amounts of microplastics than previously thought and especially of small microplastics (Cózar et al., 2014[68]; Eriksen et al., 2014[71]). With current data and sampling methodologies, it is impossible to determine with confidence whether this gap exists due to methodological issues, or whether other factors (e.g. biofouling, degradation, transport via marine currents, ingestion by marine species) may be contributing to the transport of microplastics away from the ocean surface (Cózar et al., 2014[68]).
- *Lack of microplastics survey data for lower compartments of the sea*. Microplastics surveys of the seafloor can be particularly complex and expensive to conduct. However, it has been suggested that the deep sea may be a large sink of microplastics, mainly due to the sinking effect of biofouling (SAPEA, 2019[13]). Hotspots of microplastics accumulation may form near the seafloor due to the influence of marine currents on the horizontal distribution of microplastics, potentially also overlapping with biodiversity hotspots (Kane et al., 2020[72]). Further field research is required to reliably assess the occurrence, distribution and risks of microplastics close to the ocean floor.

1.4.2. Freshwater environments

Several recent studies have also pointed to freshwaters as important microplastics sinks. Microplastics have now been observed in the surface waters and sediment of lakes and rivers, as well as in drinking water (Free et al., 2014[73]; Koelmans et al., 2019[74]; Castañeda et al., 2014[75]; Wang et al., 2017[76]; Eriksen et al., 2013[77]). Key pathways of microplastics pollution to freshwaters are terrestrial run-off and wastewater effluent, as well as mismanaged plastic waste.

Observed microplastics concentrations in freshwater environments vary widely depending on the sampling location. Table 1.5 presents microplastics concentrations from selected studies looking at microplastics in freshwaters (Koelmans et al., 2019[74]). For surface waters of lakes and rivers, some studies report concentrations significantly higher than the average observed concentrations for the ocean surface, while others report relatively low numbers. In general, the different methodologies employed (e.g. sieve sizes) render results difficult to compare and aggregate in order to draw general conclusions on the degree of MP pollution of different freshwater bodies.

Microplastics contamination of water destined for human consumption has also been reported (Kosuth, Mason and Wattenberg, 2018[78]; Mintenig et al., 2019[79]; Schymanski et al., 2018[80]). In general, groundwater resources are generally well protected from contamination and drinking water treatment removes most microplastics (Koelmans et al., 2019[74]). However, further research is required to assess potential routes of microplastics contamination of drinking water (e.g. the distribution stage) and the potential for human health risks (WHO, 2019[81]).

Table 1.5. Concentrations of microplastics in freshwater milieus

Type	Location	Results reported (average concentrations, particles / litre)	Lower size bound (µm)
Groundwater	Germany	0-0.007	3
Reservoir, surface waters and sediments	China	1.6-12.6	48
Lake, surface waters	China	0.9-2.8; 1.3-4.7	50
Urban surface waters	China	1.6-8.9	50
River	Switzerland, France, Germany, Netherlands	0.0056	300
Lake, surface waters	USA	0.00026	333

Source: (WHO, 2019[81]).

Box 1.3. Non-aquatic environmental sinks of microplastics

Non-aquatic environmental media (soil, air) can also be considered microplastics sinks.

Soil

Sludge and fertiliser application are key entry pathways into terrestrial environments, predominantly for synthetic fibres and other microplastics present in municipal wastewaters. Microplastics have been detected in agricultural fields in North America (1 microfibre per gram) (Zubris and Richards, 2005[82]), Mexico (0.87 particles per gram) (Huerta Lwanga et al., 2017[83]) and China (7.10 – 42.96 particles per gram) (Zhang and Liu, 2018[84]). Current knowledge indicates that microplastics entering soil through sludge may persist for a long time after the interruption of sludge application (Zubris and Richards, 2005[82]; Browne et al., 2011[59]). Additionally, atmospheric transport and road side deposition of microplastics, the use of intentionally-added microplastics in agriculture (e.g. seed coatings, controlled release fertilisers) and the degradation of plastic items employed in agriculture (e.g. agricultural mulch films) may also substantially contribute to terrestrial microplastics pollution.

In general, microplastics pollution of terrestrial habitats is a new field of research. Sampling methodologies are still under development, and significant data and knowledge gaps persist on the quantity, distribution and potential degradation of microplastics in soil. Further research is required in this field, especially with regards to microplastics persistence in the top layers of soils, penetration in lower levels, potential leakage into groundwater or rivers and the hazards posed to terrestrial species and ecosystems.

Air

Similarly, knowledge of airborne microplastics remains limited. Significant quantities of microplastics have been identified in atmospheric fallout (i.e. dust and particulate matter) in Paris, Hamburg and Dongguan (China) (Dris et al., 2016[32]; Klein and Fischer, 2019[85]; Cai et al., 2017[86]), as well as in protected areas of the United States (Brahney et al., 2020[87]). Commonly sampled airborne microplastics are those released during the use of garments and from road transport activity (see Chapter 2). Recent evidence indicates that airborne microplastics can travel for long distances and that air deposition may play a significant role in the pollution of remote and pristine areas (Allen et al., 2019[88]; Evangeliou et al., 2020[89]). Overall, knowledge of the abundance and concentrations of airborne microplastics remains limited, especially with regards to smaller microplastics and nanoplastics, and further research is required in this area.

1.5. Environmental and human health impacts

Emerging knowledge on the ubiquitous environmental presence of microplastics raises concerns for the hazards that these may pose to the health of ecosystems and humans. The next sections summarise findings on microplastics exposure levels (Section 1.5.1) and the health hazards posed by the toxicity of the particles (Section 1.5.2) and present an assessment of the risk implications for ecosystem and human health (Section 1.5.3). It is important to note that a significant challenge in the assessment of risks associated with microplastics is that the word is employed as an umbrella term to describe a vast array of particles with different physico-chemical characteristics and different potential for eco-toxicological effects. A discussion of specific environmental and health concerns associated with microplastics originating from the use of textiles and tyres is also included in Chapter 2.

1.5.1. Exposure

Aquatic species

Microplastics contamination has been documented for several marine and freshwater species, including planktonic organisms (Cole et al., 2017[90]), mussels and crustaceans (De Witte et al., 2014[91]; Farrell and Nelson, 2013[92]), freshwater and marine fish species (Jabeen et al., 2017[93]; Lusher, McHugh and Thompson, 2013[94]), marine mammals (Fossi et al., 2016[95]; Hernandez-Milian et al., 2019[96]), marine birds (Verlis, Campbell and Wilson, 2013[97]; van Franeker et al., 2011[98]), as well as for some terrestrial species such as earthworms (Rillig, 2012[99]). The main exposure route for wildlife is through ingestion, either due to the direct ingestion of microplastics or the ingestion of contaminated species.

Exposure to *direct* microplastics ingestion may be highly variable across different habitats and species, mainly due to differences in feeding strategies and variation in microplastics characteristics and concentrations across different feeding habitats. Particle size may be the most important factor in determining ingestion incidence (Andrady, 2011[17]). Smaller microplastics are more likely to be mistakenly ingested as prey, especially by small invertebrates at the bottom of the food chain and by filter feeders, i.e. species which strain food from the surrounding waters indiscriminately, such as small and medium invertebrates (e.g. planktons) and certain large mammals (e.g. baleen whales) (Fossi et al., 2012[100]; Wright, Thompson and Galloway, 2013[101]; GESAMP, 2015[11])[7]. There is also growing concern that certain selective feeders, i.e. species which have the ability to selectively ingest food such as copepods (a type of small crustacean), may selectively ingest plastic particles containing chemicals sorbed from the surrounding environment, due to their resemblance to prey (Procter et al., 2019[102]; Lusher, Hollman and Mendoza-Hill, 2017[103]).

Microplastics ingestion can also occur *indirectly* via the ingestion of contaminated species. The transfer across steps of the ecosystem food chain, known as trophic transfer, amplifies the exposure risk to all species in the food chain. Although indirect microplastics ingestion has been documented only for a few species (e.g. mussels, crabs, herring, captive seals) (Diepens and Koelmans, 2018[104]; Farrell and Nelson, 2013[92]; Lusher, McHugh and Thompson, 2013[94]; Nelms et al., 2018[105]), evidence of a large occurrence of microplastics in organisms at the bottom of the food chain (e.g. planktons) and recurrent inconsistencies between the types of microplastics retrieved in organisms and those commonly found in their habitats, point to a potentially large contribution of indirect ingestion to total microplastics exposure of aquatic organisms (SAPEA, 2019[13]).

Humans

Freshwater and marine microplastics contamination may contribute to increasing human exposure to microplastics, via the ingestion of commercial seafood. Microplastics have been documented in the digestive tract of several types of mussels and fish destined for human consumption (Van Cauwenberghe and Janssen, 2014[106]). These, especially when consumed without removing the digestive tract, may constitute a significant exposure route to humans (Lusher, Hollman and Mendoza-Hill, 2017[103]). The presence of microplastics has also been documented in several other contaminated food and beverages, such as tap and bottled water (Kosuth, Mason and Wattenberg, 2018[78]; Mintenig et al., 2019[79]), beer (Liebezeit and Liebezeit, 2014[107]), sea salt (Iñiguez, Conesa and Fullana, 2017[108]) and edible fruit and vegetables (Oliveri Conti et al., 2020[109]). Further, humans may also be exposed to the *inhalation* of airborne microplastics present both in indoor and outdoor environments (Dris et al., 2017[110]; Gasperi et al., 2017[111]).

According to Cox et al. (2019[112]), the estimated daily intake for adult women and men in the United States is of 126 and 142 particles, respectively, for ingested microplastics, and 132 and 170 particles respectively for inhaled microplastics. Conversely, a second study concluded that the largest source of microplastics acquisition is by far the ingestion of contaminated food and beverages, while the inhalation of microplastics represents a negligible exposure route (WWF, 2019[113]). More recently, microplastics have also been sampled in the human placenta, raising concerns on the levels of human exposure to MPs and the potential impacts on foetus development (Ragusa et al., 2021[114]). Overall, further data is needed in order to produce reliable and methodologically valid assessments of human exposure to microplastics via multiple exposure routes.

1.5.2. Toxicity of microplastics

Toxicity of microplastics to species, humans and ecosystems is defined as the combination of:

- the *physical toxicity* of the uptaken particles, i.e. the adverse health effects caused by the transition or permanence of particles in organisms;
- *the chemical toxicity*, i.e. the adverse health effects caused by the chemicals present in the ingested or inhaled microplastics; and
- the *pathogen toxicity*, i.e. the potential of microplastics to act as a vector of microbial communities (WHO, 2019[81]).

Physical toxicity

In aquatic species, the majority of the ingested microplastics are likely to be directly excreted. Yet, systemic exposure to microplastics ingestion may cause several physical injuries such as internal inflammation and abrasion, or blockages of the gastrointestinal tract. Laboratory experiments have shown that high exposure to microplastics may result in reduced feeding efficiency, starvation, reduced growth rates, physical deterioration and increased mortality rates (Wright, Thompson and Galloway, 2013[101]).

The physical toxicity of ingested microplastics on humans remains largely unknown: current knowledge is largely based on inference from observed impacts on marine and terrestrial organisms. Over 90% of ingested microplastics are thought to pass through the gastrointestinal system without being retained (Smith et al., 2018[115]; EFSA CONTAM Panel, 2016[116]). Factors affecting the clearance/retention rate are likely to be the size, shape and polymer and chemical composition of microplastics. It is believed that only very small (<1.5 µm) microplastics may be retained and transferred into the lymphatic system and human organs, although the mechanisms and impacts of microplastics uptake remain unknown (EFSA CONTAM Panel, 2016[116]). Still, systemic exposure to microplastics ingestion may lead to localised effects on the immune system, inflammation of the gut and intestine irritation (EFSA CONTAM Panel, 2016[116]; WHO, 2019[81]). Overall, further research is required in order to reliably assess the physical toxicity associated with the ingestion of microplastics, and especially of nanoplastics, on humans (WHO, 2019[81]).

Similarly, only a small portion of the inhaled microplastics is expected to reach the lungs (Gasperi et al., 2017[111]). The inhalation of air pollutants may be facilitated by the small size of particles, as well as by compromised clearance mechanisms or respiratory functions at the individual level (Prata, 2018[117]).

Chronic exposure to high concentrations of microplastics has been shown to lead to a higher prevalence of respiratory irritation, chronic respiratory symptoms, restrictive pulmonary function abnormalities, and possibly also to reproductive toxicity and carcinogenicity (Gasperi et al., 2017[111]; Pimentel, Avila and Lourenco, 2008[118]).

Chemical toxicity

Microplastics are generally found in the environment as complex mixes of different chemicals. Several chemical additives are combined with plastic polymers during manufacturing to enhance a number of desirable properties of the final plastic product (e.g. resistance to UV, biodegradation, oxidation, heat and optical brightness and colour) (OECD, 2018[119]).[8] Microplastics are also prone to sorbing persistent organic pollutants (POPs) and heavy metals from aquatic or aerial environments.

Chemicals present in microplastics may leach out following ingestion and pose hazards to the health of aquatic organisms and humans (Rochman et al., 2019[14]; SAPEA, 2019[13]). Additives such as Bisphenol A, PCBs, phthalates and some brominated flame retardants are suspected endocrine disruptors, i.e. chemicals with thyroid-disrupting effects (WHO, 2019[81]). Other known or suspected health effects of hazardous chemicals added during plastic production include carcinogenicity, reproductive health effects, developmental toxicity and mutagenicity (i.e. the induction of a transmittable change in one's genetic material). For chemicals and metals sorbed once plastics is released into the environment, potential effects on marine biota may include altered feeding behaviour, endocrine disruption, liver toxicity, tumour promotion and reduced survival (GESAMP, 2016[19]). Generally, complex equilibria dependent on the relative concentrations of pollutants in each compartment will determine absorption/desorption rates and the exposure levels for organisms (GESAMP, 2015[11]).

Pathogen toxicity

Microplastics may also act as transfer media for invasive species and virus-bearing organisms potentially harmful to ecosystems and human health. The surface of macro- and micro- plastics in aquatic environments is an ideal habitat for diverse bacterial assemblages to attach and colonize (Frère et al., 2018[120]; WHO, 2019[81]). As microplastics and pathogens are both commonly found in wastewater treatment plants, this joint exposure may increase the potential for pathogens to colonize the surface of microplastics. Documented microbial communities include those formed by pathogens commonly present in sewage as well as microorganisms able to degrade plastic polymers (Curren and Leong, 2019[121]). These may be transferred to humans via contaminated food and beverages, potentially causing imbalances in microbial communities present in the organism or spreading antibiotic resistance (SAPEA, 2019[13]; WHO, 2019[81]).

1.5.3. Environmental and human health risks and knowledge gaps

Risk assessments have been carried out in order to scientifically evaluate the adverse ecological and health impacts resulting from microplastics pollution of aquatic media. Risks are generally assessed as a function of *hazard* and *exposure*. Humans and other living species commonly ingest particles of different types and origins, and the presence of microplastics in the environment does not necessarily imply a risk for the health of organisms. Conversely, the inherent toxicity of a particle may result in health risks only under specific conditions, such as the surpassing of certain exposure levels or the vulnerability of specific species to ingesting microplastics (WHO, 2019[81]).

Available risk assessments for microplastics in aquatic environments indicate that average concentration levels lead to limited ecological risks, although adverse effects may already be occurring in certain highly polluted coastal waters or beaches (Besseling et al., 2019[122]; Burns and Boxall, 2018[123]; Everaert et al., 2018[124]). Based on the available evidence, the Science Advice for Policy by European Academies

Working Group (2019[13]) concluded that continued microplastics emissions and increases in concentration levels in different environmental media may lead to widespread ecological impacts in the near future and recommended action “to reduce, prevent and mitigate” microplastics pollution in order to reduce risks. At the same time, the group of experts highlighted the need for more data on microplastics occurrence, fate, exposure levels and modes of toxicity (including sorption mechanisms for chemicals) in order to produce higher-quality risk assessments.

Similar conclusions can be drawn with regards to risks posed specifically to human health. While physical toxicity of particles has been observed in aquatic species, research efforts have yet to determine if this may also occur in humans and what the critical exposure levels may be (SAPEA, 2019[13]). Although it is now established that microplastics can act as a vector of toxic chemicals to humans, current evidence suggests that present concentration levels of microplastics are not a major exposure pathway relative to other existing ones (SAPEA, 2019[13]). Conservative estimates of the exposure to microplastics through ingestion of a portion of seafood are 7 µg of microplastics, which would contribute to less than 0.2% of the average total dietary exposure to Bisphenol A, PCBs and PAHs (EFSA CONTAM Panel, 2016[116]; SAPEA, 2019[13]). With regards to pathogen toxicity, current evidence suggests that microplastics do not yet constitute a significant exposure route to pathogens potentially harmful to human health, relatively to other potential transfer media (e.g. contamination of water pipes, inadequate wastewater treatment) (WHO, 2019[81]). The recent WHO (2019[81]) assessment of the potential human health impacts of microplastics in drinking water concluded that there is no evidence to indicate a human health concern, advised for a reduction in plastic pollution to mitigate exposure levels and called for further research to more accurately inform risk assessments.

Overall, further research and better exposure data and toxicity assessments are required in order to adequately identify and assess risks for human health. Future research needs are summarised in Box 1.4.

Box 1.4. Limitations and further research needs

To improve the quality of risk assessments, further research is required on:

- *Microplastics occurrence and exposure levels.* The lack of high-quality estimates of microplastics concentrations in different aquatic compartments limits our understanding of exposure levels for biota and humans. More data is especially needed to adequately quantify exposure to smaller microplastics and nanoplastics, which can be ingested more easily and which are believed to pose a higher risk of health hazards to wildlife and humans (SAPEA, 2019[13]). The standardisation of microplastics definitions and analytical methods for sampling and characterisation can help to accelerate research in this area and facilitate the comparison of results.
- *Fate of microplastics and persistence in organisms.* Laboratory experiments carried out on certain aquatic species have documented the uptake of microplastics as well as their transfer to tissues and body liquids (Van Cauwenberghe, Claessens and Janssen, 2013[125]; Van Cauwenberghe et al., 2015[126]). The presence of microplastics in organisms is thought to be temporary, however the mechanisms of uptake, accumulation, and excretion of microplastics in humans and other species remain largely unknown (GESAMP, 2015[11]).
- *Concentration thresholds for health risks.* Substantial knowledge gaps persist also with regards to the concentration levels that lead to adverse health consequences. Laboratory experiments usually employ unrealistically high concentration levels and thus cannot reproduce the relationship between exposure levels and adverse effects as it may occur in the natural environment (GESAMP, 2016[19]).

1.6. Possible future trends

1.6.1. Plastics production, use and disposal

Plastics production is projected to continue to increase, causing concern for the projected leakage of plastics and the potential amplification of macro- and micro- plastics pollution. This is for two reasons in particular:

1. The increase in plastics production in recent years has been mostly driven by the packaging sector, which now constitutes almost 40% of all plastics production (Geyer, Jambeck and Law, 2017[2]). Packaging and other single-use plastics are discarded soon after use, significantly contributing to the generation of plastic waste.
2. The largest increases in plastic waste generation are expected in regions where waste management is poor. Figure 1.6 presents projections for the top twenty coastal countries by mass of mismanaged plastic waste in 2025: eighteen of them mismanaged more than 50% of their plastic waste in 2010 (Jambeck et al., 2015[5]). As their waste management systems may not develop at a sufficiently quick rate to deal with the additional amounts of plastic waste generated, this may lead to larger quantities of plastic waste dispersed into the environment.

Figure 1.6. Top 20 coastal countries ranked by mass of mismanaged plastic waste in 2025

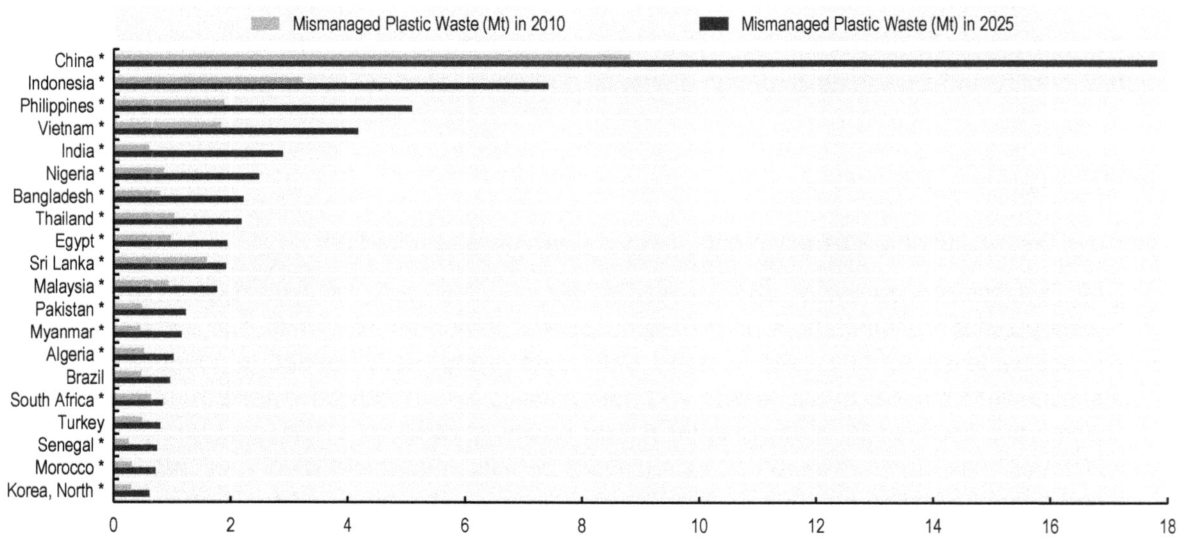

Note: * indicates countries where more than 50% of plastic waste is currently mismanaged
Source: Based on data from (Jambeck et al., 2015[5])

Current trends in plastics production and disposal, combined with the lack of effective solid waste management systems in several parts of the world, suggest that flows of mismanaged plastics to the oceans will continue to contribute to the generation of secondary microplastics in years to come. Source-reduction policies (e.g. bans and taxes on single-use plastic goods) remain limited in scope, while clean-up initiatives are expensive, remove only plastics from the surface of the oceans or from beaches and can only be sufficiently effective in the presence of emission reductions (The Ocean Cleanup[127]).

Furthermore, plastics debris already present in the environment will continue to be a source of microplastics (Andrady, 2011[17]). Microplastics constitute over 90% of the 5.25 trillion plastic particles currently present in the oceans' surface, but only a small portion of the total floating plastics in terms of mass, implying that there are still large quantities of marine plastic litter which may fragment into microplastics in future years (Eriksen et al., 2014[71]; Lebreton, Egger and Slat, 2019[128]).[9] Overall, projections based on current trends in the production of plastics find that microplastics concentrations in the surface of marine waters will increase 50-fold by 2100, to 9.6-48.8 particles per m^3 (Everaert et al., 2018[124]).

1.6.2. Projected trends in microplastics emissions

Recent industry and policy-led efforts may result in a reduction in selected microplastics emissions. Improved waste management practices, policies on frequently littered single use plastics and bans on the use of microbeads in industrial applications for which natural alternatives exist have been at the focus of policy action on plastics and microplastics pollution until now. Several countries have introduced legislation to restrict the manufacture, sale and/or import of personal care and cosmetic products containing microbeads (Canada, 2017[129]; France, 2017[130]; GOV.UK, 2018[131]; Italy, 2017[132]; New Zealand, 2017[133]; United States, 2015[134]). Approved national bans generally target microbeads intentionally added to rinse-off cosmetics, which roughly account for more than two thirds of all microbeads releases from products (ECHA, 2019[10]).[10] The European Chemical Agency (ECHA) has also proposed an EU-wide restriction to cover a wide range of microplastics intentionally-added to products, including in PCCPs, paints, coatings, detergents, maintenance products, medical and pharmaceutical applications and products used in agriculture and horticulture. ECHA (2019[10]) estimates that the restriction could result in emission reductions of more than 400 thousand tonnes of microplastics over 20 years. With regards to plastic pellets, emerging industry-led and international initiatives to prevent spillages may also curb their discharge into the environment (Operation Clean Sweep, (PlasticsEurope, 2017[22]; Marine Litter Solutions, 2011[23])).

However, releases of use-based secondary microplastics, which remain largely outside of the scope of policy frameworks in place in OECD countries, are expected to significantly increase in future years, in line with market trends and economic growth. Trends in the textile sector indicate that textile production, consumption and disposal is likely to continue to increase in line with GDP growth. At current trends, an estimated 175 Mt of clothing could be sold in 2050 (EMF, 2017[135]). In particular, the employment of synthetic fibres is expected to continue to increase, in line with current consumption trends, practices associated with the concept of “fast fashion” and the growth in textile markets in developing countries in East and South East Asia (TextileExchange, 2020[136]). While the higher uptake of synthetic fibres in textile manufacturing offers numerous economic and environmental benefits (e.g. lower costs relative to natural fibres, a reduced need for resource-intensive cotton production), in the absence of mitigation action this will contribute significantly to the intensification of microplastics pollution. It is estimated that, at current trends, 22 Mt of synthetic microfibres will have entered the oceans by 2050 (EMF, 2017[135]).

Emissions of microplastics from vehicle tyres are also expected to increase in future years, in line with GDP growth and trends in road transport. Market data projections indicate steady increases in the production of vehicles in the next decades, mainly driven by increases in production in China and India (EC, 2017[137]). Current trends in the composition of the vehicle fleet also show a continued tendency towards a higher proportion of larger and heavier vehicles, which generally lead to higher tyre tread wear (Andersson-Sköld et al., 2020[138]). Furthermore, climate policies and stricter controls on exhaust emissions (e.g. GHG emissions) will not necessarily contribute to the reduction of non-exhaust emissions (e.g. tyre and brake particles) (OECD, 2020[139]). On the contrary, a higher uptake of electric vehicles could lead to higher emissions of microplastics, mainly due to the heavier weight of EVs relatively to their traditional counterparts.

References

Allen, S. et al. (2019), "Atmospheric transport and deposition of microplastics in a remote mountain catchment", *Nature Geoscience*, Vol. 12/5, pp. 339-344, http://dx.doi.org/10.1038/s41561-019-0335-5. [88]

Andersson-Sköld, Y. et al. (2020), *Microplastics from tyre and road wear - A literature review*, Swedish National Road and Transport Research Institute (VTI). [138]

Andrady, A. (2011), "Microplastics in the marine environment", *Marine Pollution Bulletin*, Vol. 62/8, pp. 1596-1605, http://dx.doi.org/10.1016/j.marpolbul.2011.05.030. [17]

Arthur, C., J. Baker and H. Bamford (2009), *Proceedings of the International Research Workshop on the Occurrence, Effects and Fate of Microplastic Marine Debris. Sept 9-11, 2008.*, NOAA Technical Memorandum NOS-OR&R-30. [9]

Baresel, C. and M. Olshammar (2019), "On the Importance of Sanitary Sewer Overflow on the Total Discharge of Microplastics from Sewage Water", *Journal of Environmental Protection*, Vol. 10, pp. 1105-1118, http://dx.doi.org/10.4236/jep.2019.109065. [29]

Barrett, J. et al. (2020), "Microplastic Pollution in Deep-Sea Sediments From the Great Australian Bight", *Frontiers in Marine Science*, Vol. 7, http://dx.doi.org/10.3389/fmars.2020.576170. [6]

Besseling, E. et al. (2019), "Quantifying ecological risks of aquatic micro- and nanoplastic", *Critical Reviews in Environmental Science and Technology*, doi: 10.1080/10643389.2018.1531688, pp. 32-80, http://dx.doi.org/10.1080/10643389.2018.1531688. [122]

Brahney, J. et al. (2020), "Plastic rain in protected areas of the United States", *Science*, Vol. 368/6496, p. 1257, http://dx.doi.org/10.1126/science.aaz5819. [87]

Browne, M. et al. (2011), "Accumulation of microplastic on shorelines woldwide: Sources and sinks", *Environmental Science and Technology*, Vol. 45/21, pp. 9175-9179, http://dx.doi.org/10.1021/es201811s. [59]

Burns, E. and A. Boxall (2018), "Microplastics in the aquatic environment: Evidence for or against adverse impacts and major knowledge gaps", *Environmental Toxicology and Chemistry*, doi: 10.1002/etc.4268, pp. 2776-2796, http://dx.doi.org/10.1002/etc.4268. [123]

Cai, L. et al. (2017), "Characteristic of microplastics in the atmospheric fallout from Dongguan city, China: preliminary research and first evidence", *Environmental Science and Pollution Research*, Vol. 24/32, pp. 24928-24935, http://dx.doi.org/10.1007/s11356-017-0116-x. [86]

California State Water Resources Control Board (2020), *Resultion NO. 2020-0021. Adoption of definition of "microplastics in drinking water"*. [12]

Canada (2017), *Microbeads in Toiletries Regulations (SOR/2017-111), 2 June 2017*, Government of Canada, http://www.canada.ca/en/health-canada/services/chemical-substances/other-chemical-substances-interest/microbeads.html (accessed on 1 August 2018). [129]

Castañeda, R. et al. (2014), "Microplastic pollution in St. Lawrence River sediments", *Journal canadien des sciences halieutiques et aquatiques*, Vol. 71/12, pp. 1767-1771, https://doi.org/10.1139/cjfas-2014-0281. [75]

Choy, C. et al. (2019), "The vertical distribution and biological transport of marine microplastics across the epipelagic and mesopelagic water column", *Scientific Reports*, Vol. 9/1, p. 7843, http://dx.doi.org/10.1038/s41598-019-44117-2. [65]

Claessens, M. et al. (2011), "Occurrence and distribution of microplastics in marine sediments along the Belgian coast", *Marine Pollution Bulletin*, Vol. 62/10, pp. 2199-2204, http://dx.doi.org/10.1016/j.marpolbul.2011.06.030. [70]

Cole, M. et al. (2017), "Microplastic Ingestion by Zooplankton", *Wasser und Abfall*, Vol. 19/3, pp. 26-29, http://dx.doi.org/10.1021/es400663f. [90]

Cole, M. et al. (2011), *Microplastics as contaminants in the marine environment: A review*, http://dx.doi.org/10.1016/j.marpolbul.2011.09.025. [66]

Cooper, D. and P. Corcoran (2010), "Effects of mechanical and chemical processes on the degradation of plastic beach debris on the island of Kauai, Hawaii", *Marine Pollution Bulletin*, Vol. 60/5, pp. 650-654, http://dx.doi.org/10.1016/j.marpolbul.2009.12.026. [40]

Cox, K. et al. (2019), "Human Consumption of Microplastics", *Environmental Science and Technology*, Vol. 53/12, pp. 7068-7074, http://dx.doi.org/10.1021/acs.est.9b01517. [112]

Cózar, A. et al. (2014), "Plastic debris in the open ocean.", *Proceedings of the National Academy of Sciences of the United States of America*, Vol. 111/28, pp. 10239-44, http://dx.doi.org/10.1073/pnas.1314705111. [68]

Curren, E. and S. Leong (2019), "Profiles of bacterial assemblages from microplastics of tropical coastal environments", *Science of The Total Environment*, Vol. 655, pp. 313-320, http://dx.doi.org/10.1016/J.SCITOTENV.2018.11.250. [121]

Dawson, A. et al. (2018), "Turning microplastics into nanoplastics through digestive fragmentation by Antarctic krill", *Nature Communications*, Vol. 9/1, p. 1001, http://dx.doi.org/10.1038/s41467-018-03465-9. [140]

De Witte, B. et al. (2014), "Quality assessment of the blue mussel (Mytilus edulis): Comparison between commercial and wild types", *Marine Pollution Bulletin*, Vol. 85/1, pp. 146-155, http://dx.doi.org/10.1016/j.marpolbul.2014.06.006. [91]

Derraik, J. (2002), "The pollution of the marine environment by plastic debris: a review.", *Marine pollution bulletin*, Vol. 44/9, pp. 842-852, http://dx.doi.org/10.1016/S0025-326X(02)00220-5. [7]

Desforges, J. et al. (2014), "Widespread distribution of microplastics in subsurface seawater in the NE Pacific Ocean", *Marine Pollution Bulletin*, Vol. 79/1-2, pp. 94-99, http://dx.doi.org/10.1016/j.marpolbul.2013.12.035. [60]

Diepens, N. and A. Koelmans (2018), "Accumulation of Plastic Debris and Associated Contaminants in Aquatic Food Webs", *Environmental Science & Technology*, doi: 10.1021/acs.est.8b02515, pp. 8510-8520, http://dx.doi.org/10.1021/acs.est.8b02515. [104]

Dris, R. et al. (2017), "A first overview of textile fibers, including microplastics, in indoor and outdoor environments", *Environmental Pollution*, Vol. 221, pp. 453-458, http://dx.doi.org/10.1016/j.envpol.2016.12.013. [110]

Dris, R. et al. (2016), "Synthetic fibers in atmospheric fallout: A source of microplastics in the environment?", *Marine Pollution Bulletin*, Vol. 104/1-2, pp. 290-293, http://dx.doi.org/10.1016/j.marpolbul.2016.01.006. [32]

EC (2018), *REPORT FROM THE COMMISSION TO THE EUROPEAN PARLIAMENT AND THE COUNCIL on the impact of the use of oxo-degradable plastic, including oxo-degradable plastic carrier bags, on the environment*. [38]

EC (2017), *GEAR 2030 Strategy 2015-2017 - Comparative analysis of the competitive position of the EU automotive industry and the impact of the introduction of autonomous vehicles*, http://dx.doi.org/10.2873/83569. [137]

ECHA (2019), *ANNEX XV Restriction Report. Proposal for a restriction - intentionally added microplastics*. [10]

EFSA CONTAM Panel (2016), "Statement on the presence of microplastics and nanoplastics in food, with particular focus on seafood", *EFSA Journal*, Vol. 14/6, p. 30, http://dx.doi.org/10.2903/j.efsa.2016.4501. [116]

EMF (2017), *A New Textile Economy: Redesigning Fashion's Future*, Ellen Macarthur Foundation, http://www.ellenmacarthurfoundation.org/publications. [135]

Eriksen, M. et al. (2014), "Plastic Pollution in the World's Oceans: More than 5 Trillion Plastic Pieces Weighing over 250,000 Tons Afloat at Sea", *PLOS ONE*, Vol. 9/12, pp. e111913-, https://doi.org/10.1371/journal.pone.0111913. [71]

Eriksen, M. et al. (2013), "Microplastic pollution in the surface waters of the Laurentian Great Lakes", *Marine Pollution Bulletin*, Vol. 77, pp. 177-182, http://dx.doi.org/10.1016/j.marpolbul.2013.10.007. [77]

Eriksen, M. et al. (2013), "Plastic pollution in the South Pacific subtropical gyre", *Marine Pollution Bulletin*, http://dx.doi.org/10.1016/j.marpolbul.2012.12.021. [61]

Essel, R. et al. (2015), *Sources of microplastics relevant to marine protection in Germany*. [56]

EU (2018), *European Strategy for Plastics in a Circular Economy*. [4]

Eunomia (2018), "Investigating options for reducing releases in the aquatic environment of microplastics emitted by (but not intentionally added in) products - Interim Report", *Report for DG Environment of the European Commission*, p. 335, http://dx.doi.org/10.1002/lsm.22016. [54]

Eunomia (2016), *Plastics in the Marine Environment*, Eunomia, http://www.eunomia.co.uk. [42]

Evangeliou, N. et al. (2020), "Atmospheric transport is a major pathway of microplastics to remote regions", *Nature Communications*, Vol. 11/1, p. 3381, http://dx.doi.org/10.1038/s41467-020-17201-9. [89]

Everaert, G. et al. (2018), "Risk assessment of microplastics in the ocean: Modelling approach and first conclusions", *Environmental Pollution*, Vol. 242, pp. 1930-1938, http://dx.doi.org/10.1016/J.ENVPOL.2018.07.069. [124]

Farrell, P. and K. Nelson (2013), "Trophic level transfer of microplastic: Mytilus edulis (L.) to Carcinus maenas (L.)", *Environmental Pollution*, Vol. 177, pp. 1-3, http://dx.doi.org/10.1016/j.envpol.2013.01.046. [92]

Fossi, M. et al. (2016), "Fin whales and microplastics: The Mediterranean Sea and the Sea of Cortez scenarios", *Environmental Pollution*, Vol. 209, pp. 68-78, http://dx.doi.org/10.1016/j.envpol.2015.11.022. [95]

Fossi, M. et al. (2012), "Are baleen whales exposed to the threat of microplastics? A case study of the Mediterranean fin whale (Balaenoptera physalus)", *Marine Pollution Bulletin*, Vol. 64/11, pp. 2374-2379, http://dx.doi.org/10.1016/j.marpolbul.2012.08.013. [100]

France (2017), *Décret n° 2017-291 du 6 mars 2017 relatif aux conditions de mise en œuvre de l'interdiction de mise sur le marché des produits cosmétiques rincés à usage d'exfoliation ou de nettoyage comportant des particules plastiques solides et des bâtonnets ouatés à usage domestique dont la tige est en plastique.* [130]

Fraunhofer Umsicht (2018), *Kunststoffe in der Umwelt: Mikro- und Makroplastik.*, https://doi.org/10.24406/uMsiCht-n-497117. [21]

Free, C. et al. (2014), "High-levels of microplastic pollution in a large, remote, mountain lake", *Marine Pollution Bulletin*, http://dx.doi.org/10.1016/j.marpolbul.2014.06.001. [73]

Frère, L. et al. (2018), "Microplastic bacterial communities in the Bay of Brest: Influence of polymer type and size", *Environmental Pollution*, Cited By :9 Export Date: 24 July 2019, pp. 614-625, http://dx.doi.org/10.1016/j.envpol.2018.07.023. [120]

Gasperi, J. et al. (2017), "Microplastics in air: Are we breathing it in?", *Current Opinion in Environmental Science & Health*, Vol. 1, pp. 1-5, http://dx.doi.org/10.1016/j.coesh.2017.10.002. [111]

GESAMP (2016), *Sources, Fate and Effects of Microplastics in the Marine Environment: Part 2 of a Global Assessment.* [19]

GESAMP (2015), *Sources, fate and effects of microplastics in the marine environment: a global assessment*, IMO/FAO/UNESCO-IOC/UNIDO/WMO/IAEA/UN/UNEP/UNDP Joint Group of Experts on the Scientific Aspects of Marine Environmental Protection), http://www.imo.org. [11]

Geyer, R., J. Jambeck and K. Law (2017), "Production, use, and fate of all plastics ever made", *Science Advances*, Vol. 3/7, p. e1700782, http://dx.doi.org/10.1126/sciadv.1700782. [2]

GOV.UK (2018), *World-leading microbeads ban takes effect*, http://www.gov.uk/government/news/world-leading-microbeads-ban-takes-effect (accessed on 22 August 2019). [131]

Gregory, M. and A. Andrady (2003), "Plastics in the marine environment", in Anthony.L. (ed.), *Plastics and the Environment*, John Wiley and Sons. [39]

He, P. et al. (2019), "Municipal solid waste (MSW)landfill: A source of microplastics? -Evidence of microplastics in landfill leachate", *Water Research*, http://dx.doi.org/10.1016/j.watres.2019.04.060. [43]

Hernandez-Milian, G. et al. (2019), "Microplastics in grey seal (Halichoerus grypus) intestines: Are they associated with parasite aggregations?", *Marine Pollution Bulletin*, Vol. 146, pp. 349-354, https://doi.org/10.1016/j.marpolbul.2019.06.014. [96]

Huerta Lwanga, E. et al. (2017), "Field evidence for transfer of plastic debris along a terrestrial food chain", *Scientific Reports*, Vol. 7/1, p. 14071, http://dx.doi.org/10.1038/s41598-017-14588-2. [83]

Hurley, R., J. Woodward and J. Rothwell (2018), "Microplastic contamination of river beds significantly reduced by catchment-wide flooding", *Nature Geoscience*, Vol. 11/4, pp. 251-257, http://dx.doi.org/10.1038/s41561-018-0080-1. [35]

IEA (2018), *The Future of Petrochemicals*, IEA, http://www.iea.org/reports/the-future-of-petrochemicals. [1]

Iñiguez, M., J. Conesa and A. Fullana (2017), "Microplastics in Spanish Table Salt", *Scientific Reports*, Vol. 7/1, http://dx.doi.org/10.1038/s41598-017-09128-x. [108]

Italy (2017), *Legge n 205 del 27 dicembre 2017. Bilancio di previsione dello Stato per l'anno finanziario 2018 e bilancio pluriennale per il triennio 2018-2020.*. [132]

IUCN (2017), *Primary microplastics in the oceans: A global evaluation of sources*, IUCN International Union for Conservation of Nature, http://dx.doi.org/10.2305/iucn.ch.2017.01.en. [55]

Iyare, P., S. Ouki and T. Bond (2020), "Microplastics removal in wastewater treatment plants: a critical review", *Environmental Science: Water Research & Technology*, Vol. 6/10, pp. 2664-2675, http://dx.doi.org/10.1039/D0EW00397B. [30]

Jabeen, K. et al. (2017), "Microplastics and mesoplastics in fish from coastal and fresh waters of China", *Environmental Pollution*, Vol. 221, pp. 141-149, http://dx.doi.org/10.1016/j.envpol.2016.11.055. [93]

Jambeck, J. et al. (2015), "Plastic waste inputs from land into the ocean", *Science*, Vol. 347/6223, pp. 768-771, http://dx.doi.org/10.1126/science.1260352. [5]

Kane, I. et al. (2020), "Seafloor microplastic hotspots controlled by deep-sea circulation", *Science*, Vol. 368/6495, p. 1140, http://dx.doi.org/10.1126/science.aba5899. [72]

Klein, M. and E. Fischer (2019), "Microplastic abundance in atmospheric deposition within the Metropolitan area of Hamburg, Germany", *Science of The Total Environment*, Vol. 685, pp. 96-103, http://dx.doi.org/10.1016/J.SCITOTENV.2019.05.405. [85]

Koelmans, A. et al. (2019), *Microplastics in freshwaters and drinking water: Critical review and assessment of data quality*, Elsevier Ltd, http://dx.doi.org/10.1016/j.watres.2019.02.054. [74]

Kosuth, M., S. Mason and E. Wattenberg (2018), "Anthropogenic contamination of tap water, beer, and sea salt", *PLoS ONE*, Vol. 13/4, http://dx.doi.org/10.1371/journal.pone.0194970. [78]

Lares, M. et al. (2018), "Occurrence, identification and removal of microplastic particles and fibers in conventional activated sludge process and advanced MBR technology", *Water Research*, Vol. 133, pp. 236-246, http://dx.doi.org/10.1016/J.WATRES.2018.01.049. [27]

Lassen, C. et al. (2016), *Microplastics Occurrence, effects and sources of releases to the environment in Denmark*, Danish Environmental Protection Agency, Copenhagen. [57]

Lebreton, L., M. Egger and B. Slat (2019), "A global mass budget for positively buoyant macroplastic debris in the ocean", *Scientific Reports*, Vol. 9/1, p. 12922, http://dx.doi.org/10.1038/s41598-019-49413-5. [128]

Lebreton, L., S. Greer and J. Borrero (2012), "Numerical modelling of floating debris in the world's oceans", *Marine Pollution Bulletin*, Vol. 64/3, pp. 653-661, http://dx.doi.org/10.1016/J.MARPOLBUL.2011.10.027. [67]

Lebreton, L. et al. (2018), "Evidence that the Great Pacific Garbage Patch is rapidly accumulating plastic", *Scientific Reports*, Vol. 8/1, http://dx.doi.org/10.1038/s41598-018-22939-w. [52]

Lebreton, L. et al. (2017), "River plastic emissions to the world's oceans", *Nature Communications*, Vol. 8/1, pp. 1-10, http://dx.doi.org/10.1038/ncomms15611. [51]

Lee, J. et al. (2013), "Relationships among the abundances of plastic debris in different size classes on beaches in South Korea", *Marine Pollution Bulletin*, Vol. 77/1-2, pp. 349-354, http://dx.doi.org/10.1016/j.marpolbul.2013.08.013. [36]

Liebezeit, G. and E. Liebezeit (2014), "Synthetic particles as contaminants in German beers", *Food Additives and Contaminants - Part A Chemistry, Analysis, Control, Exposure and Risk Assessment*, Vol. 31/9, pp. 1574-1578, http://dx.doi.org/10.1080/19440049.2014.945099. [107]

Li, W., H. Tse and L. Fok (2016), "Plastic waste in the marine environment: A review of sources, occurrence and effects", *Science of The Total Environment*, Vol. 566-567, pp. 333-349, http://dx.doi.org/10.1016/J.SCITOTENV.2016.05.084. [47]

Lusher, A., P. Hollman and J. Mendoza-Hill (2017), *Microplastics in fisheries and aquaculture : status of knowledge on their occurrence and implications for aquatic organisms and food safety*, FAO. [103]

Lusher, A., M. McHugh and R. Thompson (2013), "Occurrence of microplastics in the gastrointestinal tract of pelagic and demersal fish from the English Channel", *Marine Pollution Bulletin*, Vol. 67/1-2, pp. 94-99, http://dx.doi.org/10.1016/j.marpolbul.2012.11.028. [94]

Lusher, A. et al. (2015), "Microplastics in Arctic polar waters: The first reported values of particles in surface and sub-surface samples", *Scientific Reports*, Vol. 5, http://dx.doi.org/10.1038/srep14947. [62]

Macfadyen, G., T. Huntington and R. Cappell (2009), *Abandoned, lost or otherwise discarded fishing gear*, Food and Agriculture Organization of the United Nations (FAO). [8]

Magnusson, K. et al. (2016), *Swedish sources and pathways for microplastics to the marine environment A review of existing data. Revised in March 2017*, https://www.ivl.se/english/ivl/publications/publications/swedish-sources-and-pathways-for-microplastics-to-the-marine-environment.html. [45]

Marine Litter Solutions (2011), *Declaration of the Global Plastics Associations for Solutions on Marine Litter*. [23]

MEPEX (2014), *Sources of microplastic-pollution to the marine environment*, MEPEX Report for Norwegian Environment Agency. [58]

Mintenig, S. et al. (2019), "Low numbers of microplastics detected in drinking water from ground water sources", *Science of the Total Environment*, Vol. 648, pp. 631-635, http://dx.doi.org/10.1016/j.scitotenv.2018.08.178. [79]

Nelms, S. et al. (2018), "Investigating microplastic trophic transfer in marine top predators", *Environmental Pollution*, http://dx.doi.org/10.1016/j.envpol.2018.02.016. [105]

New Zealand (2017), *Waste Minimisation (Microbeads) Regulations 2017*. [133]

NIVA (2018), *Microplastics in road dust – characteristics, pathways and measures. Revised in 2020.*, Norwegian Institute for Water Research. [33]

Nizzetto, L., M. Futter and S. Langaas (2016), *Are Agricultural Soils Dumps for Microplastics of Urban Origin?*, American Chemical Society, http://dx.doi.org/10.1021/acs.est.6b04140. [31]

Obbard, R. et al. (2014), "Global warming releases microplastic legacy frozen in Arctic Sea ice", *Earth's Future*, Vol. 2/6, pp. 315-320, http://dx.doi.org/10.1002/2014EF000240. [63]

OECD (2020), *Non-exhaust Particulate Emissions from Road Transport: An Ignored Environmental Policy Challenge*, OECD Publishing, Paris, https://dx.doi.org/10.1787/4a4dc6ca-en. [139]

OECD (2018), *Improving Markets for Recycled Plastics: Trends, Prospects and Policy Responses*, OECD Publishing, Paris, https://dx.doi.org/10.1787/9789264301016-en. [119]

OECD (2017), *Diffuse Pollution, Degraded Waters: Emerging Policy Solutions*, OECD Studies on Water, OECD Pubilishing, Paris, https://doi.org/10.1787/9789264269064-en. [34]

OECD (2015), "Wastewater treatment", in *Environment at a Glance 2015: OECD Indicators*, OECD Publishing, Paris, https://dx.doi.org/10.1787/9789264235199-10-en. [26]

Oliveri Conti, G. et al. (2020), "Micro- and nano-plastics in edible fruit and vegetables. The first diet risks assessment for the general population", *Environmental Research*, Vol. 187, p. 109677, http://dx.doi.org/10.1016/j.envres.2020.109677. [109]

Pimentel, J., R. Avila and A. Lourenco (2008), "Respiratory disease caused by synthetic fibres: a new occupational disease.", *Thorax*, Vol. 30/2, pp. 204-219, http://dx.doi.org/10.1136/thx.30.2.204. [118]

PlasticsEurope (2017), *PlasticsEurope Operation Clean Sweep*, http://www.opcleansweep.eu/wp-content/uploads/2017/09/OCS_Report2017.pdf. [22]

Praagh, M., C. Hartman and E. Brandmyr (2019), *Microplastics in Landfill Leachates in the Nordic Countries*, Nordic Council of Ministers, Copenhagen, http://dx.doi.org/10.6027/TN2018-557. [44]

Prata, J. (2018), "Airborne microplastics: Consequences to human health?", *Environmental Pollution*, Vol. 234, pp. 115-126, https://doi.org/10.1016/j.envpol.2017.11.043. [117]

Procter, J. et al. (2019), "Smells good enough to eat: Dimethyl sulfide (DMS) enhances copepod ingestion of microplastics", *Marine Pollution Bulletin*, Vol. 138, pp. 1-6, http://dx.doi.org/10.1016/J.MARPOLBUL.2018.11.014. [102]

Ragusa, A. et al. (2021), "Plasticenta: First evidence of microplastics in human placenta", *Environ Int*, Vol. 146, p. 106274, http://dx.doi.org/10.1016/j.envint.2020.106274. [114]

Richardson, K. et al. (2018), "Understanding causes of gear loss provides a sound basis for fisheries management", *Marine Policy*, Vol. 96, pp. 278-284, http://dx.doi.org/10.1016/J.MARPOL.2018.02.021. [53]

Rillig, M. (2012), "Microplastic in terrestrial ecosystems and the soil?", *Environ. Sci. Technol.*, Vol. 46/12, pp. 6453-6454, http://dx.doi.org/10.1021/es302011r. [99]

Rochman, C. et al. (2019), "Rethinking microplastics as a diverse contaminant suite", *Environmental Toxicology and Chemistry*, doi: 10.1002/etc.4371, pp. 703-711, http://dx.doi.org/10.1002/etc.4371. [14]

SAPEA (2019), *A Scientific Perspective on Micro-Plastics in Nature and Society*, Science Advice for Policy by European Academics, http://dx.doi.org/10.26356/microplastics. [13]

Sato, T. et al. (2013), "Global, regional, and country level need for data on wastewater generation, treatment, and use", *Agricultural Water Management*, Vol. 130, pp. 1-13, http://dx.doi.org/10.1016/J.AGWAT.2013.08.007. [25]

Schmidt, C., T. Krauth and S. Wagner (2017), "Export of Plastic Debris by Rivers into the Sea", *Environmental Science & Technology*, Vol. 51/21, pp. 12246-12253, http://dx.doi.org/10.1021/acs.est.7b02368. [50]

Schymanski, D. et al. (2018), "Analysis of microplastics in water by micro-Raman spectroscopy: Release of plastic particles from different packaging into mineral water", *Water Research*, Vol. 129, pp. 154-162, http://dx.doi.org/10.1016/j.watres.2017.11.011. [80]

Smith, M. et al. (2018), *Microplastics in Seafood and the Implications for Human Health*, NLM (Medline), http://dx.doi.org/10.1007/s40572-018-0206-z. [115]

Talvitie, J. et al. (2017), "Solutions to microplastic pollution – Removal of microplastics from wastewater effluent with advanced wastewater treatment technologies", *Water Research*, Vol. 123, pp. 401-407, http://dx.doi.org/10.1016/j.watres.2017.07.005. [28]

TextileExchange (2020), *Preferred Fiber Materials - Market Report 2020*, TextileExchange, https://textileexchange.org/wp-content/uploads/2020/06/Textile-Exchange_Preferred-Fiber-Material-Market-Report_2020.pdf. [136]

The Ocean Cleanup (2019), *The Ocean Cleanup*, https://theoceancleanup.com/. [127]

Thompson, R. et al. (2004), "Lost at Sea: Where Is All the Plastic?", *Science*, Vol. 304/5672, p. 838, http://dx.doi.org/10.1126/science.1094559. [18]

UNEP (2018), *Mapping of global plastics value chain and plastics losses to the environment (with a particular focus on the marine environment)*, Ryberg, M., Laurent, A., Hauschild, M. [20]

UNEP (2016), *Global Waste Management Outlook*, United Nations, New York, https://dx.doi.org/10.18356/765baec0-en. [49]

UNEP (2016), *Marine plastic debris and microplastics. Global lessons and research to inspire action and guide policy change*, UNEP, http://hdl.handle.net/20.500.11822/7720. [41]

UNEP (2015), *Biodegradable plastics and marine litter : misconceptions, concerns and impacts on marine environments*, United Nations Environment Programme. Global Programme of Action for the Protection of the Marine Environment from Land-based Activities. [15]

United States (2015), *Microbead-Free Waters Act of 2015*. [134]

Van Cauwenberghe, L., M. Claessens and C. Janssen (2013), "Selective uptake of microplastics by a marine bivalve (Mytilus edulis)", *Communications in Agricultural and Applied Biological Sciences*, Vol. 78/1, pp. 25-27. [125]

Van Cauwenberghe, L. et al. (2015), "Microplastics are taken up by mussels (Mytilus edulis) and lugworms (Arenicola marina) living in natural habitats", *Environmental Pollution*, Vol. 199, pp. 10-17, http://dx.doi.org/10.1016/J.ENVPOL.2015.01.008. [126]

Van Cauwenberghe, L. and C. Janssen (2014), "Microplastics in bivalves cultured for human consumption", *Environmental Pollution*, Vol. 193, pp. 65-70, http://dx.doi.org/10.1016/j.envpol.2014.06.010. [106]

van Franeker, J. et al. (2011), "Monitoring plastic ingestion by the northern fulmar Fulmarus glacialis in the North Sea", *Environmental Pollution*, Vol. 159/10, pp. 2609-2615, http://dx.doi.org/10.1016/J.ENVPOL.2011.06.008. [98]

Van Sebille, E. et al. (2015), "A global inventory of small floating plastic debris", *Environmental Research Letters*, Vol. 10/12, http://dx.doi.org/10.1088/1748-9326/10/12/124006. [69]

Veerasingam, S. et al. (2016), "Influence of 2015 flood on the distribution and occurrence of microplastic pellets along the Chennai coast, India", *Marine Pollution Bulletin*, http://dx.doi.org/10.1016/j.marpolbul.2016.05.082. [37]

Verlis, K., M. Campbell and S. Wilson (2013), "Ingestion of marine debris plastic by the wedge-tailed shearwater Ardenna pacifica in the Great Barrier Reef, Australia", *Marine Pollution Bulletin*, Vol. 72/1, pp. 244-249, http://dx.doi.org/10.1016/J.MARPOLBUL.2013.03.017. [97]

Wagner, M. and S. Lambert (2018), *Freshwater Microplastics: Emerging Environmental Contaminants?*, The Handbook of Environmental Chemistry 58, http://dx.doi.org/1978-3-319-61615-5. [16]

Wang, W. et al. (2017), "Microplastics pollution in inland freshwaters of China: A case study in urban surface waters of Wuhan, China", *Science of the Total Environment*, Vol. 575, pp. 1369-1374, https://doi.org/10.1016/j.scitotenv.2016.09.213. [76]

Wessel, C. et al. (2016), "Abundance and characteristics of microplastics in beach sediments: Insights into microplastic accumulation in northern Gulf of Mexico estuaries", *Marine Pollution Bulletin*, Vol. 109/1, pp. 178-183, http://dx.doi.org/10.1016/j.marpolbul.2016.06.002. [64]

WHO (2019), *Microplastics in drinking water*, World Health Organisation. [81]

World Bank (2018), *What a Waste 2.0 : A Global Snapshot of Solid Waste Management to 2050.* [48]

World Bank (2017), *Population, total*, https://data.worldbank.org/indicator/SP.POP.TOTL. [46]

World Economic Forum (2016), "The New Plastics Economy: rethinking the future of plastics". [3]

Wright, S., R. Thompson and T. Galloway (2013), "The physical impacts of microplastics on marine organisms: A review", *Environmental Pollution*, Vol. 178, pp. 483-492, http://dx.doi.org/10.1016/J.ENVPOL.2013.02.031. [101]

WWAP (2017), *The United Nations world water development report 2017. Wastewater: the untapped resource*, United Nations World Water Assessment Programme. [24]

WWF (2019), *No Plastic in Nature: assessing plastic ingestion from nature to people*, Dalberg Advisors, http://www.newcastle.edu.au/. [113]

Zhang, G. and Y. Liu (2018), "The distribution of microplastics in soil aggregate fractions in southwestern China", *Science of The Total Environment*, Vol. 642, pp. 12-20, http://dx.doi.org/10.1016/J.SCITOTENV.2018.06.004. [84]

Zubris, K. and B. Richards (2005), "Synthetic fibers as an indicator of land application of sludge", *Environmental Pollution*, Vol. 138/2, pp. 201-211, http://dx.doi.org/10.1016/j.envpol.2005.04.013. [82]

Annex 1.A. Degradation definitions

Annex Table 1.A.1. Degradation definitions

Term	Definition
Degradation	The partial or complete breakdown of a polymer as a result of e.g. UV radiation, oxygen attack, biological attack. This implies alteration of the properties, such as discolouration, surface cracking and fragmentation
Biodegradation	Biological process of organic matter, which is completely or partially converted to water, CO2/methane, energy and new biomass by microorganisms (bacteria and fungi).
Mineralisation	Defined here, in the context of polymer degradation, as the complete breakdown of a polymer as a result of the combined abiotic and microbial activity, into CO2, water, methane, hydrogen, ammonia and other simple inorganic compounds
Biodegradable	Capable of being biodegraded.
Compostable	Capable of being biodegraded at elevated temperatures in soil under specified conditions and time scales, usually only encountered in an industrial composter (standards apply)
Oxo-degradable	Containing a pro-oxidant that induces degradation under favourable conditions. Complete breakdown of the polymers and biodegradation still have to be proven.

Source: (UNEP, 2015[15]), Biodegradable plastics and marine litter: misconceptions, concerns and impacts on marine environments

Notes

[1] The fate of microplastics washed off by stormwater is discussed separately in the next section.

[2] A list of degradability definitions is given in Annex 1.A.

[3] See e.g. US Code of Federal Regulations 40 CFR 258.61 1991 and EU Council Directive 1999/31/EC.

[4] In addition to being sources of degradation-based synthetic microfibres, lost or discarded fishing gear may also result in the continued catching of non-target species (including protected species) the entanglement of marine wildlife, and damage to natural habitats as well as fishing vessels (Richardson et al., 2018[53]).

[5] Notably, some publications assume that microplastics from road transport activity are largely transported into the marine environment. However, as discussed in more detail in Chapter 2, recent studies focusing on tyre and road wear emissions suggest that the road surface, nearby soil and water streams, and air are also primary sinks of microplastics.

[6] Digestive fragmentation has been suggested as an additional generation route for secondary microplastics, especially for smaller microplastics and nanoplastics (Dawson et al., 2018[140]).

[7] Large filter-feeding mammals need to swallow hundreds cubic meters of seawater per day in order to capture plankton. Thus, they are suspected to ingest large quantities of microplastics both directly and via trophic transfer from preys (Fossi et al., 2012[100]; Wright, Thompson and Galloway, 2013[101]).

[8] Additives may constitute between 1% and more than a half of the total weight content of plastics (OECD, 2018[119]).

[9] For instance, it is estimated that microplastics larger than 0.5 mm constitute only 8% of total plastic mass in the Great Pacific Garbage Patch (about 6.4 metric tons of microplastics), the large accumulation of floating plastics located in the North Pacific Ocean (Lebreton et al., 2018[52]).

[10] The EU ban on oxo-degradable plastics also seeks to minimise microplastics generation (EC, 2018[38]).

2 A typology of microplastics released from textiles and tyres

This chapter traces a typology for microplastics released from textile products and vehicle tyres. It outlines their generation mechanisms, presents knowledge over their fate and the associated environmental and human health risks and pinpoints key entry points for mitigation action.

2.1. Introduction

Microfibre shedding and tyre wear are processes regularly occurring during the use of textile products and vehicle tyres. As textiles are worn and washed, mechanical abrasion occurring in their structure causes the detachment and loss of fibres. Similarly, during normal transport activity, the friction between vehicle tyres and the road surface results in the abrasion of the tyre tread and the emission of particles. In general, the emission of microfibres and tyre wear particles may occur during (and be influenced by) all stages of the lifecycle of products, as summarised in Figure 2.1.

This Chapter summarises current knowledge on the characteristics, environmental fate, and environmental and human health impacts of textile-based microfibres (Section 2.2) and tyre-based microplastics (Section 2.3). Where the data is available, it provides an assessment of where in the lifecycle of products emissions occur and which are the key influencing factors.

Figure 2.1. Losses of microplastics at different stages of the lifecycle of tyres and textiles

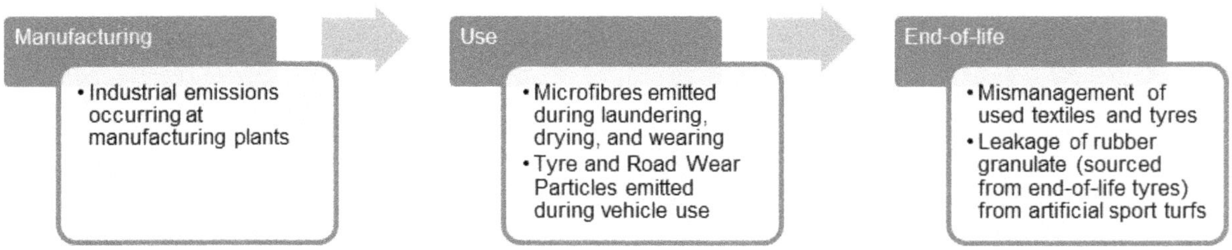

Source: Author

2.2. Emissions of textile-based microfibres: nature, drivers and consequences

The textile industry is considered one of the most polluting in the world. Harmful chemicals, high-energy use, water consumption, textile waste generation, transportation and the use of non-biodegradable packaging materials are responsible for the resource heavy and polluting lifecycle of textiles and clothing. The European Environment Agency (EEA) (2019[1]) estimates that, in the EU, supply chain pressures of clothing, footwear and household textiles are the fourth highest pressure category for the use of primary raw materials and water, second highest for land use and the fifth highest for greenhouse gas emissions. Overall, the apparel and footwear industries contribute to 8% of global GHG emissions (Quantis, 2018[2]).

In particular, the stages of textile manufacturing (detailed in Section 2.2.2) may bear high environmental consequences. About 3500 substances are used in textile production, of which 750 have been classified as hazardous for human health and 440 as hazardous for the environment (KEMI, 2014[3]). Fibre production and wet textile processing especially are associated with environmental pressures from high consumption of energy, non-renewable feedstock to make synthetic fibres, fertilisers to grow cotton, chemicals employed in dyeing and finishing treatments and water, as well as from land use (UNEP, 2020[4]).

The high and growing demand for resource input into textile manufacturing raises concerns over the environmental impacts that continued increases in production and consumption may have. Annual clothing sales are projected to more than triple and reach 160 Mt by 2050 (EMF, 2017[5]). The use of and demand for polyester-based clothing in particular has been growing exponentially since its creation and synthetic fibres currently account for two thirds of overall fibre input into textile and apparel production, as presented in Table 2.1. Approximately 59 Mt of plastics (15% of total global production) were employed in the textile manufacturing sector in 2015 (Geyer, Jambeck and Law, 2017[6]). Annual production of plastic-based clothing is expected to more than double between 2015 and 2050 (EMF, 2017[5]).

In this context, the release of microfibres from synthetic clothing is one emerging reason of concern. Synthetic microfibres have been reported in significant quantities at all depths of the marine environment (Browne et al., 2011[7]; Desforges et al., 2014[8]; Obbard et al., 2014[9]; Thompson et al., 2004[10]; Woodal et al., 2014[11]) as well as in marine organisms (Lusher, McHugh and Thompson, 2013[12]). In addition to the washing, wear and tear of synthetic clothing, microfibres sampled in the oceans may originate from a variety of other sources, such as the disintegration of fishing gear, ropes and packaging materials. Yet, the laundering of synthetic textile products alone is estimated to account for 7-35% of total microplastics releases (see Table 1.4).

Table 2.1. Overview of main textile types in production

Fibre type	Resource base	Textile type	% of total textile production
Natural	Plant-based	Cotton	23.2%
		Others: hemp, linen, etc.	5.9%
	Animal-based	Wool	1.0%
		Others: down, silk	<1.0%
Semi-synthetic	Cellulose-based	Viscose (rayon)	5.1%
		Others: Acetate, Lyocell, Modal, Cupro	1.3%
Synthetic	Petroleum-derived mostly	Polyester	52.2%
		Polyamide (nylon)	5.0%
		Others: acrylics, modacrylics, elastane, etc.	5.7%

Source: (TextileExchange, 2020[13])

2.2.1. Characteristics, fate and environmental and human health risks

Fibre shedding is a natural propensity of all fabrics. As textiles are produced and used, mechanical abrasion occurring in their structure causes the detachment and loss of fibres from fabrics. Fibre shedding may occur at (and be influenced by) all stages of the lifecycle of textile products, as follows:

- *Manufacturing*: it is likely that the emission of microfibres starts at the materials sourcing and manufacturing stages, although the extent of microfibre emissions is difficult to quantify with currently available data. Additionally, the choice of manufacturing practices is largely responsible for determining the tendency of fabrics to emit microfibres at later stages of their lifecycle.
- *Use*: wearing, washing, drying of textiles and other stages of maintenance and care may deteriorate the textile structure and contribute to microfibre shedding.
- *End-of-life*: it is possible that textiles also release microfibres at the end-of-life phase, if mismanaged into the environment, or possibly following reuse and recycling practices.

The mechanism and location of emission may determine the fate of the microfibres, as illustrated in Figure 2.2. Microfibres released from textiles enter marine and freshwaters mainly via municipal and industrial wastewaters and via dry and wet deposition. In OECD countries, conventional wastewater treatment technologies can be fairly effective at capturing a large percentage of the emitted fibres, yet, the sheer volumes of wastewaters processed imply that significant amounts of microfibres make their way into aquatic bodies. Once in the environment, synthetic microfibres are known to persist and accumulate, potentially leading to a number of ecological risks, as already discussed in Chapter 1. Microfibres (both synthetic and cellulose-based) have been largely sampled in oceans, freshwaters (Driedger et al., 2015[14]; Lahens et al., 2018[15]; Suaria et al., 2020[16]), as well as in soils where wastewater sludge has been applied (Liu et al., 2019[17]; Zhang and Liu, 2018[18]) and in air (Brahney et al., 2020[19]; Dris et al., 2016[20]).

Figure 2.2. Emission of microplastics during the lifecycle of textiles and relative pathways

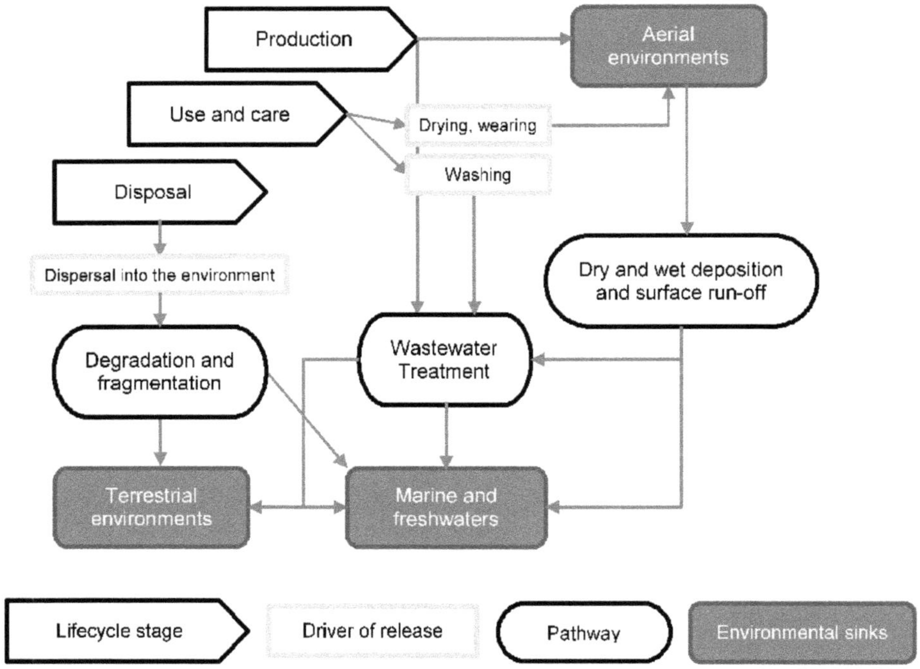

Source: Adapted from (Henry, Laitala and Klepp, 2019[21])

The presence of airborne microfibres that can be inhaled also adds to total human exposure. Textile microfibres, both cellulose-based and synthetic, have been sampled both in indoor (1-60 fibres/m3) and outdoor (0.3-1.5 fibres/m3) environments (Dris et al., 2017[22]). Recent simulations indicate that inhalation may commonly occur (Vianello et al., 2019[23]), potentially leading to inflammation and health problems (Gasperi et al., 2017[24]; Pauly et al., 1998[25]; Prata, 2018[26]). Chronic exposure to microfibres has shown to lead to a higher prevalence of respiratory irritation, chronic respiratory symptoms, restrictive pulmonary function abnormalities and possibly also to reproductive toxicity and carcinogenicity (Gasperi et al., 2017[24]; Goldberg and Thériault, 1994[27]; Zuskin, Valic and Bouhuys, 1976[28]; Pimentel, Avila and Lourenco, 2008[29]). Yet, available evidence mainly comes from research carried out in industrial settings and may not be representative of ordinary exposure to textile microfibres. Further research is required in order to close the persisting knowledge gaps, in particular to identify critical exposure levels at which adverse health effect may occur (Gasperi et al., 2017[24]).

A major reason of concern with regards to microfibre pollution relates to the potential for microfibres, both synthetic and cellulose-based, to act as transport media for chemical substances employed in textile manufacturing into the environment. These chemicals, and especially those employed during wet processing stages (e.g. finishing treatments, dyeing), bring substantial advantages to apparel products, such as increased durability and a larger range of dyeing colours (EMF, 2017[5]). Yet, certain chemicals employed in the industry are known or suspected to be associated with adverse health effects, such as carcinogenicity, hormone disruption and reproductive toxicity. Textile/apparel manufacturing practices, regular washing, as well as microfibre leakage may release these substances into the environment, potentially posing risks to aquatic ecosystems and human health.

The EU REACH Regulation classifies as Substances of Very High Concern (SVHCs) several chemicals that may be employed in textile, apparel and footwear manufacturing, such as polycyclic aromatic hydrocarbons (PAHs), chlorinated aromatic hydrocarbons, phthalates, azo-dyes and chlorinated and/or brominated flame retardants, perfluorooctane sulfonate (PFOS) and perfluorooctanoic acid (PFOA) (EU,

2006[30]; Istituto Superiore di Sanità, 2020[31]). n recent years, several regulatory efforts and industry-led initiatives have emerged to report the use of hazardous substances in textile manufacturing and minimise their releases, as detailed in Box 2.1. Yet, persisting gaps in transparency over the chemicals utilised during manufacturing create challenges for the adequate evaluation of the health hazards posed to ecosystems and human health (EMF, 2017[5]).

Box 2.1. Emerging legislation and industry-led initiatives to tackle the release of hazardous substances during the lifecycle of textile products

Fashion brands selling products in Europe and North America are subject to a number of restrictions on the chemical content of products. REACH Regulation 1907/2006 on the Registration, Evaluation, and Authorisation and Restriction of Chemicals restricts the use of substances identified as harmful (Substances of Very High Concern) in products manufactured in or imported into Europe. Similarly, in the US, the Toxic Substances Control Act (TSCA) requires companies to report, record and carry out testing on the chemical content of products placed on the market.

Further, as a response to emerging legislation and increasing public pressure, several voluntary industry-led initiatives were developed. Notably, the textile and apparel industry has developed the Zero Discharge of Hazardous Chemicals (ZDHC) Manufacturing Restricted Substances List (MRSL) to define a harmonised approach to managing harmful and hazardous chemicals in the sector. This evidence-based document provides a list of priority chemicals to be phased out and specifies a maximum concentration for each substance and serves as an industry-wide reference in multiple initiatives (ZDHC, 2015[32]). The OECD Due Diligence Guidance for the Garment and Footwear sector, for instance, recommends that companies adopt and implement an evidence-based common MRSL to address the risk of harmful chemicals in their products and supply chains (OECD, 2018[33]).

Cellulose-based fibres and the relevance of a holistic approach to microfibre pollution

Although cellulose-based (i.e. natural and semi-synthetic) fibres are expected to biodegrade quickly if released into aquatic media, emerging evidence suggests that these are commonly present in aquatic habitats (Dris et al., 2018[34]; Sanchez-Vidal et al., 2018[35]; Stanton et al., 2019[36]) and wildlife species (Compa et al., 2018[37]; Remy et al., 2015[38] Lusher, McHugh and Thompson, 2013[12]). Recent studies suggest that past research may have largely overlooked their presence of cellulose-based microfibres in the environment, potentially also leading to an overestimation of the contribution of synthetic textiles to marine microplastics pollution (Suaria et al., 2020[16]). In fact, there seems to be a considerable mismatch between the share of fibres in textile production (of which over two thirds are synthetic) and the types of microfibres polluting the environment, with 60-80% of microfibres sampled in the oceans and in marine organisms being of cellulosic origin (Suaria et al., 2020[16]).

The widespread occurrence of cellulose-based fibres in the environment calls for further research with reliable characterisation of the polymer in order to assess the occurrence, degree of persistence and toxicity of different types of microfibres present in the environment. At the same time, current evidence (and uncertainties) may justify taking a holistic approach to microfibre mitigation, as characterised by two elements: a) a comprehensive and life-cycle assessment of the environmental impacts of textiles and b) a focus on finding solutions to mitigate risks associated with microfibre shedding (for all textile types). This is for several reasons:

- It is possible that the risks associated with microfibre pollution may not be limited to synthetic fibres. As indicated above, knowledge gaps persist with regards to the degree of persistence and accumulation of non-plastic fibres in the environment. Further, cellulose-based fibres may also act as a transfer media for harmful chemicals. For natural fibres, it has been speculated that a more rapid biodegradation may increase the bioavailability of chemical additives once microfibres are ingested by aquatic organisms (Zhao, Zhu and Li, 2016[39]). For airborne microfibres, it has also been suggested that the adverse effects of chronic exposure to cellulose-based fibres may not be significantly different than for synthetic ones (Prata, 2018[26]).

- Determining whether clothing sheds microfibres of synthetic content is not straightforward in practice. Blended textiles (e.g. polyester/cotton blends) are very common (for instance to enhance certain characteristics of the final product) and fabrics made out of natural fibres are often treated with synthetic coatings during wet processing.
- More broadly, there is a strong case for finding ways to work with synthetic materials, as substitution away from synthetic fibres in textile and apparel manufacturing may not be a viable microplastics mitigation solution at scale. Natural alternatives are limited and cannot always provide the same performance capabilities of synthetic materials. Further, the lifecycle of textiles produced from natural fibres also bears significant adverse consequences on the environment, in particular in terms of high energy and water consumption, land use and the release of chemicals harmful to the environment (UNEP, 2017[40]).

2.2.2. Industrial emissions occurring during manufacturing

The stages of textile and garment manufacturing are associated with high risks for environmental and climate impacts. Industrial emissions from textile manufacturing plants have been long scrutinised, in particular with regards to the release of potentially harmful chemicals into the environment, such as certain flame retardants and chemical coatings applied to textile products during manufacturing. As the issue of microplastics pollution gained increasing scientific and policy attention, recently concerns have also emerged over the contribution of industrial emissions to microfibre pollution.

The stages of textile and apparel manufacturing are detailed in Table 2.2. Fabrics are manufactured from fibres or yarns, i.e. continuous strands of fibres, via different technologies. Several wet processing activities may be performed on fabrics to enhance the appearance and performance of the final product. These include preparatory treatments, dyeing processes and functional mechanical or chemical finishing treatments. The make-up is the last step before selling in retail or whole trade and consumer use.

Several stages of textile and garment manufacturing may contribute to the emission of microfibres into sewage waters or into the surrounding aerial environment. In particular, the processes involved in fibre processing, yarn manufacturing and fabric construction are known to lead to fibre mechanical stress and material losses (WRAP, 2019[41]). Fibre emission may also occur during the production of garments (e.g. during cutting, sewing and the application of finishing treatments), as a result of the removal of impurities and sizing, although this is less documented. WRAP (2019[41]) estimates that in the UK 168 thousand tonnes of material is lost each year during the production of clothing (per 1.1 Mt of clothing consumed annually), although it is unclear what percentage of this material loss is emitted as microfibres.

Recently, research has also been undertaken to quantify microfibres released into sewage waters. Available evidence is very limited, but suggests that textile manufacturing plants regularly emit microplastics into wastewaters. A study conducted in Sweden detected concentrations of 100-450 microfibres per litre of industrial effluent from five textile production facilities (Jönsson and Landin, 2018[42]). The detected microfibres were mainly of synthetic origin, although cotton and viscose fibres were also reported in large quantities for certain production plants. Research conducted in China found average concentrations of 16-334 (synthetic and natural-based) microfibres per litre in wastewaters discharged from textile printing and dyeing facilities (Xu et al., 2018[43]).

Although the contribution of the textile and apparel manufacturing stages to overall microfibre releases is difficult to assess due to a lack of reliable data and monitoring, there are concerns that this might be substantial. Firstly, considering the magnitude of the textile and apparel industry and the amounts of wastewaters being discharged during manufacturing, it is likely that even modest amounts of microplastics being released per litre of industrial effluent could result in significant amounts of fibres entering the environment. Secondly, the majority of textile and apparel production takes place in emerging economies, where the lower rates of connectedness to wastewater infrastructure and the lower levels of treatment (relatively to OECD countries) might potentially imply that a higher share of the industrial microfibre emissions reach water bodies.[1]

Table 2.2. Key steps in the production of textiles and garments

Relevant industrial sectors	Manufacturing stage	Description and examples of processes employed
Chemical industry, farmers and growers of raw natural materials	Raw material and fibre production	This stage includes the extraction/production and processing of fibres, which are the raw material used in the manufacture of textiles. They are usually differentiated according to several characteristics, such as strength, length, fineness, elasticity and the presence of irregularities.
Textile sector	Yarn formation	Yarns are usually formed from filament and staple fibres via spinning. Texturizing can be carried out on man-made filament fibres to simulate the appearance of natural fibres
	Fabric manufacturing	Fabrics are usually formed via *weaving*, i.e. the interlacing of yarns, or *knitting*, i.e. the interlocking in series of loops made from one or more yarns.
	Textile finishing[1]	Textile finishing includes a series of processes aimed at enhancing the appearance, durability and serviceability of fabrics. *Preparatory treatments* are carried out to remove impurities and prepare the fabric for following treatments. Examples are desizing (a removal of the sizing agents), the removal of impurities, washing, scouring (treatment with hot alkali) and bleaching. *Dyeing* is the process of colouring textiles as a whole. *Printing* applies colour only to specific areas to create patterns. *Functional finishing processes* achieve additional effects and characteristics of the textile. *Mechanical* finishes may be employed to improve the smoothness, roughness, or shining characteristics, while *chemical* finishes may add softening, water repellent, antimicrobial, or fire retardant properties.
Apparel sector	Garment fabrication	The *make-up* of apparel products is the last step before these are ready to be distributed and used by consumers. Commonly employed processes included the cutting and sewing of fabrics and the assembling of textile parts and other additional components.
Brands, retail sector	Product distribution and retail	Products are warehoused and sold

Note: 1: Colouring and finishing treatments can be carried out at all steps in the textile chain, but are usually done on fabrics.
Source: Adapted from (OECD, 2019[44])

2.2.3. Emissions occurring during use

The use phase has been identified as a major source of microfibre emissions. Several stages of the use phase – i.e. wearing, washing and drying – may contribute to mechanical abrasion occurring in the structure of fabrics and lead to the detachment of fibres. Current research has focused on the laundering of synthetic garments, where the series of mechanical and chemical actions aimed at cleaning textile products contribute to the generation and emission of loose fibres.[2] Several series of laboratory washing tests have been carried out in recent years to measure the degree of microfibre shedding from garments with different characteristics and under different washing conditions. These generally tend to employ a variety of test conditions and methods for microfibre measurement, which limits the comparability of studies and the generalisation of findings (Jönsson et al., 2018[45]). Yet, test washings have allowed the identification of certain factors that may lead to a higher or lower fibre shedding during laundering processes. These can be grouped in two categories:

- *Textile and garment characteristics.* The microfibre shedding rate during use is dependent on the degree of fibre strength and resistance to abrasion of the product. These are influenced by a variety of design and manufacturing factors, including textile composition and fibre characteristics, yarn and textile structures and garment manufacturing processes. For instance, polyester fleece and microfleece fabrics are known for being particularly prone to fibre shedding: a single fleece jacket may shed up to 250,000 fibres per laundry wash (Hartline et al., 2016[46]).

- *Product maintenance and care*. In general, laundering methods that minimise the degree of mechanical abrasion (e.g. low-temperature laundry washes and the use of softener liquid) are associated with a preservation of the integrity of textile yarns and a lower fibre shedding. The type of washing machine may also influence the degree of mechanical stress occurring in the textile structure. Drying practices, and tumble drying in particular, are likely to also influence the emission of microfibres.

Although knowledge gaps persist with regards to the relative importance of factors driving microfibre release, several mitigation options implementable at the production and use stage of textile products can already be drawn based on the available knowledge. These are presented and assessed in Chapter 3.

2.3. Emissions of tyre-based microplastics: nature, drivers and consequences

Microplastics may be emitted at all stages of the tyre lifecycle, as follows:

- *Manufacturing*: although it is possible that microplastics are generated and released as by-products during the manufacturing of tyres, there is a lack of data to verify whether this is the case. Also, manufacturing practices influence the tendency of tyres to undergo abrasion during regular use.
- *Use*: Tyre and Road Wear Particles (TRWP) are emitted during regular vehicle use due to the friction occurring between tyres and the road surface;
- *End-of-life management*: the mismanagement of tyres into the environment may potentially lead to microplastics generation and leakage. Also, certain recycling options for end-of-life tyres (e.g. the use of tyre rubber granulate used as infill in artificial sport turfs) potentially constitute a further source of microplastics into the environment.

2.3.1. Tyre and Road Wear Particles

Characteristics, fate and environmental and human health risks

During normal transport activity, the friction between vehicle tyres and the road surface results in the abrasion of the tyre tread and the emission of particles. As road pavement materials tend to also agglomerate within the tyre material, the emitted particles are generally referred to as Tyre and Road Wear Particles (TRWP). In general, TRWP are composed of a complex mixture of tyre tread material (e.g. synthetic and natural rubber, silica, oil, carbon black, sulphur compounds, zinc oxide), road pavement material (e.g. polymer modified bitumen), road marking[3] particles, brake wear particles and other airborne elements that commonly deposit on pavements (Kreider et al., 2010[47]).

Recent studies have attempted to quantify emissions of TRWP from road vehicles occurring during road transport activity, based either on emission factors for different vehicle categories and road transport activity data, or from average tyre wear rates and data on the number of tyres in use (Kole et al., 2015[48]; Lassen et al., 2016[49]; Wagner et al., 2018[50]; Magnusson et al., 2016[51]). Although estimates of the contribution of tyre wear to microplastics pollution differ, approximately 0.81 kg of emissions per capita are released from vehicle tyres annually, with the highest per capita releases occurring in the United States (Kole et al., 2017[52]). National emissions may differ based on the local context: for instance, in Germany the largest contributions to TRWP emissions come from heavy vehicles (trucks, buses) and driving on highways, while in the United States total emissions from passenger cars and trucks are roughly equivalent, and two-thirds of emissions occur in urban environments, mainly due to the higher urban travel distances in North America compared to European countries (Wagner et al., 2018[50])

At the point of emission, TRWP may become suspended in air or deposit on road surfaces and nearby soil. Additionally, the action of rain events may disperse or flush emitted TRWP into nearby water streams. The physical characteristics of the emitted particles, and in particular their size, may be important determinants of their environmental fate (Unice et al., 2019[53]). TRWP are generally elongated in shape (i.e., cigar-shaped) and are well below 1 mm in length[4] (Unice et al., 2019[54]). A portion of TRWP (1-10% in mass) is emitted in the fine particulate matter size range (< 10 µm) and contributes to ambient air pollution (see Box 2.2). Larger particles are typically deposited on the road surface or on nearby soil. The majority of TRWP tend to be heavier than water (particles have an average density of 1.8 g/cm3) (Unice et al., 2019[54]) and so they may be prone to sedimentation if dispersed into aquatic environments (Parker-Jurd et al., 2019[55]; NIVA, 2018[56]). It is also relevant to note that, following release into the environment, TRWP may undergo ageing processes that affect their physical and chemical properties and ultimately their fate. Recent studies suggest that further research is required to understand the extent of these changes in the composition and properties of TRWP in order to accurately model their environmental fate (Klöckner et al., 2020[57]; Unice et al., 2015[58]).

Tracing the fate of the emitted TRWP is crucial in order to assess exposure routes and the associated health risks, as well as to identify potential hotspots where the implementation of end-of-pipe capture solutions could be prioritised. A number of factors may influence how the particles will spread into different environmental media following emission. Airborne particles can either be deposited on the road surface, or be transported via wet and dry deposition, potentially far away from point sources (Parker-Jurd et al., 2019[55]; Magnusson et al., 2020[59]). For instance, it has been suggested that atmospheric transport may significantly contribute to the long-distance transport of airborne TRWP and other non-exhaust emissions into the marine environment and remote regions such as the Arctic, where the particles may possibly pose additional climatic risks of increased light-absorption and enhanced snow and ice melting (Evangeliou et al., 2020[60]).

Available modelling estimates of the spatial distribution of TRWP emissions suggest that a large portion of the emitted particles is expected to deposit on roads or in nearby soil (Figure 2.3). Road runoff, wind and street cleaning may contribute to the removal of these larger particles from the road and their potential dispersal into the environment. Where roads are not connected to stormwater systems, TRWP will drain off with rain into adjacent land or water streams (Andersson-Sköld et al., 2020[61]). Where stormwater systems are present, the fate of TRWP will depend on the specific treatment technologies in place (i.e. direct discharge into a recipient, stormwater treatment facilities, or a WWTP). The amount of TRWP reaching surface waters largely depends on the local conditions (e.g. presence of drains for road runoff, the type of road, the intensity of rainfall). Where urban surface runoff is collected and treated prior to discharge, approximately 11-22% of TRWP is expected to reach surface waters directly or via the sewerage system (Verschoor et al., 2016[62]; Wagner et al., 2018[50]). The type of road infrastructure may also affect the fate of the emitted particles: for instance, in Netherlands half of the emitted particles remain incorporated into porous asphalt, a type of road pavement widely employed in Dutch highways that is prone to absorbing particles (Verschoor et al., 2016[62]).[5]

Only a limited number of studies have looked at the environmental presence of TRWP, typically in road dust and stormwater runoff. A key barrier to larger and more reliable environmental quantification of TRWP is the availability of appropriate analytical methods. Conventional methods used for the sampling and characterisation of microplastics are not easily adaptable to TRWP, while methods well-adapted to TRWP are costly and time-consuming (Andersson-Sköld et al., 2020[61]). There are concerns that inadequate and different analytical methods for sampling and characterisation may be underestimating the amount of (or falsely confirming presence of) TRWP in the natural environment and their overall contribution to microplastics pollution (Parker-Jurd et al., 2019[55]). Harmonised methods for sampling, sample preparation and analysis of TRWP are required to allow for further environmental sampling and for better consistency and comparability between different studies.

Figure 2.3. Overview of available studies modelling the environmental fate of TRWP

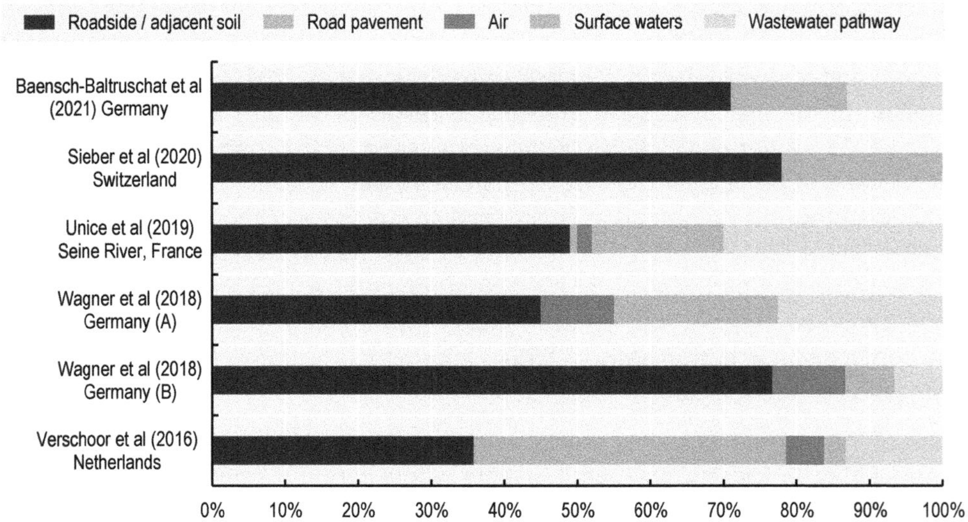

Notes: Comparisons are difficult to make as different studies included different sets of environmental compartments and/or had different objectives. All studies modelled annual emissions of TRWP. Sieber et al. (2020[63]) also calculated the accumulation of tyre-based microplastics for Switzerland over a period of 30 years (1988–2018) and included the emissions and fate of microplastics lost from artificial sports turfs. Baensch-Baltruschat et al. (2021[64]) did not include airborne emissions (which they considered to be 5% of total emissions). Wagner et al. (2018[50]) proposed two scenarios: scenario (A) assumes that 50% of TRWP deposited on road surfaces are mobilised via surface runoff, while scenario (B) assumes that only 15% are mobilised.

Source: Author's elaboration based on (Baensch-Baltruschat et al., 2021[64]; Sieber, Kawecki and Nowack, 2020[63]; Unice et al., 2019[54]; Verschoor et al., 2016[62]; Wagner et al., 2018[50])

Available microplastics surveys indicate that tyre wear may be a significant contributor to the emission of microplastics into surface waters, potentially to a larger extent than previously estimated. A study completed around the San Francisco Bay area found that nearly half of all microplastics contained in stormwater discharge were suspected TRWP (Sutton et al., 2019[65]). A recent study conducted in the United Kingdom found a large presence of TRWP at key entry points into the marine environment (wastewater treatment effluent, stormwater runoff and wind), possibly several orders of magnitude greater than that of synthetic microfibres (Parker-Jurd et al., 2019[55]). Overall, further field data is needed to improve our understanding of the transport processes and sinks of TRWP and to validate and complement the available model estimates.

Only a limited number of studies have assessed the potential environmental and human health impacts of TRWP and further research is required to adequately assess risks. Some of the chemicals used in the manufacture of tyres, road marking products and polymer modified bitumen are hazardous to human health and the environment, however there is limited knowledge about the extent to which these substances are released from microplastics (Andersson-Sköld et al., 2020[61]). Research that informs toxicological considerations is based on the use of TWP, i.e. tyre wear particles that are created in laboratory conditions, rather than particles sampled from the environment.[6] The majority of available studies assessed the (acute and chronic) toxicity of leachates from TWP on aquatic organisms: while some showed no toxicity on freshwater and sediment dwelling species (Marwood et al., 2011[66]; Panko et al., 2013[67]), others observed adverse health effects (Halle et al., 2020[68]; Tian et al., 2021[69]). As with other microplastics, the ingestion of TRWP is a key exposure route for aquatic wildlife (Khan, Halle and Palmqvist, 2019[70]; Redondo-Hasselerharm et al., 2018[71]; Wik et al., 2009[72]), however large knowledge gaps persist with regards to the potential health hazards posed. A recent study by Halle et al. (2021[73]) showed that TRWP in the aquatic environment may affect acute mortality and long-term growth.

Overall, further research is required both to assess the toxicity of the ingested particles and to improve our understanding of the associated hazards in realistic environmental scenarios (Halle et al., 2020[68]). With regards to risks for human health, the most researched exposure route for adverse health impacts is the inhalation of non-exhaust emissions, as outlined in Box 2.2. However, little is known with regards to the risks posed to human health by TRWP via ingestion, relatively to other microplastics.

Box 2.2. Impacts of non-exhaust emissions on air quality and human health

Air pollution is a major environmental and human health risk, to which road transport emissions significantly contribute. Emissions of particulate matter (PM) from motor vehicles originate from two main sources: tailpipe exhaust and the degradation of vehicle parts and the road surface (OECD, 2020[74]). The latter are defined as non-exhaust PM emissions and comprise all airborne particulate emissions generated by the wear of vehicle parts (mainly tyres and brake pads) and of the road surface, as well as by the resuspension of road dust.

Tyre wear significantly contributes to non-exhaust emissions and air pollution. Estimates of the contribution of tyre tread wear to total particulate matter range from 0.1 to 10% for PM10 and 1–7% for PM2.5 (Andersson-Sköld et al., 2020[61]; Panko, Kreider and Unice, 2018[75]). Additional contributors to non-exhaust emissions are the wear of road surfaces and of brake pads and the resuspension of particles on the road surface (OECD, 2020[74]). Brake wear particles are emitted as a result of the abrasion occurring between stationary brake pads and the vehicle rotor during braking. They tend to be smaller in size and approximately 50% of brake wear particles become airborne at the point of emission (Grigoratos and Martini, 2015[76]).

It is now well established that the inhalation of fine PM and the associated metals and combustion products (PAHs) negatively affects human health. Exposure to PM, and in particular to PM2.5, is associated with increased risks of cardiovascular, respiratory and developmental conditions, as well as an increased risk of overall mortality (OECD, 2020[74]). The oxidative stress induced by the metals and organic compounds found in PM emissions is considered to be a main biological mechanism responsible for these negative health impacts (OECD, 2020[74]). In light of the hazards posed by certain polycyclic aromatic hydrocarbons (PAHs), the EU has placed a restriction on the use of 8 PAHs in tyres and extender oils via the REACH regulation (Annex XVII.50).

Influence factors

Tyre abrasion can cause an overall mass loss of up to 10% during the lifetime of a tyre (Grigoratos et al., 2018[77]). A variety of local factors may influence the amount of tyre tread material lost per kilometre travelled. These can be grouped in four categories (ETRMA, 2018[78]):

- *tyre characteristics*: size, tread depth, construction, tyre pressure and temperature, contact patch area, chemical composition, accumulated mileage;
- *vehicle characteristics*: weight and size, distribution of loads, location of driving wheels, wheel alignment, engine power, mechanical/electronic braking system, suspension type and conditions;
- *driving behaviour*: speed, acceleration/deceleration, frequency and extent of braking, cornering;
- *road surface characteristics*: pavement type, porosity, maintenance, weather conditions.

While current knowledge does not allow for a precise estimate of tyre wear rates, some general trends can be derived with regards to the influence of different factors on tyre wear. For instance, it is estimated that these are highest for heavier vehicles (e.g. buses, trucks and lorries) than for passenger cars. Further research is required in particular to assess and quantify the relative impact of each influence factor on tyre wear in real-life conditions. Several mitigation options implementable at the production and use stage of tyres can already be drawn based on the available knowledge over the drivers of TRWP emission. These are discussed in Chapter 3.

2.3.2. Management of end-of-life tyres (ELTs)

Tyres are typically replaced when they are no longer suitable for use due to wear or damage. Tyres may be re-used when they have been only partially worn and sufficient residual tread depth remains, or otherwise may be retreaded into new tyres. When neither reuse nor retreading is possible, scrap or End-of-Life Tyres (i.e. tyres which can no longer be used for their original purpose) may be employed for material recovery and civil engineering applications, or incinerated for energy recovery (WBCSD, 2019[79]).

Dumping and improper disposal of used tyres remain an issue in several countries. In general, the degree of recovery and the performance of ELT management is dependent on the existence and level of maturity of formal management systems. Landfilling of old tyres is illegal in several OECD countries (e.g. in the European Union, the US State of California)[7]. Generally, landfilling is considered an undesirable disposal option for tyres due to their slow degradation, the potential to cause damage to landfill liners and the intrinsic value of tyre materials. Yet, it is likely that in several emerging economies where formal management schemes are not in place, significant amounts of tyres are abandoned, landfilled, or stockpiled. In addition to wasting potentially valuable resources, the mismanagement of tyres contributes to several local environmental and human health risks, such as the risk of stockpile fires, the potential for old tyres to act as a breeding ground for disease-carrying mosquitos and hazards associated with chemical leachate.

Several OECD countries have introduced ELT management schemes to facilitate the separate collection and environmentally sound handling of used tyres, such as Extended Producer Responsibility systems and take-back obligation schemes. These resulted in an overall improvement of collection rates for used tyres, as well as fostered the development of the ELT recycling industry and the proliferation of solutions to close material loops in the sector. For instance, in the Flanders, the EPR system in place has contributed to decreasing the amounts of dumped tyres almost to zero (OECD, 2016[80]). Further, the regular flow of used tyres guaranteed by the management scheme in place has allowed for the development of a market for recycling tyres and tyre materials and a reduction of total tyre materials disposed via incineration from energy recovery.

In recent years, concerns emerged with regards to the potential for microplastics to leak from certain material recovery applications for ELTs. This is discussed below.

Leakage of rubber granulate from artificial sport turfs

A common method for material recovery from end-of-life tyres is shredding for the production of rubber granulate, i.e. small particles to be used in a variety of industrial applications. Rubber granulate can be manufactured from ELTs as well as from rubber derived from other sources (e.g. virgin elastomer alternatives such as EPDM rubber and TPE) and usually has a size between 0.5 and 2.5 mm (Eunomia, 2018[81]). A common application of rubber granulate is use as infill for artificial sport turfs. The use of rubber granulate as infill material offers several advantages compared to natural alternatives, such as durability, resistance to varying weather conditions, good shock absorbance and safety characteristics, low costs, as well as a lower need for virgin materials (Magnusson et al., 2016[51]).

Some recent studies have pointed to artificial turfs as an additional source of microplastics discharge into surrounding soil and surface drains, due to the emission of rubber granulate mainly caused by transport off the pitch during use (e.g. by athletes) or during maintenance and the effect of weather events (RIVM, 2018[82]). Initial estimates for Sweden found that approximately 2-3 tonnes of microplastics per football field may be lost yearly, suggesting that rubber infill may constitute a major source of microplastics pollution (Kole et al., 2017[52]). It is now recognised that several factors influence the overall volume of infill material (e.g. compaction) and that past figures may have largely overestimated the extent of microplastics leakage from artificial sport turfs. Still, a more recent study conducted in Denmark estimated the infill material loss (due to contact with athletes, snow clearance and rain water discharges) to be 300-730 kg/year per field (Løkkegaard, Malmgren-Hansen and Nilsson, 2018[83]). For Sweden, new calculations estimate that around 550 kg/year from an average football field, which would imply yearly national losses of 475 tonnes of microplastics (Swedish EPA, 2019[84]).

In response to recent findings, several OECD countries have mandated research projects and calls for evidence to fill knowledge gaps on the composition, leakage, exposure pathways and potential hazards of rubber granulate used in artificial sport pitches. A recent mass flow study in Switzerland demonstrated that about 3% of rubber-based particles entering the environment is released as granules (and 97% as TRWP) (Sieber, Kawecki and Nowack, 2020[63]). Further research is required to better assess the environmental risks associated to the use of rubber granulate as infill material in sport pitches, and in particular to further investigate the potential for release of hazardous substances via ELT-derived rubber granulate (ANSES, 2018[85]). An additional source of microplastics pollution which also requires further investigation is the use of rubber granulate in moulded rubber granule surfaces, such as fall protections and multicourts present in playgrounds.

References

Andersson-Sköld, Y. et al. (2020), *Microplastics from tyre and road wear - A literature review*, Swedish National Road and Transport Research Institute (VTI). [61]

ANSES (2018), *Scientific and technical support on the possible risks related to the use of materials derived from the recycling of used tyres in synthetic sports grounds and similar uses*. [85]

Baensch-Baltruschat, B. et al. (2021), “Tyre and road wear particles - A calculation of generation, transport and release to water and soil with special regard to German roads”, *Science of The Total Environment*, Vol. 752/141939, https://doi.org/10.1016/j.scitotenv.2020.141939. [64]

Brahney, J. et al. (2020), “Plastic rain in protected areas of the United States”, *Science*, Vol. 368/6496, p. 1257, http://dx.doi.org/10.1126/science.aaz5819. [19]

Browne, M. et al. (2011), “Accumulation of microplastic on shorelines woldwide: Sources and sinks”, *Environmental Science and Technology*, Vol. 45/21, pp. 9175-9179, http://dx.doi.org/10.1021/es201811s. [7]

Compa, M. et al. (2018), “Ingestion of microplastics and natural fibres in Sardina pilchardus (Walbaum, 1792) and Engraulis encrasicolus (Linnaeus, 1758) along the Spanish Mediterranean coast”, *Marine Pollution Bulletin*, Vol. 128, pp. 89-96, https://doi.org/10.1016/j.marpolbul.2018.01.009. [37]

Desforges, J. et al. (2014), “Widespread distribution of microplastics in subsurface seawater in the NE Pacific Ocean”, *Marine Pollution Bulletin*, Vol. 79/1-2, pp. 94-99, http://dx.doi.org/10.1016/j.marpolbul.2013.12.035. [8]

Driedger, A. et al. (2015), *Plastic debris in the Laurentian Great Lakes: A review*, http://dx.doi.org/10.1016/j.jglr.2014.12.020. [14]

Dris, R. et al. (2017), “A first overview of textile fibers, including microplastics, in indoor and outdoor environments”, *Environmental Pollution*, Vol. 221, pp. 453-458, http://dx.doi.org/10.1016/j.envpol.2016.12.013. [22]

Dris, R. et al. (2018), "Synthetic and non-synthetic anthropogenic fibers in a river under the impact of Paris Megacity: Sampling methodological aspects and flux estimations", *Science of The Total Environment*, Vol. 618, pp. 157-164, https://doi.org/10.1016/j.scitotenv.2017.11.009. [34]

Dris, R. et al. (2016), "Synthetic fibers in atmospheric fallout: A source of microplastics in the environment?", *Marine Pollution Bulletin*, Vol. 104/1-2, pp. 290-293, http://dx.doi.org/10.1016/j.marpolbul.2016.01.006. [20]

EEA (2019), *Textiles in Europe's circular economy*. [1]

EMF (2017), *A New Textile Economy: Redesigning Fashion's Future*, Ellen Macarthur Foundation, http://www.ellenmacarthurfoundation.org/publications. [5]

ETRMA (2018), *Way Forward Report*. [78]

EU (2006), *REACH Regulation 1907/2006 on the Registration, Evaluation, and Authorisation and Restriction of Chemicals*. [30]

Eunomia (2018), "Investigating options for reducing releases in the aquatic environment of microplastics emitted by (but not intentionally added in) products - Interim Report", *Report for DG Environment of the European Commission*, p. 335, http://dx.doi.org/10.1002/lsm.22016. [81]

Evangeliou, N. et al. (2020), "Atmospheric transport is a major pathway of microplastics to remote regions", *Nature Communications*, Vol. 11/1, p. 3381, http://dx.doi.org/10.1038/s41467-020-17201-9. [60]

Gasperi, J. et al. (2017), "Microplastics in air: Are we breathing it in?", *Current Opinion in Environmental Science & Health*, Vol. 1, pp. 1-5, http://dx.doi.org/10.1016/j.coesh.2017.10.002. [24]

Geyer, R., J. Jambeck and K. Law (2017), "Production, use, and fate of all plastics ever made", *Science Advances*, Vol. 3/7, p. e1700782, http://dx.doi.org/10.1126/sciadv.1700782. [6]

Goldberg, M. and G. Thériault (1994), "Retrospective cohort study of workers of a synthetic textiles plant in quebec: II. Colorectal cancer mortality and incidence", *American Journal of Industrial Medicine*, doi: 10.1002/ajim.4700250613, pp. 909-922, http://dx.doi.org/10.1002/ajim.4700250613. [27]

Grigoratos, T. et al. (2018), "Experimental investigation of tread wear and particle emission from tyres with different treadwear marking", *Atmospheric Environment*, Vol. 182, pp. 200-212, https://doi.org/10.1016/j.atmosenv.2018.03.049. [77]

Grigoratos, T. and G. Martini (2015), "Brake wear particle emissions: a review", *Environmental Science and Pollution Research*, Vol. 22/4, pp. 2491-2504, http://dx.doi.org/10.1007/s11356-014-3696-8. [76]

Halle, L. et al. (2021), "Tire wear particle and leachate exposures from a pristine and road-worn tire to Hyalella azteca: Comparison of chemical content and biological effects", *Aquatic Toxicology*, Vol. 232, p. 105769, http://dx.doi.org/10.1016/j.aquatox.2021.105769. [73]

Halle, L. et al. (2020), *Ecotoxicology of micronized tire rubber: Past, present and future considerations*, Elsevier B.V., http://dx.doi.org/10.1016/j.scitotenv.2019.135694. [68]

Hartline, N. et al. (2016), "Microfiber Masses Recovered from Conventional Machine Washing of New or Aged Garments", *Environ. Sci. Technol.*, Vol. 50, p. 11532−11538, https://doi.org/10.1021/acs.est.6b03045. [46]

Henry, B., K. Laitala and I. Klepp (2019), "Microfibres from apparel and home textiles: Prospects for including microplastics in environmental sustainability assessment", *Science of The Total Environment*, Vol. 652, pp. 483-494, https://doi.org/10.1016/j.scitotenv.2018.10.166. [21]

Istituto Superiore di Sanità (2020), *Rapporti ISTISAN 20/10 - Chimica, moda e salute.* [31]

Jönsson, C. and R. Landin (2018), *Report no. 18004. Investigation of the occurrence of microplastics from the waste water at five different textile production facilities in Sweden*, Swerea IVF. [42]

Jönsson, C. et al. (2018), "Microplastics Shedding from Textiles—Developing Analytical Method for Measurement of Shed Material Representing Release during Domestic Washing", *Sustainability*, Vol. 10/7, p. 2457, http://dx.doi.org/10.3390/su10072457. [45]

KEMI (2014), *Chemicals in textiles – Risks to human health and the environment*, http://www.kemi.se/files/8040fb7a4f2547b7bad522c399c0b649/report6-14-chemicals-in-textiles.pdf (accessed on 26 November 2019). [3]

Khan, F., L. Halle and A. Palmqvist (2019), "Acute and long-term toxicity of micronized car tire wear particles to Hyalella azteca", *Aquatic Toxicology*, Vol. 213, p. 105216, http://dx.doi.org/10.1016/j.aquatox.2019.05.018. [70]

Klöckner, P. et al. (2020), "Characterization of tire and road wear particles from road runoff indicates highly dynamic particle properties", *Water Research*, Vol. 185, p. 116262, https://doi.org/10.1016/j.watres.2020.116262. [57]

Kole, P. et al. (2015), *Autobandenslijtstof: een verwaarloosde bron van microplastics?*. [48]

Kole, P. et al. (2017), "Wear and Tear of Tyres: A Stealthy Source of Microplastics in the Environment.", *International journal of environmental research and public health*, Vol. 14/10, http://dx.doi.org/10.3390/ijerph14101265. [52]

Kreider, M. et al. (2010), "Physical and chemical characterization of tire-related particles: Comparison of particles generated using different methodologies", *Science of The Total Environment*, Vol. 408/3, pp. 652-659, http://dx.doi.org/10.1016/J.SCITOTENV.2009.10.016. [47]

Lahens, L. et al. (2018), "Macroplastic and microplastic contamination assessment of a tropical river (Saigon River, Vietnam) transversed by a developing megacity", *Environmental Pollution*, Vol. 236, p. 661−671, https://doi.org/10.1016/j.envpol.2018.02.005. [15]

Lassen, C. et al. (2016), *Microplastics Occurrence, effects and sources of releases to the environment in Denmark*, Danish Environmental Protection Agency, Copenhagen. [49]

Liu, X. et al. (2019), "Transfer and fate of microplastics during the conventional activated sludge process in one wastewater treatment plant of China", *Chemical Engineering Journal*, Vol. 362, pp. 176-182, https://doi.org/10.1016/j.cej.2019.01.033. [17]

Løkkegaard, H., B. Malmgren-Hansen and N. Nilsson (2018), *Mass balance of rubber granulate lost from artificial turf fields, focusing on discharge to the aquatic environment. A review of literature.*, https://www.genan.eu/wp-content/uploads/2020/02/Teknologisk-Institut_Mass-balance-of-rubber-granulate-lost-from-artificial-turf-fields_May-2019_v1.pdf. [83]

Lusher, A., M. McHugh and R. Thompson (2013), "Occurrence of microplastics in the gastrointestinal tract of pelagic and demersal fish from the English Channel", *Marine Pollution Bulletin*, Vol. 67/1-2, pp. 94-99, http://dx.doi.org/10.1016/j.marpolbul.2012.11.028. [12]

Magnusson, K. et al. (2016), *Swedish sources and pathways for microplastics to the marine environment A review of existing data. Revised in March 2017*, https://www.ivl.se/english/ivl/publications/publications/swedish-sources-and-pathways-for-microplastics-to-the-marine-environment.html. [51]

Magnusson, K. et al. (2020), *Atmosfäriskt nedfall av mikroskräp*, http://urn.kb.se/resolve?urn=urn:nbn:se:naturvardsverket:diva-8436. [59]

Marwood, C. et al. (2011), "Acute aquatic toxicity of tire and road wear particles to alga, daphnia, and fish", *Ecotoxicology*, Vol. 20/2079, https://doi.org/10.1007/s10646-011-0750-x. [66]

NIVA (2018), *Microplastics in road dust – characteristics, pathways and measures. Revised in 2020.*, Norwegian Institute for Water Research. [56]

Obbard, R. et al. (2014), "Global warming releases microplastic legacy frozen in Arctic Sea ice", *Earth's Future*, Vol. 2/6, pp. 315-320, http://dx.doi.org/10.1002/2014EF000240. [9]

OECD (2020), *Non-exhaust Particulate Emissions from Road Transport: An Ignored Environmental Policy Challenge*, OECD Publishing, Paris, https://dx.doi.org/10.1787/4a4dc6ca-en. [74]

OECD (2019), *Due Diligence on Upstream Production*, https://mneguidelines.oecd.org/OECD-Garment-Forum-2019-session-note-Due-diligence-on-upstream-production.pdf. [44]

OECD (2018), *OECD Due Diligence Guidance for Responsible Supply Chains in the Garment and Footwear Sector*, OECD Publishing, Paris, https://dx.doi.org/10.1787/9789264290587-en. [33]

OECD (2016), *Extended Producer Responsibility: Updated Guidance for Efficient Waste Management*, OECD Publishing, Paris, https://doi.org/10.1787/9789264256385-en. [80]

Panko, J. et al. (2013), "Chronic toxicity of tire and road wear particles to water- and sediment-dwelling organisms", *Ecotoxicology*, Vol. 22, pp. 13–21, https://doi.org/10.1007/s10646-012-0998-9. [67]

Panko, J., M. Kreider and K. Unice (2018), "Review of Tire Wear Emissions", in *Non-Exhaust Emissions*, Elsevier, http://dx.doi.org/10.1016/b978-0-12-811770-5.00007-8. [75]

Parker-Jurd, F. et al. (2019), *Investigating the sources and pathways of synthetic fibre and vehicle tyre wear contamination into the marine environment*, Report prepared for the Department for Environment Food and Rural Affairs (project code ME5435). [55]

Pauly, J. et al. (1998), "Inhaled cellulosic and plastic fibers found in human lung tissue", *Cancer Epidemiology Biomarkers and Prevention*, Vol. 7/5, pp. 419-428. [25]

Pimentel, J., R. Avila and A. Lourenco (2008), "Respiratory disease caused by synthetic fibres: a new occupational disease.", *Thorax*, Vol. 30/2, pp. 204-219, http://dx.doi.org/10.1136/thx.30.2.204. [29]

Prata, J. (2018), "Airborne microplastics: Consequences to human health?", *Environmental Pollution*, Vol. 234, pp. 115-126, https://doi.org/10.1016/j.envpol.2017.11.043. [26]

Quantis (2018), *Measuring fashion - Insights from the Environmental Impact of the Global Apparel and Footwear Industries study*, https://quantis-intl.com/measuring-fashion-report-2018/. [2]

Redondo-Hasselerharm, P. et al. (2018), "Ingestion and Chronic Effects of Car Tire Tread Particles on Freshwater Benthic Macroinvertebrates", *Environmental Science and Technology*, Vol. 52/23, pp. 13986-13994, http://dx.doi.org/10.1021/acs.est.8b05035. [71]

Remy, F. et al. (2015), "When Microplastic Is Not Plastic: The Ingestion of Artificial Cellulose Fibers by Macrofauna Living in Seagrass Macrophytodetritus", *Environmental Science & Technology*, Vol. 49/18, pp. 11158-11166, http://dx.doi.org/10.1021/acs.est.5b02005. [38]

RIVM (2018), *Verkenning milieueffecten rubbergranulaat bij kunstgrasvelden*, Verschoor, A. J., Bodar, C.W.M., Baumann, R.A., http://dx.doi.org/10.21945/RIVM-2018-0072. [82]

Sanchez-Vidal, A. et al. (2018), "The imprint of microfibres in southern European deep seas", *PLOS ONE*, Vol. 13/11, pp. e0207033-, https://doi.org/10.1371/journal.pone.0207033. [35]

Sieber, R., D. Kawecki and B. Nowack (2020), "Dynamic probabilistic material flow analysis of rubber release from tires into the environment", *Environmental Pollution*, Vol. 258, p. 113573, https://doi.org/10.1016/j.envpol.2019.113573. [63]

Stanton, T. et al. (2019), "Freshwater and airborne textile fibre populations are dominated by 'natural', not microplastic, fibres", *Science of the Total Environment*, Vol. 666, p. 377−389, https://doi.org/10.1016/j.scitotenv.2019.02.278. [36]

Suaria, G. et al. (2020), *Microfibers in oceanic surface waters: A global characterization*, Oceanography, http://advances.sciencemag.org/. [16]

Sutton, R. et al. (2019), *Understanding Microplastic Levels, Pathways and Transport in the San Francisco Bay Region*, San Francisco Estuary Institute, SFEI-ASC Publication No. 950., https://www.sfei.org/sites/default/files/biblio_files/Microplastic%20Levels%20in%20SF%20Bay%20-%20Final%20Report.pdf. [65]

Swedish EPA (2019), *Microplastics in the Environment 2019*, http://www.naturvardsverket.se/Om-Naturvardsverket/Publikationer/ISBN/6900/978-91-620-6957-5/. [84]

TextileExchange (2020), *Preferred Fiber Materials - Market Report 2020*, TextileExchange, https://textileexchange.org/wp-content/uploads/2020/06/Textile-Exchange_Preferred-Fiber-Material-Market-Report_2020.pdf. [13]

Thompson, R. et al. (2004), "Lost at Sea: Where Is All the Plastic?", *Science*, Vol. 304/5672, p. 838, http://dx.doi.org/10.1126/science.1094559. [10]

Tian, Z. et al. (2021), "A ubiquitous tire rubber–derived chemical induces acute mortality in coho salmon", *Science*, Vol. 371/6525, p. 185, http://dx.doi.org/10.1126/science.abd6951. [69]

UNEP (2020), *Sustainability and Circularity in the Textile Value Chain: global stocktaking*, https://wedocs.unep.org/20.500.11822/34184. [4]

UNEP (2017), *Exploring the potential for adopting alternative materials to reduce marine plastic litter*, United Nations Environment Programme. [40]

Unice, K. et al. (2015), “Experimental methodology for assessing the environmental fate of organic chemicals in polymer matrices using column leaching studies and OECD 308 water/sediment systems: Application to tire and road wear particles.”, *Science of the Total Environment*, Vol. 533, pp. 476–487, https://doi.org/10.1016/j.scitotenv.2015.06.053. [58]

Unice, K. et al. (2019), “Characterizing export of land-based microplastics to the estuary - Part I: Application of integrated geospatial microplastic transport models to assess tire and road wear particles in the Seine watershed”, *Science of The Total Environment*, Vol. 646, pp. 1639-1649, https://doi.org/10.1016/j.scitotenv.2018.07.368. [54]

Unice, K. et al. (2019), “Characterizing export of land-based microplastics to the estuary - Part II: Sensitivity analysis of an integrated geospatial microplastic transport modeling assessment of tire and road wear particles”, *Science of the Total Environment*, Vol. 646, pp. 1650-1659, https://doi.org/10.1016/j.scitotenv.2018.08.301. [53]

Verschoor, A. et al. (2016), *Emission of microplastics and potential mitigation measures. Abrasive cleaning agents, paints and tyre wear*, RIVM Report 2016-0026. [62]

Vianello, A. et al. (2019), “Simulating human exposure to indoor airborne microplastics using a Breathing Thermal Manikin”, *Scientific Reports*, Vol. 9/1, p. 8670, http://dx.doi.org/10.1038/s41598-019-45054-w. [23]

Wagner, S. et al. (2018), “Tire wear particles in the aquatic environment - A review on generation, analysis, occurrence, fate and effects.”, *Water Res* 139, pp. 83-100, http://dx.doi.org/doi:10.1016/j.watres.2018.03.051. [50]

WBCSD (2019), *Global ELT Management – A global state of knowledge on regulation, management systems, impacts of recovery and technologies*. [79]

Wik, A. et al. (2009), “Toxicity assessment of sequential leachates of tire powder using a battery of toxicity tests and toxicity identification evaluations”, *Chemosphere*, Vol. 77/7, pp. 922-927, http://dx.doi.org/10.1016/j.chemosphere.2009.08.034. [72]

Woodal, L. et al. (2014), “The deep sea is a major sink for microplastic debris.”, *Royal Society Open Science*, Vol. 1, p. 140317−140317. [11]

WRAP (2019), *Textile derived microfibre release: Investigating the current evidence base*, Prepared by Resource Futures. [41]

Xu, X. et al. (2018), “Pollution characteristics and fate of microfibers in the wastewater from textile dyeing wastewater treatment plant”, *Water Science & Technology*, Vol. 78/10, pp. 2046-2054, https://doi.org/10.2166/wst.2018.476. [43]

ZDHC (2015), *Manufacturing Restricted Substances List*, Zero Discharge of Hazardous Chemicals Programme, http://www.roadmaptozero.com/fileadmin/pdf/MRSL_v1_1.pdf (accessed on 12 May 2021). [32]

Zhang, G. and Y. Liu (2018), “The distribution of microplastics in soil aggregate fractions in southwestern China”, *Science of The Total Environment*, Vol. 642, pp. 12-20, http://dx.doi.org/10.1016/J.SCITOTENV.2018.06.004. [18]

Zhao, S., L. Zhu and D. Li (2016), “Microscopic anthropogenic litter in terrestrial birds from Shanghai, China: Not only plastics but also natural fibers”, *Science of The Total Environment*, Vol. 550, pp. 1110-1115, https://doi.org/10.1016/j.scitotenv.2016.01.112. [39]

Zuskin, E., F. Valic and A. Bouhuys (1976), "Byssinosis and airway responses due to exposure to textile dust", *Lung*, Vol. 154/1, pp. 17-24, http://dx.doi.org/10.1007/BF02713515. [28]

Notes

[1] As illustrated in Figure 1.4, releases into the environment of microfibres emitted during product use are particularly high in emerging economies (including major textile manufacturing countries such as China and India), mainly due to the lower rates of connectedness and treatment of wastewaters and the larger population sizes.

[2] All washing methods are expected to contribute to fibre release, but there is limited knowledge on fibre release occurring during practices such as hand washing, steaming, or dry cleaning.

[3] Road markings consist of plastic polymers, pigments, fillers and additives (Andersson-Sköld et al., 2020[61]).

[4] The size range for TRWP was estimated to span from 4μm to 280 μm, with the mode centred around 50 μm (Kreider et al., 2010[47]).

[5] This is not the rule in most other OECD countries. Porous asphalt is used in 95% of Dutch roads but only in 1% of roads in most other EU countries (Eunomia, 2018[81]). To maintain its functionality, porous asphalt pavements require regular street sweeping, which removes debris and pollutants (including TRWP).

[6] Some studies have investigated risks associated with rubber granulate used as infill material. This is discussed in Section 2.3.2.

[7] Council Directive 99/31/EC of 26 April 1999 on the landfill of waste ("Landfill Directive") introduces a ban on the disposal in landfills of shredded and whole waste tyres, excluding tyres used as engineering material. The California Code of Regulations, Title 14, establishes that waste tyres may not be landfilled in a solid waste disposal facility, unless they are permanently reduced in volume prior to disposal.

3 Mitigation technologies and best practices

This chapter documents and assesses available best practices and technologies that can be employed to mitigate the release of microplastics from textiles and tyres into the environment. The chapter follows a life-cycle approach, discussing options implementable at the design and manufacturing, use and end-of-life phases, as well as options for the end-of-pipe capture of microplastics.

3.1. Introduction

The present chapter aims to provide a stocktake of knowledge and techniques currently available to mitigate the leakage of microfibres and TRWP into the environment. These include several mitigation best practices, actions and technologies implementable during different stages of the lifecycle of textile products and vehicle tyres, as outlined in Figure 3.1. The chapter is structured as follows: Sections 3.2 and 3.3 present and assess the available mitigation best practices and technologies that can be implemented throughout the lifecycle of textile products and tyres (design and manufacturing, use and end-of-life), while Section 3.4 documents and assesses options for the end-of-pipe capture of microplastics.

Figure 3.1. Overview of microplastics mitigation entry points and actions (for textiles and tyres)

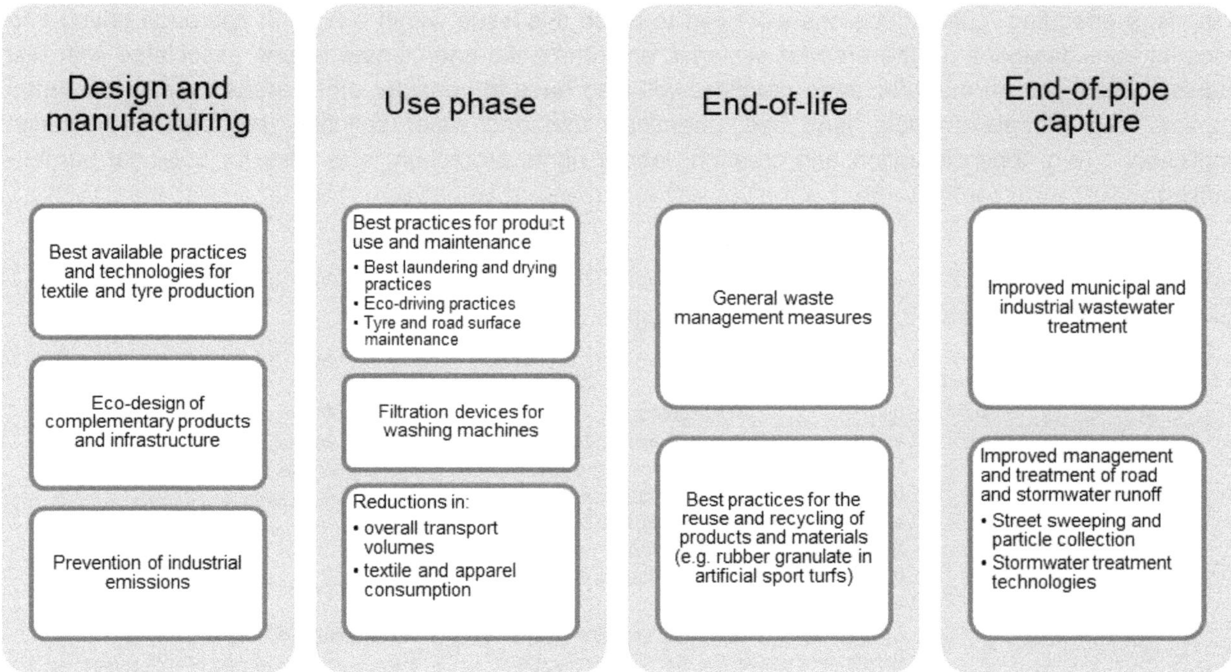

Source: Authors' own elaboration

3.2. Technologies and best practices implementable during the textile lifecycle

The sections below report and assess relevant best practices and mitigation technologies applicable throughout the lifecycle of textiles. Best practices and relevant mitigation technologies implementable at the design and manufacturing stage are discussed in Section 3.2.1, including also eco-design options for the detergent and washing machine industries and potential mitigation solutions for industrial emissions. Section 3.2.2 assesses mitigation actions implementable at the use stage, i.e. the uptake of best use practices and of mitigation technologies, while Section 3.2.3 outlines relevant end-of-life measures to prevent the leakage of textile waste into the environment as well as measures to extend the lifecycle of garments and reduce waste generation. Where knowledge is available, considerations on costs and potential trade-offs or synergies with other environmental objectives are also discussed.

3.2.1. Product design and manufacturing

Best practices and technologies for textile design and manufacturing

The textile design and manufacturing phase holds a large potential for microfibre mitigation, as it offers the opportunity to reduce overall microfibre release at source and to mitigate emissions into a variety of entry-pathways, including emissions into air occurring during wearing and everyday use (De Falco et al., 2020[1]). Several parameters in textile manufacturing influence the amounts of microfibres released during use, from the choice of fibre and yarn type, the fabric structure, the finishing treatments employed and the post-manufacturing processes. Table 3.1 presents and assesses a number of preferable parameters and processes for textile production in line with microfibre mitigation, as identified by available research.

Although the objective of this section is to assess and compare best practices aimed at minimising microfibre shedding, policy decisions will need to place this issue within a holistic approach taking into account considerations on the broader systemic environmental and climate issues associated with fast fashion. Decisions on manufacturing practices will also have to consider other areas for environmental impacts (e.g. climate impacts, land use, chemicals use and water pollution, resource use), social implications (e.g. jobs disruption and creation, labour rights protection) and risks for potential burden-shifting.

Table 3.1. Overview of best practices and technologies relevant for the minimisation of microfibre shedding and implementable during textile design and manufacturing

Mitigation measure	Relevant stages	Best practices / technologies	
		Description	Benefits (+) and Disadvantages (-)
Optimisation of fibre, yarn and fabric characteristics	Yarn formation	Yarns made of *continuous filaments* (fibres of indefinite length) are to be preferred to yarns made of short staple fibres since short fibres can more easily slip away due to the mechanical actions of washing and wearing (De Falco et al., 2020[1]; Carney Almroth et al., 2018[2]; Dalla Fontana, Mossotti and Montarsolo, 2020[3]).	+ Easy implementation + Also prevents the release of microfibres to air + Less expensive production process + Fibre production method already increasing in use - Leads to changes in fabric properties
	Yan and fabric formation	*Compact yarn and fabric structures*, like highly twisted yarns and woven fabrics, are preferable to looser textile structures, such as poorly twisted yarns and knitted fabrics (De Falco et al., 2020[1]; Carney Almroth et al., 2018[2]; Yang et al., 2019[4]).	+ Textile features already in use + Also prevents the release of microfibres to air - Leads to changes in fabric properties - Higher production costs
Optimisation of the finishing treatments applied	Textile finishing	*Protective coatings*: the application of a thin layer on the surface of the fabric can protect the fabric from the mechanical and chemical stresses it undergoes during a washing process (EU MERMAIDS, 2015[5]). Coatings have been developed on polyamide fabrics with an efficiency of more than 80% in microfibres reduction by using pectin (De Falco et al., 2018[6]) and biodegradable polymers (De Falco et al., 2019[7]).	+ Also prevents the release of microfibres to air + Opportunity to substitute with less-hazardous finishings and implement circular practices + Extended fabric lifetime - Leads to changes in fabric properties - Certain textile auxiliaries can contribute to chemical pollution and should be avoided - Implementation and costs strongly depend on the type of treatment developed
		The avoidance of mechanical finishing treatments napping, raising, shearing and brushing, which are employed to obtain textile surfaces composed of loose short cut fibres and are thus associated with higher shedding (Sillanpaa and Sainio, 2017[8]; Cai et al., 2020[9]; Pirc et al., 2016[10]; Roos, Levenstam Arturin and Hanning, 2017[11]), could mitigate microfibre emissions.	+ Also prevents industrial emissions of microfibres + Also prevents the release of microfibres to air - Where the processes are unavoidable (e.g. for the production of fleece, pile, velvet), microfibre removal and collection may be required

Mitigation measure	Relevant stages	Best practices / technologies	
		Description	Benefits (+) and Disadvantages (-)
Best garment manufacturing and post-manufacturing practices	Fabrication and tailoring	*Laser cutting* should be preferred over scissor cutting to prevent the release of microfibres from the edge of the fabrics (Roos, Levenstam Arturin and Hanning, 2017[11]; Cai et al., 2020[9]).	+ Better efficiency and cost saving + Technology already in use + Lower industrial waste generation (Nayak and Padhye, 2016[12])
	Post-manufacturing / distribution	*Removal of microfibres* via pre-washing: the amount of microfibre released from synthetic fabrics is greater in the first washes. This is likely to be partially due to the fibre residuals from manufacturing processes. Preliminary controlled industrial washing of the textile/garment has been proposed as a mitigation measures, implementable at the end of the production phase or before distribution (EU MERMAIDS, 2015[13]).	+ Also prevents the release of microfibres to air + Already occurring in certain cases - Variable and potentially high costs - Difficult to implement where manufacture takes place abroad in emerging economies - Requires the presence of adequate wastewater treatment systems

Notes: Napping is done to obtain a fuzzy effect on the fabric surface, by raising the loose fibres (raising) and then cutting the raised nap to a uniform height (shearing) (EU MERMAIDS, 2015[13]). Brushing is a finishing treatment where brushes or other abrading devices are used to remove loose threads and enhance the final appearance of garments.
Source: Authors' own elaboration

Research has identified several manufacturing processes in line with microplastics mitigation that are already widely employed in textile manufacturing, such as the use of *continuous filaments, compact structures and laser cutting*. For instance, the production of staple fibres has been decreasing in recent years in favour of continuous filaments, whose production costs less than staples (The Fiber Year, 2017[14]). However, trade-offs with desirable garment characteristics or with other environmental benefits may pose a barrier to their large-scale deployment. For instance, the use of continuous filaments and compact structures, in line with lower microfibre shedding, will affect the characteristics of the final product, in addition to also requiring higher chemical use and water consumption during manufacturing (e.g. in the case of woven fabrics which require sizing and desizing processes) (Shaker et al., 2016[15]). Similarly, a shift away from knitted and towards woven fabrics could not be easily achieved: knitted fabrics represent 57% of the world market (compared to 32% for woven fabrics) (The Fiber Year, 2017[14]) and are produced at significantly lower costs than woven ones (Shaker et al., 2016[15]). Further research could explore the relevance of increasing the use of knitted fabrics with more compact features, such as highly twisted yarns.

The application of *finishing treatments* that create protective coatings against microfibre shedding is a key mitigation solution, yet still in the developmental phases. A promising option in terms of efficiency, costs and implementation feasibility is a coating based on pectin, a natural polysaccharide that can be recovered from waste of the agricultural and food industries at a low cost. Washing tests of fabrics treated with pectin-based coatings showed a microfibre reduction effectiveness of about 90% (De Falco et al., 2018[16]). The coating is applied on fabrics with a treatment similar to padding, a process already commonly used in industrial finishing treatments.

Coatings based on biodegradable polymers (e.g. polylactic acid and polybutylene succinate-co-butylene adipate) also showed a promising mitigation effectiveness, although currently their application may be costly and challenging to scale up at industrial level (De Falco et al., 2019[7]). Coatings based on protein-based materials inspired by squids have also been proposed, yet the production costs for the raw material could be high and their effectiveness after repeated washing cycles remains unclear (Pena-Francesch and Demirel, 2019[17]). Overall, protective coatings offer a promising technological mitigation option implementable at industrial scale during the production of textiles, however further research and testing is required in order to assess its effectiveness, implementation costs, application feasibility on different types of fabrics, compatibility with textile manufacturing processes (e.g. dyeing) and durability.

As microfibre shedding tends to decrease in subsequent washing cycles[1], *prewashing of synthetic fabrics* has been proposed as a potentially effective mitigation measure. The main benefit of the prewashing practice at industrial level is that it provides retailers and/or consumers with products with a lower tendency to shed microfibres. Where adequate wastewater treatment systems are in place, the highest quantities of microfibres released at the beginning of fabric lifetime would be more efficiently retained at the end of manufacturing. Further, the practice could be also useful to remove microfibres from manufacturing processes entrapped in the fabrics, as well as other chemical residuals (Cesa et al., 2020[18]; Cai et al., 2020[9]; Belzagui et al., 2019[19]).

Removing microfibres at the production stage[2] can be a strategic and cost-effective option to tackle the issue of microfibre shedding as upstream as possible (before these are channelled into different environmental pathways) while also synergistically targeting industrial emissions of microfibres and other pollutants. However, prewashing may be associated with high implementation costs and a variable mitigation potential. Depending on the local context, the effective implementation of this practice may require the update of the current industrial wastewater treatment infrastructure with technologies able to retain microfibres with adequate efficiency. Thus, this mitigation best practice may be challenging and costly to implement in SMEs in emerging economies, where the majority of textile manufacturing takes place. In light of these challenges, it has been suggested that policy could also envision that the pre-washing of textile products manufactured abroad takes place in the importing country under controlled conditions. In sum, pre-washing has a high mitigation potential, however further tests are required to evaluate its implementation feasibility at different entry points (i.e. textile manufacturing, fabric manufacturing, or retail), as well as to further investigate whether the decrease in microfibre emissions occurs independently from the specific characteristics of different fabrics.

In general, as point-source emissions are easier to manage than diffuse ones, the design and manufacturing of textiles and garments generally offers large opportunities for cost-effective reductions in microfibre emissions. However, persisting knowledge gaps pose a barrier to the development and implementation of the identified mitigation best practices and technologies. Further research is currently required to more reliably assess the cost-effectiveness and implementation feasibility of the available mitigation options, as well as to evaluate the potential trade-offs with the preservation of desirable environmental benefits or garment characteristics.[3]

The lack of standardised methodologies and the lack of transparency along the textile value chain have been identified as key barriers to the investigation and implementation of best manufacturing practices. Firstly, the lack of common measurement standards for microfibre shedding renders test results difficult to compare and aggregate, limiting possibilities to draw conclusions on the manufacturing parameters which influence microfibre shedding during use. Secondly, the complex and geographically dispersed nature of textile and apparel value chains provides challenges to the adequate provision of product information further downstream (Niinimäki et al., 2020[20]). Knowledge and data gaps in the manufacturing history of fabrics (e.g. production steps, chemicals used, etc.) pose challenges to the evaluation of the effect of specific production processes on microfibre release and, therefore, to the identification of best design and manufacturing practices. For these reasons, collaboration between researches and textile industries could be beneficial and instrumental in accelerating research and industrial-scale deployment (see Chapter 5).

Prevention of industrial emissions

As outlined in Chapter 2, microfibres were found in relevant concentrations in industrial wastewater (Xu et al., 2018[21]) and in water and sediments sampled in textile industrial areas (Deng et al., 2020[22]). Given there is currently insufficient information to reliably quantify and characterise the release of microfibres occurring during manufacturing, there is a need for textile producers to collect data on industrial microfibre emissions in order to adequately inform mitigation action.

It has been suggested that in-line vacuum systems could be added to capture loose fibres via air filtration and exhaustion after processes such as brushing, sanding and raising (Carney Almroth et al., 2018[2]). The EU MERMAIDS project recommended to handle carefully mechanical finishings which generate many loose microfibres, such as napping (EU MERMAIDS, 2015[13]). Textile manufacturing facilities could be fitted with treatment systems of water and air dedicated to the removal of microfibres, although such systems have not yet been developed or presented. Implementation steps are expected to be long and potentially to bear high costs for the textile industry, given the existing technological barriers. Options for the improved treatment of industrial wastewater effluents are discussed in Section 3.4.1.

Best practices for the production of laundry detergents and washing machines

Detergent and washing machine manufacturers may also be important players in the mitigation of microfibre emissions. Available research has identified several entry points for the identification of best practices for microfibre pollution mitigation implementable during the production of detergents and washing machines, as summarised in Table 3.2.

Table 3.2. Overview of microfibre mitigation actions relevant for detergent and washing machine manufacturers

Industrial sector	Best practices / technologies	
	Description	Benefits (+) and Disadvantages (-)
Detergent production	Focusing production on *liquid light duty detergents*, since heavy-duty detergents are more aggressive and cause a greater release of microfibres, especially powder ones (EU MERMAIDS, 2015[13]).	+ Better fabric care - Possible additional production costs for the relevant industry - Possible additional carbon footprint and costs for transportation
	Developing detergents *effective at low temperatures and during short washing cycles* (Cotton et al., 2020[23]).	+ Synergic action with the best practice for laundry of low washing temperature and time - Possible additional production costs for the relevant industry
	Research and development for new additives to improve the mitigation effect of detergent products on microfibre release during the washing cycle.	+ By preventing fibre breakage, the fabric care is improved and the textile life prolonged. - Possible additional production costs for the relevant industry
Washing machine production	Development of built-in filtration systems that retain microfibres.	+ Compared to external filtration systems, the correct functioning of the machine could be better controlled. - Possible additional production costs for the relevant industry
	Preference for *front-load washing machines* over top-load ones. Top-load washing machines usually have central agitators that spin to rub textiles against each other in order to wash them, likely causing higher abrasion of garments and higher fibre release compared to the rotating drum of front-load washing machines (Hartline et al., 2016[24]).	+ Better fabric care - Costs of production conversion for top-load machines manufactures
	Development of washing machines that use *lower volumes of water* (Kelly et al., 2019[25]; Lant et al., 2020[26]).	+ Lower water consumption - Possible higher production costs for the industry

Source: Authors' own elaboration

The use of detergents and softeners can influence the microfibre shedding degree of clothing and also directly contribute to the release of intentionally-added microplastics. The development of products aligned with the prevention of fibre loss, such as detergents that are effective at low temperatures and during short laundry cycles, while also efficiently cleaning the fabric, can potentially contribute to microplastics pollution mitigation, although solutions may take time to be developed. It will be crucial that new detergents and additives do not contain intentionally-added microplastics or harmful substances available for release into the environment. A synergic action between innovation in detergent production and in the application of finishing treatments during textile manufacturing should also be taken into consideration to ensure that the laundry cycle does not provoke the detachment of coatings and that an overall microfibre reduction effect is achieved.

At the level of washing machines production, there is scope for adapting the design of products in order to help mitigate the generation and emission of microfibres during laundering. However, currently, there are no reports of washing machines available on the market with a tested effectiveness in mitigating microfibre emissions.[4] Washing machines able to both maintain the correct functioning of the machine and mitigate microfibre releases into wastewaters (e.g. via built-in filtration systems) may take time to be developed and tested.

In both cases, the implementation of these mitigation actions may take time and could bear substantial costs for the relevant industries, from R&D to manufacturing, potentially also resulting in higher consumer prices. However, as for textile design and manufacturing, the development of solutions at the industry level can hold large potential for mitigation as well as for easier implementation and monitoring via adequate policy intervention.

3.2.2. Textile use stage

Best practices for maintenance and care

The use of garments contributes to microfibre pollution in two ways: it causes the release of microfibres into air (De Falco et al., 2020[1]; Dris et al., 2017[27]) and it causes fabric abrasion and tear that can lead to microfibre emissions during washing. Although further research is required in order to correlate practices aimed at improving fabric durability with microfibre release, several practices aligned with adequate textile care and improved durability of fabrics are expected to also minimise microfibre generation during laundering and drying, as summarised in Table 3.3. These include reducing the frequency of washing cycles, washing full loads and at low temperatures, preferring liquid to powder detergents, using fabric softeners (except for fabrics which can be damaged by the use of softeners, such as outdoor apparel) and avoiding tumble-drying.

Key barriers to implementation are a lack of consumer awareness and knowledge on the environmental consequences of microfibre pollution, as well as on the available mitigation measures. As reported in previous sections, scientific consensus over the relative effectiveness of these practices remains uncertain, also due to the absence of standardised methodologies to quantify microfibre release. Further research is required in order to gather more and conclusive data on the parameters that influence the release of microfibres during the laundering, drying and wearing of textiles. The good outcome of such investigations will also depend on the level of collaboration between relevant stakeholders and industrial sectors.

Further research is also needed to understand how the tendency of garments to emit microfibres changes over their lifetime, particularly to understand whether there is a threshold beyond which older garments start releasing higher amounts of microfibres. Several studies have found that the release of microfibres decreases during subsequent washing cycles (Cai et al., 2020[28]; Carney Almroth et al., 2018[2]; Cesa et al., 2020[18]; Belzagui et al., 2019[19]; De Falco et al., 2019[29]; Napper and Thompson, 2016[30]; Pirc et al., 2016[10]; Sillanpaa and Sainio, 2017[8]), however this trend has mainly been observed with new garments and might differ with clothes that have been worn. One study mechanically aged some garments and found that they released more microfibres than new ones (Hartline et al., 2016[24]). Tests conducted in real household conditions found relevant quantities of microfibres released, however these cannot give indications of potential trends over the lifecycle of garments (Galvão et al., 2020[31]; Lant et al., 2020[26]).

Table 3.3. Overview of best practices to minimise microfibre shedding implementable during textile washing and drying

Use stage	Best practice: Description	Best practice: Benefits (+) and Disadvantages (-)
Washing	Fabrics should be *washed less frequently* and only when it is required by the level of dirt (EU MERMAIDS, 2015[32]; Napper, Barrett and Thompson, 2020[33]).	+ Lower energy and water consumption + Better maintenance and longer lifetime of garments.
	The use of detergent favours the release and transport of microfibres (De Falco et al., 2019[29]; Yang et al., 2019[4]; Carney Almroth et al., 2018[2]). *Liquid detergents* should be preferred over powder ones, which are generally more harmful to textiles and enhance microfibre release[1] (EU MERMAIDS, 2015[32]; De Falco et al., 2018[16]).	+ Better fabric care by avoiding friction - Effect on the production of detergent manufacturers with related costs to adjust their products
	Fabric softeners should be used to mitigate fibre-to-fibre friction occurring during washing and reduce fibre shedding. It has been estimated that the use of softeners reduces microfibre release by 35% (De Falco et al., 2018[16]).	+ Better maintenance and longer lifetime of garments. - Additional costs for consumers - Not suitable for all textiles types (e.g. outdoor apparel)
	Employing laundry programs that use less volumes of water and *washing full loads of textiles* reduces microfibre shedding (EU MERMAIDS, 2015[32]; Lant et al., 2020[26]; Kelly et al., 2019[25]). Although more research is required in this area, it is believed that high water-volume-to-fabric ratio results in a greater wettability of the fabric and consequentially higher detachment of microfibers from the yarns (De Falco et al., 2018[16]).	+ Lower energy and water consumption - Potential trade-offs with the effectiveness of the cleaning process.
	Low washing temperatures, shorter laundry cycles and low mechanical action (i.e. centrifuge, spin) minimise the stress mechanisms that fabrics undergo during washing (De Falco et al., 2018[16]; Hartline et al., 2016[24]; Lant et al., 2020[26]; EU MERMAIDS, 2015[32]; Yang et al., 2019[4]; Zambrano et al., 2019[34]; Dalla Fontana, Mossotti and Montarsolo, 2020[3]).	+ Lower energy and water consumption + Reduced colour loss and dye transfer to wastewaters (Cotton et al., 2020[23]) + Better maintenance and longer lifetime of garments.
Drying	The usage of *tumble dryers* is likely to enhance fibre release. Pirc et al. (2016[10]) found that during tumble drying a fleece shirt released on average 3.5 times the number of fibres released during washing. Other researchers also hypothesized that non-natural drying and over-drying could cause fabric damage and increased microfibre release (Cesa et al., 2020[18]). However, the impact of tumble-drying on microfibre release may vary depending on the textile composition and structure, and further research is required to assess it.	+ Lower energy and water consumption - Additional costs for tumble-dryer manufacturers to find mitigation alternatives.

Notes: 1: This may be due to the presence in powder detergents of inorganic compounds insoluble in water that cause more friction with textiles, or to the higher pH of powder detergents compared to liquid ones (De Falco et al., 2018[16]).
Source: Authors' own elaboration

Capturing and filtration devices implementable at the level of washing machines

Several capturing and filtration devices have been developed to reduce microfibre release during washing processes. The majority of existing technologies are available to consumers on the market and include devices to be added to the drum of the washing machine (in-drum capturing devices), external filtration systems to be positioned at the end of the drainpipe (add-on external filters) and built-in filters. Selected examples are described in Table 3.4 according to their type, effectiveness (in terms of % of weight reduction of microfibres released) and key characteristics.

In general, several issues need to be taken into account when considering mitigation technological solutions implementable during the use phase of garments. Additional costs for the consumer are a primary concern, as also are the degree of additional maintenance required and the ease of use. In terms of user-friendliness, particular attention has been given to the need to find solutions which prevent mishandling, for instance via the rinsing of the filter in the sink and the dispersal of microfibres into household sewage. Additional concerns are the potential trade-offs that may arise with other environmental benefits, such as the energy efficiency of the laundering process, the environmental footprint of the lifecycle of filters (e.g.

production, collection, reuse or recycling, disposal) as well as their durability and the need to ensure the adequate disposal of the retained microfibres (Herweyers et al., 2020[35]).

Table 3.4. Overview of capturing and filtration devices for microfibres

Type	Name	Description	Effectiveness	Cost	Benefits (+) and Disadvantages (-)
In-drum devices	Cora Ball	Laundry ball with stalks to catch fibres (Cora Ball, 2020[36])	31% (Napper, Barrett and Thompson, 2020[33]); 5% (McIlwraith et al., 2019[37]);	USD $ 37.99	+ Ease of use (added directly to the drum with clothing) + Could reduce overall shedding - Cannot be used with delicates - Tedious cleaning process
	Guppyfriend washing bag	A polyamide 6.6 50×74 cm washing bag	86% (Guppyfriend, 2020[38]); 54% (Napper, Barrett and Thompson, 2020[33]);	€ 29.75	+ Could reduce overall shedding + Protects fabrics during washing, potentially extending their lifetime + Low price - Can limit the maximum washing load
Add-on external filters	Lint LUV-R Septic SAV-R and MicroPlastics LUV-R	Filters made of a stainless steel mesh with hole diameters of 1580 µm (Lint LUV-R) or 150 µm (MicroPlastics LUV-R)	65% (Lint LUV-R Septic SAV-R) and 87% (MicroPlastics LUV-VR) (Environmental Enhancements, 2020[39]); 80% (McIlwraith et al., 2019[37]); 29% (Napper, Barrett and Thompson, 2020[33]); 65-74% (Browne, Ros and Johnston, 2020[40]); 1	USD $ 145 (Lint LUV-R Septic SAV-R) USD $ 180 (MicroPlastics LUV-R)	- Unclear cleaning and maintenance
	PlanetCare	Filter based on a cartridge to be replaced after approximately 20 wash cycles	90% (Planet Care), 79% (Slovenian National Institute of Chemistry), 73% (National Research Council of Italy, Institute for Polymers, Composites and Biomaterials) (PlanetCare[41]); 25% (Napper, Barrett and Thompson, 2020[33]); 2	€ 9.95 (monthly subscription) € 139.50 (for 13 cartridges)	+ Easy installation (Swedish EPA, 2018[42]) - Used cartridges need to be sent back to the producers
	Filtrol	Reusable mesh filter with replaceable filter bag (Filtrol, 2020[43])	89% (Athey et al., 2019[44]);	USD $ 139.99	+ Easy installation - Does not retain the smallest particles (Swedish EPA, 2018[42]) - Cannot be used with fabric softeners or excessive amount of detergent
	Indikon-1	Filter based on a cartridge to be replaced after about 100 washes	81% 3	N/A	+ Easy maintenance: the unit tells the consumer when to change the cartridge - Used cartridges needs to be sent back to the producers
Built-in filters	XFiltra	Prototype filter designed to perform three actions: filtration, pump and de-watering	90% (Xeros Technologies, 2020[45]) 78% (Napper, Barrett and Thompson, 2020[33])	N/A	+ Removes the need for the user to purchase, install and operate an external filter unit. + No need for cartridge replacement - Unclear maintenance needs for consumers

Notes: The table only presents a selection of examples for which sufficient information was retrieved, however additional filtration devices may exist on the market or be in the phase of development. The information on the technologies presented also only reflects the state of knowledge at the time of writing.

1: Different versions of the Lint LUV-R (Septic SAV-R and MicroPlastics LUV-VR) filter were tested by the studies presented.

2: Similarly, different versions of the Planet Care filter were tested during its developing phase.

3: Information provided by Avril Greenaway, Cleaner Seas Group, on 4 February 2021

Key advantages of filtration devices are their commercialisation, availability for implementation and ongoing continued technological improvement. However, their use remains on a voluntary basis by the consumer, so it is difficult to control their uptake and assess their effectiveness in real-life conditions, especially where more delicate cleaning and maintenance operations are required. Furthermore, the majority of these devices have been conceived for use in household applications rather than at large scale (e.g. in industrial or commercial laundering facilities), although several models could be easily adapted to allow for larger water flows.[5]

Common barriers and issues to be addressed in order to allow the broader implementation of filtering technologies include:

- *The lack of standardised test methods to assess and compare the effectiveness of available devices.* While some filters have been independently tested, a clear and reliable picture of their effectiveness and durability is not yet available. The dimensional range of the microfibres retained by filter devices needs to be investigated further. It is essential to develop standardised test methods to compare the effectiveness of filters and to assess their compatibility with washing machines and with textile laundering processes.
- *The need for further research on the potential trade-offs and synergies* with other best practices and technologies for microfibre mitigation. For instance, although using the Guppyfriend bag can ensure better fabric care, it could potentially lead consumers to wash full loads less frequently.
- *The need for the provision of information on adequate maintenance practices.* For some in-drum filters currently on the market, it is recommended that these are cleaned when fibres or entanglements are visible. Where maintenance or replacement of parts by the consumer is required, inadequate handling could potentially cause clogging or malfunctioning in the washing machine.
- *The lack of endorsement by the washing machine industry.* As external filtration systems have not yet been endorsed by washing machine manufacturers, the compatibility of these devices with different types and brands of washing machines cannot be determined yet. Also, the impacts of these technological solutions on the normal functioning of the machine, notably in terms of energy/water consumption and cleaning effectiveness, are neither clear nor well documented.
- *The need for the adequate disposal of microfibres*. It should be ensured that the disposal of microfibres, which are small in size and can be easily dispersed, is handled carefully. For instance, the PlanetCare and Indikon-1 filters use a cartridge that needs to be replaced after a certain number of washes and require customers to return the full cartridges so that these can be handled correctly. Both companies aim to reuse or recycle the used cartridges, although public information of how this aim is achieved is not yet available.

Drawing from these elements, an assessment of considerations relevant for the design of policies that mandate the adoption of filtering technologies for washing machines is included in Chapter 4.

3.2.3. Textile end-of-life stage

The current system of textile and fashion consumption is responsible for the production of more than 92 Mt of textile waste per year (Niinimäki et al., 2020[20]). The recovery of materials at the end of the life cycle of products is very low: it is estimated that 87% of the total fibre input in textile manufacturing is landfilled or incinerated and less than 1% of the materials used in textile manufacturing are recycled at the end of the lifecycle of products (EMF, 2017[46]).

Little information is currently available on the contribution of the end-of-life of textiles to overall microfibre releases. Since the mismanagement of plastic waste contributes to the emission of microplastics (see Section 1.2.2), it is likely that the inadequate management of textile waste contributes to the release of microfibres to both water and air. It is unclear to what extent recycling and reuse practices are aligned with microfibre mitigation objectives. For instance, fibre grinding, i.e. a recycling process where fibres are ground to be used in other applications such as construction, could require further evaluation with regards to microfibre release and the potential need for mitigation solutions at recycling facilities. With regards to garments made out of recycled fibres, available evidence does not provide a clear picture of trends in microfibre release in comparison with garments made of virgin fibres (Roos, Levenstam Arturin and Hanning, 2017[11]; De Falco et al., 2019[29]; Özkan and Gündoğdu, 2021[47]; De Falco et al., 2020[48]). With regards to reuse, further research is also required to ascertain whether and to what extent ageing garments have a higher tendency to shed fibres (see Section 3.2.2).

In general, further research is needed to adequately assess the impact of reuse and recycling practices on microfibre generation. Yet, given available knowledge, it is likely that the environmental benefits of reusing (or recycling) garments outweigh the potential additional microfibre leakage associated with the use of old (or recycled) garments. Reductions in textile production and waste generation, also achievable by extending the useful life of products and by keeping materials within the economy, can significantly reduce environmental impacts associated with the handling and transportation of textile waste and the demand for virgin materials.

Textile waste generation could be prevented or reduced via a number of measures, such as:

- *Reductions in pre-consumer textile waste generation*. Between 10% and 30% of the fabric used in the manufacturing process is wasted. Additionally, incinerating unsold garments remains a common practice. Pre-production waste generation could be reduced by slowing down manufacturing rates and improving the accuracy of production via better communication between design and manufacturing (which are often in different geographical locations) (Niinimäki et al., 2020[20]). Regulatory measures can also be introduced to ban the destruction of unsold merchandise (see for instance (France, 2020[49])).
- *Extended lifetime of garments and reductions in post-consumer textile waste generation*. A key barrier in the reduction of textile waste are practices associated with the concept of "fast fashion" (i.e. cheap manufacturing, massive production and continuous proposal of new, short-lived garments) which encourage fast disposal (Niinimäki et al., 2020[20]). Today, clothes are more and more underutilised: it is estimated that in the past 15 years, the average number of times a piece of garment is used before being thrown away has decreased by 36% (EMF, 2017[46]). Several options exist to extend the lifetime of clothing and textile materials, including creating markets for second-hand clothing. Efficient and dedicated textile collection systems are required to support reuse practices and to ensure that garments maintain their quality over their extended lifetime. Emerging business models such as product-service systems, supplier take-back schemes and sharing platforms, can play a large role in increasing the utilisation of garments and steering textile consumption towards higher sustainability (UNEP, 2020[50]).
- *Improved textile recycling*. Several recycling practices exist for textiles and garments: conversion to cleaning and wiping rags, fibre recovery for use in new yarns, fibres re-spinning into new filaments and feedstock recycling (i.e. the polymer is broken down to its original monomers) (Piribauer and Bartl, 2019[51]). The presence of separate collection is a necessary prerequisite to enable recycling, especially to enable the larger uptake of higher value recycling opportunities. For instance, legislation in place in the EU obliges member states to collect textile waste separately by 2025 and ensure that waste collected separately is not incinerated or landfilled (EEA, 2019[52]). Measures aimed at encouraging eco-design could also facilitate end-of-life management and efficient recycling of garments, for instance by avoiding the use of multi-material textiles, which are more challenging to recycle efficiently.

3.3. Technologies and best practices implementable during the tyre lifecycle

The sections below report and assess relevant best practices and mitigation technologies applicable along the lifecycle of tyres. Section 3.3.1 discusses relevant mitigation options implementable during the design and manufacturing of tyres as well as of roads and vehicles. Section 3.3.2 assesses mitigation actions implementable during the use phase, i.e. the uptake of good practices for tyre use and maintenance and eco-driving practices, as well as broader actions aimed at reducing overall vehicle kilometres travelled. Section 3.3.3 focuses on the end-of-life phase and outlines relevant best practices for the maintenance of artificial sports turfs.

3.3.1. Product design and manufacturing

Mitigation technologies and best practices related to material design intend to reduce the tyre wear rate. This can be achieved either by optimising tyre tread and road pavement characteristics or by reducing vehicle weight (Table 3.5).

Table 3.5. Overview of mitigation actions relevant for TRWP and implementable during product design and manufacturing

Mitigation action	Description	Advantages (+) and Disadvantages (-)
Optimisation of tyre tread characteristics and dimensions	Tyre characteristics influence the tyre tread wear rate. The optimisation of tyre design in line with lower tyre tread wear, without compromising on other relevant characteristics of tyres, is expected to substantially reduce TRWP generation.	+ Potentially high impact + Potential prolonged lifetime of tyres + No time-intensive adaptation of infrastructure needed - Currently, trade-offs with safety concerns and other desirable characteristics of tyres - Requirements for tyre design depend also on vehicle type
Optimisation of road design and road surface characteristics	Since the characteristics of roads (i.e. the road design, the texture of the pavement and the types of road markings employed) influence wear, these could be optimised to allow for lower tyre tread wear rates.	+ Potentially high impact + Reduction in noise levels - High costs and limited implementation potential (for road pavement replacement) - Trade-offs with safety and durability concerns - Further research required in some areas (e.g. road pavement optimisation with regards to tyre wear)
Reduction in vehicle weight	A shift towards lighter vehicles (or a reversal of trends towards heavier ones) can reduce TRWP generation.	+ No changes in infrastructure required + Lower fuel consumption - Vehicle weight depends in part on consumer preferences - Transition into e-mobility may lead to an increase in average vehicle weight and TRWP generation

Source: (Andersson-Sköld et al., 2020[53]; OECD, 2020[54]; Pohrt, 2019[55])

Optimisation of tyre tread characteristics and dimensions

Tyre characteristics, such as the dimension and the mechanical properties of the tread, influence the tyre wear rate. Mitigation measures may target an increase in stiffness ratio between tread and carcass. For instance, a wider tread and a low tread sea volume could result in decreased TRWP generation (Klüppel, 2014[56]). Wider tyres exert less pressure against the road surface and cause less abrasion, although this is partially offset by the larger contact area with the road surface. In general, wider tyres are expected to have slightly lower abrasion rates compared to narrow tyres (Pohrt, 2019[55]).

Efforts are ongoing to improve the *eco-design of tyres* in line with microplastics mitigation. These generally entail optimising design parameters to enhance resistance to abrasion, as well as replacing potentially hazardous chemicals employed during production in order to minimise the toxicity of emitted TRWP. Improvements in material design should not only respond to safety concerns but also ensure tyre durability resulting in longer tyre life, potentially reducing the resource requirements for tyre production. Tyres are designed to achieve a balance between safety and environmental performances, such as abrasion, braking, wet grip, rolling resistance and noise. With current technologies, these performance characteristics are variously antagonistic to each other. The development of innovative solutions in tyre design will be required in order to see significant reductions in the rate of tyre wear whilst preserving high standards in other performance areas. Policy interventions could be considered to incentivise or mandate the development of low abrasion tyre tread materials (see Chapter 4).

Tyre type and dimension are usually selected according to the vehicle type. Global car markets have witnessed a trend towards larger and wider tyres (which are generally in line with lower tyre tread wear), yet this came with concurrent increases in the average vehicle weight and power (which generally lead to higher tyre wear) (Li, 2018[57]). As the share of e-mobility in the vehicle fleet is expected to increase in the near future, tyre design may be adapted to minimise tyre wear. Certain recent innovations aim to reduce rolling resistance and increasing the vehicle mileage in order to reduce overall tyre tread wear (Continental, 2019[58]). The use of airless tyres, which cannot be operated with incorrect pressure conditions (see Section 3.3.2), may also contribute to reducing emissions in the future.

Optimisation of road design and road surface characteristics

The design of road infrastructure and the characteristics of traffic impact tyre wear by influencing the conditions in which vehicles are operated. *Road design characteristics* (e.g. curves, hills) can be optimised so as to mitigate TRWP generation. For instance, tyre wear abrasion that occurs at curves may be reduced by increasing the roadway inclination in curves (Klüppel, 2014[56]). Another influencing factor is the extent to which road features lead to frequent and large speed changes, for instance due to the presence of traffic lights (Andersson-Sköld et al., 2020[53]). Further, the choice of *road markings* (and of the application method) can also mitigate the rate of wear (Andersson-Sköld et al., 2020[53]). Not only different types of road markings are wear-resistant to different degrees, but they also may directly contribute to microplastics pollution. Lastly, as damaged road pavements may lead to higher tyre wear, adequate *road surface maintenance* could substantially contribute to TRWP mitigation. Key stakeholders involved in the partial or full implementation of optimised road pavement and infrastructure characteristics are road authorities and municipalities as well as the construction industry.

The *structure of the road pavement* also affects tyre and road wear. Coarser textures are expected to cause higher road wear compared to smoother surfaces and asphalt roads generally cause a lower wear rate than concrete pavements (Pant and Harrison, 2013[59]). The roughness of the pavement micro-texture is the main driver of wear in the road surface, while the macro-texture has a minor influence (Andersson-Sköld et al., 2020[53]). In general, there is a trade-off between improved resistance to road wear and safety: the micro-texture may be adapted to reduce tyre wear, however this might lead to reduced friction and thereby safety.

Several studies are ongoing to address this conflict and test innovative pavements optimised for lower tyre and road wear. For example, the Danish Road Directorate has been working on developing a road pavement that reduces the rolling resistance between vehicles and road pavements, to explore solutions to reduce road transport GHG emissions. Tested pavements have shown a reduction in rolling resistance, resulting in reduced fuel consumption, without significant compromises on safety requirements and durability (Pettinari, Lund-Jensen and Schmidt, 2016[60]).

Although the implementation of such road pavements is associated with higher costs, it also leads to a lower noise level and it may benefit from higher acceptability by municipalities, road authorities and the public (Pettinari, Lund-Jensen and Schmidt, 2016[60]). This technology is not yet state-of-the-art and further research and development is needed, in particular to improve durability, before implementation will be possible. Once innovative road pavements are available, it may be advisable to apply these in areas with particularly high tyre wear abrasion rates, for instance on congested roads or on high-speed motorways. For the time being, given the well-known relationship between the state of road surfaces and rolling resistance, adequate road maintenance to preserve smooth and even surfaces can be an effective strategy to reduce the production of TRWP (ETRMA, 2018[61]).

Reductions in vehicle weight

As vehicle weight increases, so does the frictional force between tyres and road surfaces and therefore the generation of TRWP. Yet, trends in the composition of the vehicle fleet show a tendency towards a higher proportion of larger and heavier vehicles (Andersson-Sköld et al., 2020[53]). Additionally, electric vehicles also tend to be heavier than their traditional counterparts, mainly due to the weight of batteries (Timmers and Achten, 2016[62]). As a result, total emissions of TRWP are projected to increase at a higher rate than the increase in traffic (Andersson-Sköld et al., 2020[53]). The higher torque (rotational force) of electric cars compared to their traditional counterparts may also lead to increased tyre wear during acceleration (Soret, Guevara and Baldasano, 2014[63]).

Reductions in vehicle weight may be achieved by the application of advanced lightweight materials in cars (Serrenho, Norman and Allwood, 2017[64]). Aluminium alloys are commonly used as replacement materials, as they provide similar performance properties as steel with lower weight (Hirsch, 2011[65]). However, these advanced materials generally require a greater amount of energy to manufacture and recycle and further research and development is required to enable their larger uptake in vehicle production (Raabe, Tasan and Olivetti, 2019[66]). More broadly, measures aimed at encouraging or incentivising the uptake of lighter vehicles as well as reducing overall volumes of road traffic (as discussed in Section 3.2.2) may significantly contribute to reductions in air pollution and in GHG emissions, while also generating co-benefits in terms of TRWP pollution mitigation (see Chapter 4 for a discussion of relevant policy instruments).

3.3.2. Tyre use stage

Mitigation actions implementable during the use phase include the optimisation of vehicle operation parameters such as tyre pressure, wheel alignment, vehicle load, vehicle speed, driving conditions, driving behaviour and reductions in total transport volumes (Table 3.6). The advantages and disadvantages of each mitigation action are discussed below. Importantly, several mitigation best practices and technologies implementable during the use phase generate numerous synergies with other relevant benefits and environmental policy objectives.

Table 3.6. Overview of mitigation actions relevant for TRWP and implementable during the use phase of tyres

	Mitigation action	Description	Advantages (+) and Disadvantages (-)
Optimising vehicle maintenance	Ensuring correct tyre pressure and/or implementing technologies to monitor it on vehicles	Since low or incorrect inflation pressure leads to greater tyre wear (Salminen, 2014[67]; Wang et al., 2016[68]; Li et al., 2011[69]), ensuring adequate tyre pressure can limit TRWP generation. Automatized monitoring systems for tyre pressure may help to ensure optimal pressure conditions.	+ Easy to implement: simple regular pressure check and no additional infrastructure required + Potentially high impact + Policy action already underway (e.g. requirements for pressure monitoring systems in the EU) (EC, 2010[70]). + Improved fuel efficiency
	Ensuring correct wheel alignment	Incorrect wheel alignment leads to higher tyre tread abrasion (and fuel consumption). Thus, regular and/or stricter checks on the alignment of vehicle wheels can mitigate TRWP generation.	+ Potentially high impact + Low costs (no additional infrastructure required) + Improves fuel efficiency - Requires regular vehicle inspections - Impact also depends on correct tyre pressure
Eco-driving	Reducing vehicle speed	The emission of TRWPs increases with speed. Speed determines the level of mechanical stress in the tyre material and thus directly influences the degree of tyre wear (Gustafsson et al., 2009[71]; Li et al., 2011[69]; Wang et al., 2016[68]). Thus, measures aimed at reducing vehicle speed, such as the introduction and enforcement of speed limits, can mitigate TRWP generation.	+ High impact + Low costs (no additional infrastructure needed) + Co-benefits with increased safety, lower fuel consumption and lower air pollution - Necessary measures require public acceptability - Policy measures require greater enforcement efforts - Potentially longer travel times

Mitigation action		Description	Advantages (+) and Disadvantages (-)
	Adapting driving behaviour	Aggressive driving styles, rapid deceleration and complete stops generate considerable amounts of TRWP compared to gradual acceleration and deceleration. Hence, a higher uptake of eco-driving practices, including with the aid of advanced driver-assistance systems, can mitigate TRWP generation.	+ High impact + Co-benefits with lower fuel consumption, lower air pollution, increased safety and reduced noise levels - High implementation barriers
Reducing traffic	Reducing traffic volumes	Reductions in vehicle traffic via policy disincentives and/or the provision of alternative transport infrastructure can reduce the overall quantities of TRWP generated.	+ Potentially high impact + Lower air pollution - Absent compensating measures, policy disincentives may generate distributional effects - Long implementation timeframe - Additional infrastructure potentially needed

Source: (Verschoor and de Valk, 2017[72]; Andersson-Sköld et al., 2020[53]; OECD, 2020[54])

Optimising vehicle maintenance: tyre pressure and wheel alignment

Maintaining optimal *pressure in vehicle tyres* throughout their use can optimise performance as well as minimise TRWP generation. If the tyre pressure is too low, internal heat generation occurs, which increases wear (Li et al., 2011[69]). Over-inflation, on the other hand, leads to uneven tyre tread wear, which can reduce the lifespan of a tyre. In OECD countries, the share of the vehicle fleet operating with suboptimal tyre pressure could be significant. For instance, it was calculated that in Sweden one in seven cars has at least one tyre with an air pressure which is 30% too low, causing higher tyre wear (Andersson-Sköld et al., 2020[53]).

Tyre pressure monitoring systems (TPMS) have been introduced on passenger cars in several OECD countries and provide one technological solution to the problem. These are electronic systems designed to monitor tyre pressure and to report real-time information to drivers when the tyre requires to be inflated. Verschoor and de Valk (2017[72]) estimated that equipping all Dutch cars with a TPMS would lead to a 14% reduction in tyre wear. Since 2014, newly registered cars in the EU are fitted with TPMSs (EC, 2010[70]). Still, as regular pressure tests are not always performed, older vehicles registered in the EU before November 2014 may operate under non-optimal tyre pressure conditions. Where measures for TPMS have been introduced, it is expected that the number of cars operating with sub-optimal tyre pressure will decrease as older cars without pressure monitoring system are removed from the market.

Incorrect *wheel alignment* may increase tyre wear rates by up to 10% (Verschoor and de Valk, 2017[72]). The share of the vehicle fleet operating with incorrect wheel alignment can also be significant: in Germany, for instance, 15% of vehicles operate with incorrect wheel alignment (Kraftfahrtbundesamt, 2019[73]). Tests on wheel alignment are generally done during the change of tyres, e.g. from summer to winter tyres. In countries or regions where seasonal changes of tyres are not required, alignment checks occur less frequently. Yet, regular testing and wheel realignment is a relevant option that can increase the lifetime of tyres (without adaptation of infrastructure) and also reduce tyre wear.

Eco-driving and traffic flow management: vehicle speed and driving behaviour

Driving behaviour is one major parameter influencing the tyre wear rate. Higher speeds, fast acceleration and fast retardation and high cornering speeds in particular are associated with increased tyre wear (Pohrt, 2019[55]). Changes of direction, congestion and high-speed roads are also generally associated with higher TRWP generation (Andersson-Sköld et al., 2020[53]).

Significant reductions in TRWP can be achieved by encouraging drivers to adopt *eco-driving practices*, i.e. maintaining lower and constant speeds. Since tyre wear rate increases by a factor of four relative to increases in speed, speed reductions hold a high mitigation potential (Pohrt, 2019[55]). Examples of specific measures include the introduction and effective enforcement of local speed limits of cornering roads as well as of motorways, measures to improve driver awareness, the use of advanced driver-assistance systems, such as cruise control and adaptive distance control and general traffic management measures.

Speed reduction will be relevant either to reduce or better enforce existing speed limits or to introduce (nationwide or local) measures where these are not present (e.g. in Germany). Implementation costs would be relatively low as only limited infrastructure would be required, however public acceptability is likely to be the main implementation barrier to the introduction or adaptation of speed limits. For this reason, it will be important to share with the public and policymakers scientific evidence on the adverse consequences of speeding in terms of potential safety and on the environmental gains which can be achieved via speed limits.

Although measures aimed at reducing speeds are primarily driven by safety concerns, a reduction of tyre wear rates can be achieved as a co-benefit, for instance as a result of smoother driving with continuous traffic flow instead of stop-and-go traffic. These measures also generate significant synergies with environmental objectives, such as reduced fuel consumption and lower emissions of CO_2 and air pollutants (e.g. NOx and particulate matter). The adoption of eco-driving practices and smart road management can reduce fuel consumption up to an average of 6.3%, with consequent reductions in CO_2 emissions (Wang and Boggio-Marzet, 2018[74]). Further evidence is required in order to quantify potential reductions in tyre wear emissions achievable via improved driver awareness and traffic management.

Reducing transport volumes

Several options exist to mitigate TRWP emissions via *overall reductions in traffic volumes*. These are not unique to TRWP generation, rather have been discussed extensively in order to respond to needs to mitigate GHG emissions and air and noise pollution, limit sealed surfaces in urban areas in order to allow rainwater to seep away and prevent floods, decrease the amount of urban space occupied by road traffic and reduce congestion.

In order to decrease transport volumes, overall higher accessibility can be delivered by increasing the role of transport modes such as public transport, cycling and walking (which generate less TRWP per capita); ultimately increasing TRWP mitigation potential while also improving other well-being (e.g. health, equity) goals (OECD, 2019[75]). The promotion of modal shifts requires adequate infrastructural investments for sustainable transport modes, for instance via the construction of advanced railroad systems to increase ridership and capacity of public transportation systems. Urban areas can also be designed in compact ways so as to reduce dependence on private vehicle travel. In general, creating proximity between people and places is key to avoiding unnecessary trips or unnecessarily long distances and to increasing the scope for active and public transport (OECD, 2019[75]).

A reduction in total traffic and total mobility should be considered a long-term goal that requires parallel adaptations of transportation systems and urban forms. Notable drawbacks of traffic reduction measures include the need for public acceptability as well as potentially high implementation costs and the potential for distributional effects. Again, these can be greatly reduced if policy and investments are refocused on the enhancement of accessibility. To the extent that traffic reduction also reduces local air pollutants and GHG emissions, policies that seek to reduce TRWP via a reduction in vehicle-kilometres travelled also have environmental health and climate mitigation co-benefits. Furthermore, by incentivising active travel and enhancing accessibility, particularly for vulnerable population, policies that generate "avoid" and "shift" effects can also bring additional health benefits as well as contribute to more equitable access to services and opportunities (OECD, 2019[75]).

A number of cities around the world have implemented traffic reduction schemes aimed at improving air quality, quality of life and safety. For example, Strasbourg, Nurnberg, Copenhagen, Vienna and Ghent have successfully implemented traffic calming measures (EC, 2004[76]). Other options may include the reallocation and re-design of streets, parking and road pricing, expansions and upgrades of public transport and active mode services, or incentives for the uptake of shared services. Such measures usually reduce vehicle traffic while promoting other modes of transport as cycling and public transport (Titos et al., 2015[77]). Although these measures are not typically implemented in order to mitigate microplastics, reductions in TRWP will occur as a co-benefit.

3.3.3. Tyre end-of-life stage

As discussed in Chapter 2, End-of-Life Tyres are commonly employed in material recovery applications, including for the production of rubber granulate used as infill in artificial sport pitches or in moulded surfaces used in playgrounds and outdoor facilities. The use of rubber granulate as infill material for sport pitches offers improved durability and resistance to varying weather conditions, good shock absorbance and safety characteristics, low costs and a lower need for virgin materials (Magnusson et al., 2016[78]). Yet, several studies have indicated that sport pitches may constitute a significant source of microplastics pollution (see Section 2.3.2).[6]

Guidelines have been developed to support the prevention of rubber granulate leakage in the design and operation of artificial turf pitches (Fidra, 2020[79]; EuRIC, 2020[80]; CEN/TR, 2020[81]). Selected options, presented in Table 3.7, include several low-cost, high-potential mitigation actions. Examples include the installation of infrastructure which prevents the emission of rubber granulate particles (e.g. side paved areas around the pitch, cattle grids and brushing stations located near the pitch entrance, drainage and filtration systems for runoff) and the routine maintenance of the pitch (EuRIC, 2020[80]; Eunomia, 2018[82]). The lack of awareness among owners and operators as well as the lack of regulatory or financial incentives may be posing barriers to a larger uptake of the identified mitigation best practices and technologies.

Table 3.7. Overview of best practices and technologies for the prevention of microplastics leakage during the operation of artificial sports pitches

Best practices and technologies	Description	Advantages (+) and Disadvantages (-)
	Design and installation	
Optimisation of pitch layout	Installation of solid side pavement around the pitch, from which scattered infill material can be easily collected.	+ Potentially high impact - Requires infrastructural changes - Mostly relevant for new pitches
Installation of physical barriers around the pitch with a board at the bottom	Physical barriers (e.g. fences, side perimeters) have proved successfully at preventing particles leaving the pitch.	- Requires additional infrastructure + Synergy effects with safety e.g. sport equipment may not fly outside the pitch
Installation of brushing stations for players' shoes and of boot cleaning mats/grates at pitch entrance points	The installation of brushing stations at the exit of the pitch can enable the cleaning of shoes and prevent the material from being carried away outside the pitch. The use of grates and/or scraper mats can also help with the removal of rubber granulate from players' shoes.	+ Low-cost structural adaptations of existing pitches + Potentially high impact + Can easily be retrofitted on existing pitches
	Maintenance	
Regular brushing and drag matting	Regular brushing and drag matting of the field ensures that the dispersed infill is returned to the field	+ Required to ensure pitch performance and player safety + Brushing also minimises compaction (and the need for additional rubber infill) + Extends lifetime of the pitch
Installation of drainage slit traps	Drainage water is collected and treated before discharge. This can be achieved via the use of traps for granulates.	+ Potentially high impact - Can be retrofitted - Requires continued maintenance in order to be effective
Separate collection and treatment of surface water	Surface water runoff is collected separately from drainage water. It can be treated to collect particulate materials	+ Potentially high impact - Requires additional infrastructure - Mostly relevant for future pitches

Best practices and technologies	Description	Advantages (+) and Disadvantages (-)
Snow clearance: use of dedicated storage areas or piling on the pitch	Removed snow should be stored in dedicated areas that allow for the collection of the infill once the snow melts. Where this is not possible, snow can be piled on (potentially winter-lined) pitches, so that microplastics mixed with snow are not dispersed.	+ Simple adaptation of the pitch operation + Prevents a deterioration in the pitch infill + High impact where snowfall is significant - Requires space for snow storage (or the temporary reduction in the pitch size).

Source: (EuRIC, 2020[80]; CEN/TR, 2020[81])

3.3.4. Comparison of mitigation options for tyre-based microplastics

Potential mitigation best practices and technologies for tyre-based microplastics are evaluated in Table 3.8 according to three criteria: mitigation potential, implementation efforts required and costs and the societal impact. In general, progress in tyre and pavement design in line with lower wear rates offers a high mitigation potential, although the development of optimised tyres and road pavements without compromises in safety, noise and durability may take some time. During the use phase, reduced vehicle speed, adapted driving behaviour and adequate maintenance of vehicle and tyres also have a high TRWP reduction potential. At the same time, since complete prevention of TRWP generation and emission cannot be achieved by optimized materials, end-of-pipe options may be important solutions to retain the emitted TRWP before these enter the environment. There, case-by-case designs may be required for the installation or adaptation of stormwater and road runoff treatment options, as discussed in Section 3.4.2.

Table 3.8. Assessment of mitigation best practices and technologies according to selected criteria

Values are assigned based on the three criteria: mitigation potential, implementation efforts required and costs, and the societal impact. The table is colour coded from red (higher barriers to implementation) to green (easier implementation and higher mitigation potential).

	Mitigation potential	Implementation efforts required and costs	Societal impact	Stakeholders
Optimisation of tyre design	High	Medium-High	Medium-Low	Tyre and car manufacturing industries
Optimisation of road design	High	Medium-High	Medium-Low	Public authorities, municipalities, road infrastructure developers
Reductions in vehicle weight	Medium-High	Medium	Medium-High	Car manufacturing industry, consumers, state
Tyre pressure optimisation	Medium-High	Low	Medium	Car and tyre manufacturing industries, consumers, public authorities
Wheel alignment optimisation	Medium	Low	Medium	Consumers, public authorities
Eco-driving and traffic flow management	High	Medium	High	Consumers, public authorities
Reductions in total transport volumes	Very High	Medium-High	High	Public authorities, municipalities, regional transport authorities, consumers
Direct particle collection and street sweeping	Medium	Medium	Low	Communities, industry
Improved stormwater management and treatment	Very High	Medium-High	Low	Public authorities, municipalities
Artificial turf pitch operation	Medium-High	Medium-Low	Low	Pitch operators, customers, municipalities

Note: End-of-pipe mitigation options relevant for TRWP are discussed in Section 3.4
Source: Authors' own evaluation based on (Andersson-Sköld et al., 2020[53]; Eunomia, 2018[82])

3.4. End-of-pipe mitigation technologies and best practices

End-of-pipe options, such as (potentially separate) wastewater and stormwater collection and treatment, constitute a last barrier to pollutants present in contaminated water sources and play a critical role in preserving water quality. The performance of end-of-pipe technologies in removing microplastics is only of recent interest and not yet fully understood. Existing treatment processes for wastewaters generally retain the majority of microplastics initially in the wastewater effluents. However, in an attempt to improve their overall performance in retaining a range of water pollutants (including microplastics), there is interest to explore ways to enhance the treatment efficiency further. Additionally, substantial quantities of microplastics enter the environment via diffuse pathways (i.e. dry and wet deposition, road and stormwater runoff). In this sense, end-of-pipe options such as improved stormwater management, generally driven by the need to manage increased runoff rates caused by urbanisation, can also contribute to the preservation of water quality.

The next sections explore existing facilities and technologies that can be adopted to enhance the capture of microplastics carried in domestic and industrial wastewaters (Section 3.4.1) and in road dust and stormwater runoff (Section 3.4.2).

3.4.1. Wastewater treatment and sewage sludge management

Treating municipal wastewaters in a wastewater treatment plant (WWTP) is the norm in OECD countries. WWTPs purify used water resources from pollutants originating from human activities and rainwater runoff before these are reintroduced into the water cycle, preventing the spread of pollutants and bacteria hazardous to human health and the environment.

Each WWTP involves selected combinations of chemical, physical and biological processes taking place simultaneously or interacting, in order to achieve a final effluent which is in line with existing regulations for water reuse or release into the environment. Depending on the stringency of the regulations in place and other location-specific characteristics (e.g. availability of space, capacity of treatment, types and concentrations of pollutants and features of the receiving water body such as the dilution capacity and sensitive uses), WWTP may be designed to have unique combinations of preliminary, primary, secondary and tertiary (and potentially additional) treatment stages. When required, old WWTPs are retrofitted (via the addition and/or replacement of some treatment units) to enable compliance with more stringent standards.

Although several knowledge gaps remain (Box 3.1), some indicative conclusions can be drawn from available data on the fate of microplastics during WWT. Table 3.9 describes the main objectives to be attained during each stage of the treatment process in a conventional setup and outlines the expected microplastics stage removal rate. Conventional WWTPs can achieve microplastics retention rates of 80-95% (by number), likely mostly attained in preliminary and primary treatment steps (e.g. screening, removal of grit and grease).[7] WWTPs with tertiary treatment[8] show only marginal higher efficiency at retaining microplastics compared to plants with only secondary treatment, although this might vary depending on the specific technologies in place (Talvitie, 2018[83]; Nikiema, Mateo-Sagasta and Saad, 2019[84]). The effectiveness of the process in terms of microplastics removal seems to be more affected by the size rather than type of the particle, with smaller particles being more difficult to remove (Lv et al., 2019[85]; Talvitie et al., 2017[86]).

Table 3.9. Conventional treatment of wastewater: objectives, performance in terms of microplastics removal and costs

	Preliminary	Primary	Secondary	Tertiary/Advanced	Disinfection
Objective	Removal of coarse particles	Removal of floatables, grit, grease, some suspended solid matter, heavy metals and other pollutants.	Removal of biodegradable organic matter and suspended solids	Removal of contaminants (e.g. nitrogen) affecting the quality or a specific use of water	Deactivation of pathogens (e.g. bacteria and viruses)
Typical processes employed	Screening to remove large items Grit removal Skimming of grease Coagulation and flocculation Primary sedimentation Flotation		Activated sludge + secondary sedimentation, Oxidation ditch Anaerobic/Anoxic/Oxic process Membrane bioreactors	Biological aerated filter (BAF) Rapid sand filter Filtering disks	Contact with chlorine, ozone, or ultraviolet radiation
Performance					
For conventional pollutants	Debris and floatable materials (depending on design target)	• BOD: 20-30% • Suspended solids: 60%-98% • Phosphorus: 60-95% • Heavy metals (varies depending on design target)	BOD and TSS: typically 85%-95% removal	• Nitrogen: 90% • Other pollutants, including heavy metals (depending on design target)	Typically over 99%
For MPs: cumulative [per stage] removal rate		42 - 82%	16 - 98% [-293%[1] - 99.7%]	79 - 99.9% [54 - 84%]	79 - 99.9% [< 1%]
Fate of microfibres	Negligible removal	Highest removal achieved during this stage, through: • Skimming for light microplastics • Filtration and gravity settling processes for heavier microplastics.	Some removal is achieved at this stage, but exact removal mechanisms are uncertain.	Could remove fine microfibres	Variable, it could cause physical and chemical alteration of microplastics
Fate of micro fragments	Negligible removal	Removed by sedimentation	Trapped in flocs and removed during the secondary sedimentation	Small particles are well removed by filtration	Variable. Could cause physical and chemical alteration of microplastics
Costs					
Investment & operational costs (US example)	*Sewer and secondary treatment plant (in the US):* Average investment and O&M costs are 3,308 and 437 USD per m^3/d, respectively (2017)			*Sewer and tertiary treatment plant (in the US):* Average investment and O&M costs are 57,534 and 6,168 USD per m^3/d, respectively (2017).	

Notes: m^3/d stands for cubic meters treated per day

1: Some WWTP do not involve secondary sedimentation (i.e. the clarification done after a secondary bioreactor) to enable the removal of the microplastics from the effluents. With sludge recirculation, microplastics concentrations actually increase in the treatment unit. In those cases, removal would be done in a tertiary filtration unit.

Source: Adapted from (Nikiema et al., 2020[87])

Box 3.1. Data limitations for assessing the microplastics removal rate of WWT processes

Associating a certain microplastics removal rate to specific parameters, such as the type of treatment process employed, can be challenging. This is for several reasons, including:

- *The quality and availability of the data.* There are concerns related to the quality of some available data on microplastics' removal in WWTPs. The majority of available studies build on one-time measures and replications are scarce. This is an issue since there could be a wide temporal and spatial variation in influent and effluent wastewater quality from one or different countries and studies.

- *The lack of standardised methods.* The lack of consistency in analytical protocols for sampling, processing and analysis limits the comparability of available studies. This poses challenges to the accurate identification of factors and treatment stages which influence the microplastics removal rate (Weis, 2020[88]). There is an important need to develop methods for the sampling and analysis of TRWP in wastewaters, for which very little information is available and no studies have been carried out so far (Andersson-Sköld et al., 2020[53]; Baensch-Baltruschat et al., 2020[89]).
- *The general complexity of the issue.* During wastewater treatment, numerous interactions may occur between various chemical and physical processes, microorganisms and other factors. These could impair or otherwise support the removal of microplastics by modifying the surface of microplastics or causing their further breakdown into smaller particles that are more difficult to remove (Lv et al., 2019[85]; Ruan et al., 2019[90]; Nikiema et al., 2020[87]).

Note: Harmonization and standardization of analytical techniques is required, including for the mesh size used for sampling, which defines the lower size limit for microplastics' detection. This is further discussed in Chapters 4 and 5.

Opportunities to improve existing municipal WWTPs in OECD countries

In OECD countries, the infrastructure in place can be considered largely effective at preventing the release of microplastics present in the wastewater influent to surface waters. Table 3.10 presents selected cases to illustrate how primary, secondary and tertiary treatment stages influence the microplastic removal rate in a number of OECD countries (and China). As illustrated, conventional secondary treatment systems remove between 86% and 99.8%[n] of microplastics in raw wastewater.

According to Murphy et al. (2016[91]), the highest microplastic removal is achieved during skimming (especially for lighter microplastics), while other authors (see for instance (Talvitie et al., 2017[92]; WHO, 2019[93])) also emphasize the important role played by filtration or gravity settling processes for the removal of heavier microplastics. The overall performance in terms of microplastics removal is mainly determined by the removal performance achieved during the primary treatment stage.

Table 3.10. Microplastics removal in selected cases with primary, secondary and tertiary treatment

	Treatment variant	Country	MP removal per stage [cumulative]	Inlet conc. (MP / L)	Notes	References
Primary treatment	Screening, grit removal, skimming and primary sedimentation	United States	78% [m]	-		(Mason et al., 2016[94])
	Screening, grit removal, primary sedimentation	France	80.6%	1,737	No chemicals used	*
	Screening, grit removal, pre-aeration and sedimentation	Finland	82% [m]	567.8		(Talvitie et al., 2017[86])
			99%	57.6		(Lares et al., 2018[95])
	Screening, aerated grit removal chamber	China	21 - 30%	0.28	Micro fragments and microfibres represent 65% and 21% of inflow microplastics, respectively	(Lv et al., 2019[85])

	Treatment variant	Country	MP removal per stage [cumulative]	Inlet conc. (MP / L)	Notes	References
Secondary treatment	Membrane Bioreactor (MBR) [1]	Spain	79.1% Microfibres: 57.7% Micro fragments: 98.8%	4.40 ± 1.01	Influent and effluent have 48.1% and 96.7% microfibres, respectively	(Bayo, López and Olmos, 2020[96])
		Finland	99.4% Microfibres: 99.1% Micro fragments: 89.9%	0.6		(Lares et al., 2018[95])
	Activated sludge [2]		88%	11.7	This study analysed micro litter	(Talvitie et al., 2017[92])
			~75% Microfibres: 1% Micro fragments: 76.4% (mix)	14.2 (microfibres) 290.7 (other microplastics)	Influent and effluent have 4.7% and 16.7% microfibres, respectively	(Talvitie et al., 2015[97])
			Around -66% [98%]	0.6	The amount of microplastics increases in the process	(Lares et al., 2018[95])
		Turkey	[74%]	26,555	WWTP treats domestic wastewater only. Average MP sizes in influent and effluent are 1.57 mm and 1.15 mm.	(Gündoğdu et al., 2018[98])
		China	77.5% [86.9%]	1.2		(Ruan et al., 2019[90])
	Oxidation ditch [3]		95% [96%]	0.22		(Lv et al., 2019[85])
	A2O process [4]		17% [-293%]	1.32		
	7 WWTPs		[90.5%]	[6.55]		(Long et al., 2019[99])
Tertiary/Advanced Treatment	Activated sludge	France	85.2% [97.1%]	337		*
	Biofiltration		72.1% [92.7%]	43		
	Membrane filtration	China	95% [79%]	1.1	Inlet conc. is 4.70 mg/L and outlet conc. is 0.03 mg/L. Removal rate is 99.7% ^{m}.	(Lv et al., 2019[85])
	BAF process	Finland	Up to 53.8% [99.9%]	1.4 (varying between 1 and 2)	Average concentration in the effluent of 2.5 MP/L (0.7 - 3.5 MP/L)	(Talvitie et al., 2017[92])
			85% [98.6 - 98.9%] Microfibres: 64% Micro fragments 87.5% (mix)	13.8 (microfibres) 68.6 (other MPs)	4.9 MP/L (for microfibres) 8.6 MP/L (for microplastics)	(Talvitie et al., 2015[97])
	Rapid sand filter	Spain	75.5% Microfibres: 53.8% Micro fragments: 95.5%	4.40 ± 1.01, with 48.1% microfibres	Outflow contains 1.08 ± 0.28 MP/L, with 90.8% microfibres	(Bayo, López and Olmos, 2020[96])
	Rapid Sand filter	France	-58.3% [90.2%]	12	Increase in MP concentrations	*
	Filtering disks		68.8% [97.1%]	16	Outflow contains 5 MP / L	*

Notes: The indicated level of performance depends on the whole process train in place, as each step has an impact on the removal of the next one, the final removal being accumulative. Performance also depends on some important design characteristics (e.g. pore size).

The removal efficiency can be obtained on a percent mass basis (indicated by ^{m}) or on a percent number basis (^{n}). The latter is employed throughout except where otherwise specified.

* Marks information gathered during the expert meeting "OECD Workshop on Microplastics from Synthetic Textiles in the Environment: Knowledge, Mitigation and Policy", held on 11 February 2020.

1: In the case of MBR, secondary and tertiary treatments are achieved in a single stage process.

2: In the case of activated sludge, secondary and tertiary treatments can be achieved in a single stage process (e.g. for low-loaded activated sludge plants).

3: This process is a variant of the conventional activated sludge treatment process. It relies on long solids retention times for the treatment.

4: This process is a variant of the conventional activated sludge treatment process. The biological reactor comprises of three separate section operating under anaerobic, anoxic and aerobic conditions

Source: Adapted from (Nikiema et al., 2020[87])

In response to more stringent regulations on water quality, several countries have seen WWTPs being retrofitted with additional treatment units in recent years. Although these advancements primarily aim to ensure that nutrient or heavy metal levels in treated effluents are within water quality standards, they may offer potential co-benefits with higher cumulative MP retention efficiencies. Given the large volumes of wastewaters treated and the possible high quantities of microplastics entering the environment via the wastewater pathway, there is scope for exploring the effectiveness of available technologies in removing microplastics to potentially inform the design of end-of-pipe capture solutions for microplastics and other micropollutants contained in wastewaters (Talvitie et al., 2017[86]).

Different tertiary technologies may offer varying microplastics mitigation potential. If processes such as Biological aerated filter (BAF) and Rapid sand filters yield inconsistent or limited results for microplastics removal (Bayo, López and Olmos, 2020[96]; OECD, 2020[100]), filtering disks, dissolved air flotation and membrane-based systems (i.e. membrane bioreactor (MBR); reverse osmosis (typically only employed for specific reuse options); membrane filtration) offer the potential for effective treatment of both microplastics and nutrients and heavy metals. With most tertiary treatment processes, there are issues reported with risk of by-passing of microfibres, due to their longitudinal shape, hence resulting in their escaping into the environment (Bayo, López and Olmos, 2020[96]). The removal of microplastics through advanced filtration may vary depending on the surface characteristics and size of microplastics: for instance, MBR has been found to be particularly effective at retaining micro fragments and MPs < 1 mm, but less so for microfibres and larger particles (Bayo, López and Olmos, 2020[96]; Lv et al., 2019[85]; Talvitie et al., 2015[97]). Furthermore, membrane defects and fouling can negatively affect their performance.

Table 3.10 illustrated examples of the use of MBR technology for microplastic removal. Membrane bioreactor (MBR) units are a well-established membrane-based technology among the most effective treatment options for microplastics. MBR offers the benefit of combining biological treatment (secondary) and membrane filtration (tertiary) in a single step. The membrane (1.0-0.01 µm) is selected based on its effectiveness at removing targeted contaminants and its durability based on the operating conditions. Currently, MBR is used for municipal or industrial wastewater treatment to enhance removal of nitrogen or hardly biodegradable compounds. Membrane technologies are costly to implement and maintain and are currently only employed where the objective is to enable water reuse in scarce areas, retrofit inefficient plants, minimise effluents in small vulnerable water bodies, or where compact installations are required. Typically, MBR is 38-53% more expensive and 25-50% more energy-intensive than use of conventional activated sludge process (Bertanza et al., 2017[101]).

Overall, risk assessments and cost-benefit analyses will need to be carried out in order to evaluate costs against the advantages offered (e.g. removal of higher levels of suspended solids or nutrient). Conventional wastewater secondary treatment processes, such as activated sludge, seem to be more cost-effective to implement than tertiary treatment processes with regards to removal of microplastics. Beyond this, knowledge remains limited and to some extent insufficient to derive conclusions on the best technology to retain microplastics.

Industrial wastewater treatment

As discussed in Section 2.2.2, the textile industry is an important potential source of microfibres. Although microplastics is not a targeted contaminant for removal during industrial wastewater treatment,[9] currently employed technologies at industrial WWTPs, where in place, may be fairly effective at retaining microplastics, with certain industrial WWTPs exhibiting microfibre removal efficiencies >85%.

Table 3.11 presents the treatment performance achieved by typical textile-based industrial WWTP in China, the world's largest producer of fabrics. In general, large microfibres are more easily removed than small microfibres (i.e. < 50µm) (Zhou, Zhou and Ma, 2020[102]). Air flotation appears to be a suitable technology for removal of low-densities microfibres. However, removal of microfibres is mostly achieved in membrane-based processes such as MBR or Reverse Osmosis (i.e. during Step 2 and Step 3, respectively). On the other hand, the several pigments found in the influent wastewater responded differently to the wastewater treatment process and the reasons for this behaviour remain unclear (Xu et al., 2018[21]; Zhou, Zhou and Ma, 2020[102]).

Table 3.11. Inlet effluent quality and treating performance of various elemental processes in removal of microfibres

Plant capacity (m^3/d)	Type of treatment	Influent concentration (microfibres/L)	Size (µm)	Details	Preliminary treatment	Secondary treatment	Tertiary treatment
500 [b]	Onsite	~12,000	~400	Processes implemented	Conditioning	MBR	Reverse Osmosis
				Cumulative removal efficiency	N/A	74.4%	84.7%
				Microfibre size	N/A	~260 µm	~225 µm
2,000 [b]	Onsite	~54,000	~600	Processes implemented	Conditioning	Anaerobic/Oxic	Air flotation
				Cumulative removal efficiency	N/A	96%	97.5%
				Microfibre size	N/A	~360 µm	~350 µm
4,000 [b]	Onsite	~1,200	~1,200	Processes implemented	Conditioning	MBR	Reverse Osmosis
				Cumulative microfibre removal efficiency	N/A	44.3%	99.5%
				Microfibre size	N/A	~300 µm	~450 µm
400,000 [b]	Offsite[1]	13,600	~450	Processes implemented	Primary treatment	Oxidation ditch	Air flotation + Ozone oxidation + activated carbon filter + rotary disk filter
				Cumulative removal efficiency	N/A	90.7%	97.4%
				Microfibre size	N/A	~270 µm	~260 µm
600,000 [b]	Offsite[2]	8,367	~600	Processes implemented	Primary treatment	Anaerobic/ Anoxic/Oxic	Denitrification filter + Fenton oxidation + air flotation
				Cumulative removal efficiency	N/A	80.9%	92.8%
				Microfibre size	N/A	~500 µm	~250 µm
30,000 [a]	Offsite[3]	333.4 ± 24.4	80% were > 30 µm, with the majority between 100 µm and 1 mm	Processes implemented	Screening + grit separation + primary sedimentation	Aeration + secondary sedimentation	Coagulation + sand filter + activated carbon filter
				Cumulative [individual] removal efficiency	76% [76%]	84% [32%]	95% [70%]

Notes: m^3/d stands for cubic meters treated per day. N/A: not available.
1: Some onsite treatment has already been carried out for 50 textile mills
2: Some onsite treatment has already been carried out for 80 textile mills
3: 95% in volume is coming from 33 printing and dyeing enterprises while the remaining 5% is domestic wastewater from residential areas.
Source: [a] (Xu et al., 2018[21]); [b] (Zhou, Zhou and Ma, 2020[102])

The range of contaminants typically targeted by WWT for industrial effluents from textile manufacturing/dyeing plants is exemplified in Table 3.12. An improved understanding of the quantities and fate of microfibres emitted during textile manufacturing processes is required in order to inform future decisions on the optimisation of industrial wastewater treatment to retain microfibres emitted during the manufacturing process. As industrial and commercial laundry facilities are also potential hotspots for microfibres in OECD countries, ad-hoc wastewater treatment may also be an effective option to mitigate microfibre pollution closer to the source of emission. For instance, a study conducted in Sweden found that wastewater treatment adjacent to industrial laundries reduced microfibre concentrations by 65-97% (Swedish EPA, 2018[103]). In general, whether further investments in WWTP upgrades are cost-effective will vary depending on the types of contaminants emitted into industrial effluents and the local conditions (e.g. the type of WWT infrastructure in place, other micropollutants present in sewage).

Table 3.12. Removal of other pollutants during treatment of industrial textile wastewater

Pollutant	Inlet concentration	Pollutant removal efficiency (%) Cumulative [individual process]		
		Primary treatment	Secondary treatment	Tertiary treatment
Chroma	342.0 mg/L	-82%	46% [70%]	85% [72%]
Chemical oxygen demand	283.4 mg/L	36%	73% [58%]	91% [68%]
Ammonium nitrogen (NH_3-N)	3.9 mg/L	28%	43% [20%]	68% [44%]
Suspended solids	207.8 mg/L	74%	93% [73%]	99% [84%]
Total phosphorus	0.3 mg/L	24%	49% [33%]	77% [56%]

Source: (Xu et al., 2018[21])

Management of sewage sludge

Sewage sludge is the by-product of wastewater treatment, i.e. the residual mixture of solids and water retained from the influent wastewater. As microplastics are captured by the wastewater treatment process, these are transferred into the sludge fraction. The situation varies according to the types of MPs present in the influent and the type of WWT infrastructure. Typically, 69-99% in number of the microplastics initially in the influent wastewater are transferred to the sludge fractions produced at different stages of the wastewater treatment process (including the preliminary stages). It has been estimated that, in Swedish WTTPs, only 40-60% of microplastics originally in the wastewater influent are transferred to the anaerobically digested sludge, although it remains unclear to what extent treatment may lead to MP degradation to a size not detectable by commonly employed analytical methods (Tumlin and Bertholds, 2020[104]). As illustrated in Table 3.13, microfibres typically represent 63-80% of microplastics in sludge, but, especially when the WWTP also receives stormwater, other types of microplastics can also be present.

Wastewater sludge is most commonly incinerated or employed in agriculture as fertiliser. In several OECD countries, land application of sludge plays a key role in enhancing soil health through enrichment with the organic matter and nutrients. However, there are concerns that, in the long term, regular application of large volumes of sludge may result in the pollution of soil with contaminants not targeted by sludge treatment, including microplastics. Generally, sludge fractions undergo thickening and dewatering to reduce the water content, and, when intended for land application, they also undergo stabilisation to reduce the risks associated with pathogens and odours from biodegradation of organic matter. These processes may cause melting or shearing in microplastics, but typically no effective removal of the particles.

Nutrient recovery is a promising option to recycle back nutrients into agriculture without potentially re-applying hazardous organic and inorganic pollutants to land. Currently, only phosphorus recovery from digested sludge is carried out in some places to recover dry struvite, which is used as a slow-release fertilizer. This enables the recovery of 40% of the total phosphorus content, which corresponds to 90% of the soluble phosphate ion, although nitrogen and organic matter are not recovered (Koga, 2019[105]). Nutrient recovery options have a large commercial potential, however currently financial sustainability is not always achieved (Koga, 2019[105]).

In general, further research is required to assess the concentrations and hazards of microplastics in sewage sludge and evaluate possible end-cf-pipe mitigation options. For the time being, a low-cost strategic way of approaching the issue may be to avoid land application for sludge fractions richer in MPs, where the adequate infrastructure for incineration is present (taking account of potential GHG emissions and other environmental impacts). Sludge microplastics contamination varies widely according to the phase of the process from where it was obtained (Table 3.13). Given the majority of microplastics are retained during the preliminary and primary stages, sludge generated during skimming or primary sedimentation, for instance, will be richer in microplastics (typically 5-10 times) than sludge from biological treatments (secondary sludge). Indeed, in most OECD countries the fate of these sludge fractions richer in microplastics is generally incineration or landfilling. In order to evaluate further options for the management of microplastics in wastewater sludge, further research is required to assess the fate of microplastics during conditioning and treatment (e.g. in digesters) as well as to evaluate the potential risks for terrestrial environments posed by sludge application on agricultural land.

Table 3.13. Composition of sludge based on its origin

Origin of sludge within a WWTP	MP concentrations (count/g)	Sludge generation (g DW per L of treated wastewater)	Share of microfibres	Share of micro fragments	References
Primary sludge only	14.9 (WW)	Variable	65%	34%	(Gies et al., 2018[106])
Activated sludge only	4.4 (WW)		82%	10%	
	113 (DW)	0.075	47%	-	(Magni et al., 2019[107])
	23.0 (DW)				(Lv et al., 2019[85])
A2O sludge only	14.9 (WW)	0.99	8% with size > 300μm		(Lee and Kim, 2018[108])
	240.3 (DW)	-	33-57%	30-46%	
Sequential Batch Reactor sludge	9.7 (WW)	0.76	24% with size > 300μm		
Media based biological process	13.2 (WW)	0.51	20% with size > 300μm.		
MBR only	27.3 (DW)		-		(Lares et al., 2018[95])

Notes: DW: dry weight; WW: wet weight.
Source: Authors

3.4.2. Management and treatment of stormwater runoff and road dust

As discussed in Chapters 1 and 2, stormwater runoff collects pollutants originating from several sources, including a range of microplastics deposited on roads and washed off by precipitation events. Although the lack of data on the concentrations of microplastics in stormwater remains a challenge, stormwater runoff is believed to be the major entry pathway into the environment for TRWP (Parker-Jurd et al., 2019[109]). Despite the knowledge gaps, several existing measures to manage stormwater can contribute to minimising microplastics runoff into water bodies. Additionally, nature-based solutions (e.g. green roofs, permeable surfaces) can avoid that rainwater and runoff further contaminate sewage.

In light of emerging evidence on the contribution of tyre and road wear to non-exhaust particulate emissions and microplastics pollution, potential mitigation measures for airborne TRWP have also recently gained policy attention (OECD, 2020[54]). Targeting pollutants present in air and road dust may prove to be a cost-effective solution to prevent stormwater contamination with TRWP. Measures such as improving urban cleaning services and installing and adequately maintaining meshes, booms or separators on drains to retain and remove microplastics can help reducing solids which would otherwise be carried away with the water (Prata, 2018[110]).

The sections below discuss selected options to i) manage road dust and collect TRWP and other road traffic-related pollutants and ii) manage and treat stormwater runoff.

Street sweeping and direct particle collection

Street sweeping can provide an effective end-of-pipe measure to collect coarse particles contained in road dust, although the practice is less effective with fine dust (OECD, 2020[54]). Different techniques are available, such as removal by air, vacuum, or mechanical action of a broom (Calvillo, Williams and Brooks, 2015[111]), which will deliver different levels of performance. The collected particulate material is transferred and retained in the waste storage tank of the street sweeping machine. Although street sweeping does not require additional infrastructure, the collected street dust requires safe disposal after collection.

Further research is required in order to allow for a reliable assessment of the effectiveness of road sweeping at retaining TRWP (Andersson-Sköld et al., 2020[53]). Current knowledge indicates that the cleaning efficiency is likely to depend on the type of pavement, the type of sweeping machine and the precipitation conditions. Available research has identified a number of best practices to optimise the efficiency of street sweeping:

- Coordinating street sweeping with weather conditions to the pavement properties can increase its effectiveness (Andersson-Sköld et al., 2020[53]). For instance, road sweeping prior to strong rain events may remove TRWP before these are flushed away with the road runoff (ETRMA, 2018[61]).
- It may be more cost-efficient to prioritise street sweeping for high-traffic roads that are not equipped with efficient runoff water collection systems. Also, street sweeping is less effective on porous asphalt than on non-porous asphalt.
- Adapting the sweeping method to the weather and road conditions may also optimise the process. For instance, tests from the city of Stuttgart have shown that using street cleaning machines in wet mode (combining sweeping and water flushing) can provide a higher level of TRWP removal than other systems (ETRMA, 2018[61]). Conversely, with dry conditions, dry vacuum sweeping may be most effective at retaining road dust particles.

Filter techniques also exist for the treatment of road runoff, such as gully pot filters and underground sedimentation facilities (see next Section), which both generally bear small footprint requirements. In the case of *gully pots*, which are already widely employed in several countries to retain sediment in road runoff and minimise problems with sediment deposition downstream, available knowledge indicates that they can offer a low-cost and effective solution to retain microplastics coming from road transport activity, yet they require regular maintenance and cleaning in order to be effective (NIVA, 2018[112]). In general, further research is required to assess the adequacy and effectiveness of different techniques at retaining TRWP and other microplastics from road runoff. There are also efforts to develop technological solutions to capture emitted particles directly at the point of emission from the vehicle tyre, although innovative technologies still require further research, development and evaluation (Smithers, 2020[113]).

Improving stormwater management and treatment

Stormwater runoff not intended to be directed to a municipal WWTP should generally be treated before release into the environment for the removal of conventional pollutants such as heavy metals, oils and other organic pollutants (including PAHs), nutrients, pathogens and solids (Liu et al., 2019[114]; Strassler and Strellec, 1999[115]). Several technologies can serve this purpose, including wetlands, retention and detention ponds and infiltration systems. These can be found in urban and non-urban areas and are designed to remove particulate material and, to some extent, dissolved contaminants.

Table 3.14 presents the advantages, disadvantages, potential co-benefits and costs of common stormwater treatment technologies discussed in this section. Although the purpose here is to evaluate options that might be well-suited for microplastics removal, it is important to note that considerations on the implementation of these solutions are generally driven by a diverse set of concerns that include water quality preservation but also flood protection, cl mate change mitigation and adaptation, or habitat creation.

Table 3.14. Advantages, disadvantages, co-benefits and costs of selected stormwater treatment technologies

Technology	Advantages	Disadvantages	Co-Benefits	Typical life-cycle cost analysis and capital costs (excluding land costs)
Retention and detention ponds	• Installed as runoff/ stormwater quantity control structure, especially with detention ponds, reduces flooding risks • Effective and efficient settlement of particulates due to long residence time • Reduction of some pollutants, especially with retention ponds	• Pond can be rendered ineffective or damaged by nuisance plants, erosion and litter accumulation • Mosquito breeding • High space requirements	• Depending on location, recreational purposes, aesthetic and amenity benefits. • Creation of new habitats for wildlife • Development of aquatic vegetation along the shoreline	• Capital costs: USD 24.3 - 27.8 /m² • Net present value: USD 26.7-41.1 /m² at year 25 and USD 27.8 – 47.4 /m² at year 50 (Canadian example) • Capital costs per m² are 20% lower than for wetlands (US example)
Infiltration systems	• Filtration removes some pollutants • Water flow control • Low risk of mosquito breeding and odour problems due to low residence time • Water capture and storage • Supports a runoff flow control strategy	• Not suitable where groundwater is a primary drinking water source • Not suitable where soils are poorly permeable or in high traffic areas (for pavement systems) • Risk of high sediment accumulation, clogging and groundwater contamination • High maintenance costs • Capture capacity is low for trenches and wells	• Concrete pavers save, over 25 years, 0.17 kg of carbon dioxide per m² of land via stormwater reductions • Water capture to restore or maintain hydrology	• Capital cost: USD 49.8 – 62.0 /m² • Net present value: USD 75.4 /m² at year 25 and CAD 93.6 /m² at year 50. (Canadian example) • Capital costs per m² are 1.5 to 4 times higher than for wetlands (US example)
Wetlands	• Pollutant reduction • Hydrological and habitat benefits • Human health benefits	• Mosquito breeding • Should be setup after a retention ponds or other systems facilitating sediment control	• Increased wildlife habitat • Increased property values • Recreational opportunities	• Capital costs average USD 86 per m² of treatment capacity (US example)

Notes: Original costs for retention ponds in Canada are: Investment cost: CAD 32.7 -37.5/m²; Net present value: CAD 35.9-55.2 /m² at year 25 and CAD 37.4 – 63.7 /m² at year 50; Original costs for permeable concrete pavers in Canada are: Investment cost: CAD 67.0 - 83.3 /m²; Net present value: CAD 101.46/m² at year 25 and CAD 125.84/m² at year 50. Exchange rate applied is 1 CAD = 0.7437 USD. (Canadian Nursery Landscape Association, 2017[116])
Source: Adapted from (Nikiema et al., 2020[87]);

Detention/retention ponds

Sedimentation ponds are artificial basins commonly employed in OECD countries to manage stormwater runoff and remove particulate material via sedimentation processes. Two main types exist: detention and retention ponds. In detention ponds, runoff is captured and detained for a period of time and then clean water is released gradually, providing water quantity and peak flow regulation and limited water quality control. In retention ponds, the system maintains a permanent pool: the captured runoff water is retained until it is released or replaced by the following runoff water. Retention systems can provide both quantity and quality control for water runoff (Strassler and Strellec, 1999[115]).

Sedimentation ponds are considered as one of the most effective stormwater management installation for removing particulate material and potentially microplastics, because the long residence time allows particles to settle. Sedimentation ponds are designed to remove particles > 63 µm with removal efficiencies > 50% (Boogaard et al., 2017[117]). However, retention is expected to vary widely due to highly variable particulate loads (NIVA, 2018[112]). To ensure performance, the system requires regular removal and appropriate disposal of retained sediments (Liu et al., 2019[118]).

Infiltration systems

Infiltration systems are a sedimentation technique designed to aid water infiltrate into the ground, while the soil, organic matter, or a membrane serves as filtering media to remove sediments from stormwater runoff. Variants include:

- *Infiltration basins*, designed to drain their accumulated water within 3 days;
- *Porous pavement systems* made of porous asphalt or porous concrete, which typically reduce runoff formation by 45% compared to a fully asphalted area; and
- *Infiltration trenches or wells*, which have limited capacity and thus are often used in combination with detention or retention ponds.

These options have the merit of enriching groundwater, although adequate monitoring is required to ensure that the process does not result in groundwater contamination. Infiltration systems are not appropriate in all locations; for instance, sufficient levels of clay are needed in soil to allow the removal of dissolved pollutants in the runoff water (Strassler and Strellec, 1999[115]). As the infiltration systems are prone to clogging, it is crucial that accumulated sediments are removed from the pond bottom at least yearly and that soil compaction is prevented. Pavement systems must undergo periodic vacuuming or jet-washing to remove sediment from the pores and be protected from excessive equipment traffic.

Wetlands

Wetlands are a commonly employed nature-based solution for stormwater management and treatment (Ziajahromi et al., 2020[119]). Wetlands are known for their ability to improve water quality via natural processes involving wetland vegetation, soils and their associated microbial assemblages to filter water as it passes through the system. Benefits of wetlands include removal of nutrients and pharmaceutical residues and the prevention of unwanted releases of untreated water (Coalition Clean Baltic, 2017[120]). For conventional contaminants, removal occurs primarily via degradation and uptake by microbes and plants or their assimilation and absorption into organic and inorganic sediments.

Wetlands may prove effective at retaining microplastics present in stormwater, although research on the topic is limited. Different wetland variants exist:

- *Constructed wetlands (CWs)* are engineered and managed wetland systems designed to mimic natural wetlands. Available investigations of the performance of CWs in removing microplastics reported removal efficiencies over 99.7% for microplastics with a size exceeding 20 µm (Coalition Clean Baltic, 2017[120]; Liu et al., 2019[114]).
- *Floating wetlands (FWs)* are also manmade ecosystems. They employ small artificial platforms that allow plants to grow on floating mats in open water where their roots spread through the floating mats and down into the water. In a recently published study, between 15% and 38% of microplastics in the sediments accumulated in a FW were found to be synthetic rubber-carbon filled particles, most likely derived from vehicle tyres (Ziajahromi et al., 2020[119]). Further research is

required to adequately assess the removal effectiveness of FWs and to allow for comparisons with other options. Furthermore, as FWs can be built from plastic materials, there may be a risk of potential contribution to microplastics pollution via the degradation of the plastic construction materials (Ziajahromi et al., 2020[119]).

Comparison of stormwater treatment options

Although further research is required to fill the persisting data and knowledge gaps on the contribution of stormwater treatment infrastructure to microplastics pollution mitigation, available data suggests that wetlands and retention ponds may be highly effective at removing microplastics from water. It is likely that careful management of retained sediments is necessary to ensure the effective control of microplastics.

Wetlands are generally cost-effective because of the low investment and maintenance costs. The costs to set-up a wetland system in the United States are USD 379-11,016 (average USD 3,441) per m^3/d treated or USD 86 per m^2 (Hunter et al., 2018[121]), although these are highly variable in different locations. The operation and maintenance cost is typically USD 3.5-40 per m^3/d treated. Normally, wetlands have indefinite lifespans and are expected to be permanent landscape. The opportunity cost of land removed from other uses (e.g. agricultural production) is not negligible: it could represent between 50% and 70% of the total implementation costs. Construction costs per volume of runoff treated for wetlands are 25% higher than for retention and detention ponds, mainly due to the plant selection and sediment forebay requirements. Infiltration basins can be significantly more expensive, with 1.5 to 4 times higher costs for installations of equivalent size (Strassler and Strellec, 1999[115]). Also, annual operation and maintenance costs represent a significant percentage of the capital expenditure: 2%-6% for retention basins and constructed wetlands, 1% or less for detention ponds and 1-20% for infiltration trenches or ponds. These costs will vary based on a number of location-specific parameters.

Stormwater management infrastructure described above offers multiple co-benefits such as enhanced availability of water (which contributes to sustainable basin management), rainwater flow management, water quantity control, as well as increases in wildlife habitat, property values and recreational opportunities. In turn, all stormwater management options cannot be easily implemented everywhere. Soil characteristics, volumes of runoff and traffic conditions will determine the most suitable solution. There may also be a case for prioritising the installation of stormwater infrastructure near pollution hotspots, such as road sections with high traffic volume, although the cost-effectiveness of this approach needs to be assessed further (Gehrke, Dresen and Blömer, 2020[122]).

The decentralisation of stormwater and road runoff treatment may also contribute to reducing the pressure on combined sewer systems and the potential for combined sewer overflows, a substantial source of diffuse pollutants, including microplastics (as discussed in Chapter 1). Adequate stormwater runoff is necessary to prevent important floods in highly populated and paved urban areas, especially as pressures from diffuse sources of water pollution intensify. Furthermore, the development of flood management strategies may provide a useful entry-point to also improve microplastics capture as a co-benefit. Conversely, solutions such as constructed wetlands could also provide a treatment solution for excess loads occurring during heavy rain events (Meyer et al., 2013[123]).

References

Andersson-Sköld, Y. et al. (2020), *Microplastics from tyre and road wear - A literature review*, Swedish National Road and Transport Research Institute (VTI). [53]

Arcelik (2018), *Arcelik Global - A Better Future For The Environment*, http://www.arcelikglobal.com/en/company/press-room/press-releases/a-better-future-for-the-environment-grundig-s-appliance-portfolio-additions/ (accessed on 30 September 2020). [125]

Athey, S. et al. (2019), *Microfiber Policy Brief*, https://rochmanlab.files.wordpress.com/2019/01/microfiber-policy-brief-2019.pdf. [44]

Baensch-Baltruschat, B. et al. (2020), "Tyre and road wear particles (TRWP) - A review of generation, properties, emissions, human health risk, ecotoxicity, and fate in the environment", *Science of the Total Environment*, Vol. 733/137823, http://dx.doi.org/10.1016/j.scitotenv.2020.137823. [89]

Bayo, J., C. López and S. Olmos (2020), "Membrane bioreactor and rapid sand filtration for the removal of microplastics in an urban wastewater treatment plant.", *Marine Pollution Bulletin*, pp. 156, 111-211. [96]

Belzagui, F. et al. (2019), "Microplastics' emissions: Microfibers' detachment from textile garments", *Environmental Pollution*, Vol. 248, pp. 1028-1035, https://doi.org/10.1016/j.envpol.2019.02.059. [19]

Bertanza, G. et al. (2017), *A comparative techno-economic-environmental assessment of full-scale CAS vs MBR technologies*, http://www.thembrsite.com/features/a-comparative-techno-economic-environmental-assessment-of-full-scale-classical-activated-sludge-vs-membrane-bioreactor-technologies/. [101]

Boogaard, F. et al. (2017), *Removal efficiency of storm water treatment techniques: standardized full scale laboratory testing*, pp. 255-262, http://dx.doi.org/10.1080/1573062X.2015.1092562. [117]

Browne, M., M. Ros and L. Johnston (2020), "Pore-size and polymer affect the ability of filters for washing-machines to reduce domestic emissions of fibres to sewage", *Plos One*, Vol. 15/6, p. e0234248. [40]

Cai, Y. et al. (2020), "The origin of microplastic fiber in polyester textiles: The textile production process matters", *Journal of Cleaner Production*, Vol. 267, p. 121970, https://doi.org/10.1016/j.jclepro.2020.121970. [9]

Cai, Y. et al. (2020), "Systematic Study of Microplastic Fiber Release from 12 Different Polyester Textiles during Washing", *Environmental Science and Technology*, Vol. 54/8, p. 4847−4855, https://doi.org/10.1021/acs.est.9b07395. [28]

Calvillo, S., E. Williams and B. Brooks (2015), *Street Dust: Implications for Stormwater and Air Quality, and Environmental Management Through Street Sweeping*, pp. 71-128. [111]

Canadian Nursery Landscape Association (2017), *Life Cycle Cost Analysis Of Natural On-site Stormwater Management Methods*, https://cnla.ca/uploads/pdf/LCCA-Stormwater-Report.pdf. [116]

Carney Almroth, B. et al. (2018), "Quantifying shedding of synthetic fibers from textiles; a source of microplastics released into the environment", *Environmental Science and Pollution Research*, Vol. 25/2, pp. 1191-1199, http://dx.doi.org/10.1007/s11356-017-0528-7. [2]

CEN/TR (2020), *CEN/TR 17519:2020 Surfaces for sports areas. Synthetic turf sports facilities. Guidance on how to minimize infill dispersion into the environment.* [81]

Cesa, F. et al. (2020), "Laundering and textile parameters influence fibres release in household washings.", *Environ. Pollut.*, Vol. 257, p. 113553, https://doi.org/10.1016/j.envpol.2019.113553. [18]

Coalition Clean Baltic (2017), *Guidance on concrete ways to reduce microplastic inputs from municipal storm water and wastewater discharges*, Coalition Clean Baltic. [120]

Cocca, M. et al. (eds.) (2020), *First Investigation of Microfibre Release from the Washing of Laminated Fabrics for Outdoor Apparel*, Springer International Publishing, Cham. [48]

Continental (2019), *E-mobility: Continental launches first tire optimized for electric buses in city traffic*, http://www.continental.com/en/press/press-releases/2019-04-08-e-mobility-169470 (accessed on 23 September 2020). [58]

Cora Ball (2020), *Cora Ball*, http://coraball.com/ (accessed on 30 September 2020). [36]

Cotton, L. et al. (2020), "Improved garment longevity and reduced microfibre release are important sustainability benefits of laundering in colder and quicker washing machine cycles", *Dyes and Pigments*, Vol. 177, p. 108120, https://doi.org/10.1016/j.dyepig.2019.108120. [23]

Dalla Fontana, G., R. Mossotti and A. Montarsolo (2020), "Assessment of microplastics release from polyester fabrics: The impact of different washing conditions", *Environmental Pollution*, Vol. 264, p. 113960, https://doi.org/10.1016/j.envpol.2020.113960. [3]

De Falco, F. et al. (2020), "Microfiber Release to Water, Via Laundering, and to Air, via Everyday Use: A Comparison between Polyester Clothing with Differing Textile Parameters", *Environ. Sci. Technol.*, Vol. 54, pp. 3288-3296, https://doi.org/10.1021/acs.est.9b06892. [1]

De Falco, F. et al. (2019), "Novel finishing treatments of polyamide fabrics by electrofluidodynamic process to reduce microplastic release during washings", *Polym. Degrad. Stab.*, Vol. 165, pp. 110-116, https://doi.org/10.1016/j.polymdegradstab.2019.05.001. [7]

De Falco, F. et al. (2019), "The contribution of washing processes of synthetic clothes to microplastic pollution", *Scientific Reports*, Vol. 9, p. 6633, https://doi.org/10.1038/s41598-019-43023-x. [29]

De Falco, F. et al. (2018), "Pectin based finishing to mitigate the impact of microplastics released by polyamide fabrics", *Carbohydr. Polym.*, Vol. 198, p. 175−180, https://doi.org/10.1016/j.carbpol.2018.06.062. [6]

De Falco, F. et al. (2018), "Evaluation of microplastic release caused by textile washing processes of synthetic fabrics", *Environmental Pollution*, Vol. 236, pp. 916-925, http://dx.doi.org/10.1016/j.envpol.2017.10.057. [16]

Deng, H. et al. (2020), "Microplastic pollution in water and sediment in a textile industrial area", *Env. Poll.*, Vol. 258, p. 113658, https://doi.org/10.1016/j.envpol.2019.113658. [22]

Dris, R. et al. (2017), "A first overview of textile fibers, including microplastics, in indoor and outdoor environments", *Environmental Pollution*, Vol. 221, pp. 453-458, http://dx.doi.org/10.1016/j.envpol.2016.12.013. [27]

EC (2010), *COMMISSION DIRECTIVE 2010/48/EU of 5 July 2010 adapting to technical progress Directive 2009/40/EC of the European Parliament and of the Council on roadworthiness tests for motor vehicles and their trailers*. [70]

EC (2004), *Reclaiming city streets for people Chaos or quality of life?*, EC-General Directorate for the Environment, https://ec.europa.eu/environment/pubs/pdf/streets_people.pdf (accessed on 14 September 2020). [76]

EEA (2019), *Textiles in Europe's circular economy*. [52]

EMF (2017), *A New Textile Economy: Redesigning Fashion's Future*, Ellen Macarthur Foundation, http://www.ellenmacarthurfoundation.org/publications. [46]

Environmental Enhancements (2020), *Environmental Enhancements Store*, https://environmentalenhancements.com/ (accessed on 30 September 2020). [39]

ETRMA (2018), *Way Forward Report*, European Tyre and Rubber Manufacturers Association, https://www.etrma.org/wp-content/uploads/2019/10/20200330-FINAL-Way-Forward-Report.pdf. [61]

EU MERMAIDS (2015), *Good Practice Guide*. [32]

EU MERMAIDS (2015), *Handbook for zero microplastics from textiles and laundry*. [13]

EU MERMAIDS (2015), *Report of the reduction of fibres loss by the use of textiles auxiliaries*. [5]

Eunomia (2018), "Investigating options for reducing releases in the aquatic environment of microplastics emitted by (but not intentionally added in) products - Interim Report", *Report for DG Environment of the European Commission*, p. 335, http://dx.doi.org/10.1002/lsm.22016. [82]

EuRIC (2020), *Implementation of best practices in synthetic turfs to avoid the release of microplastics from rubber granulate into the environment*, European Recycling Industries' Confederation, https://www.euric-aisbl.eu/position-papers/item/350-implementation-of-best-practices-in-synthetic-turfs-to-avoid-the-release-of-microplastics-from-rubber-granulate-into-the-environment. [80]

Fidra (2020), *Guidelines for Designers and Procurement Specialists*, Fidra, http://www.fidra.org.uk/artificial-pitches/cleaner-pitch-guidelines/ (accessed on 24 September 2020). [79]

Filtrol (2020), , https://filtrol.net/ (accessed on 30 September 2020). [43]

France (2020), *LOI n° 2020-105 du 10 février 2020 relative à la lutte contre le gaspillage et à l'économie circulaire*, http://www.legifrance.gouv.fr/eli/loi/2020/2/10/TREP1902395L/jo/texte. [49]

Galvão, A. et al. (2020), "Microplastics in wastewater: microfiber emissions from common household laundry", *Environmental Science and Pollution Research*, Vol. 27, pp. 26643–26649, https://doi.org/10.1007/s11356-020-08765-6. [31]

Gehrke, I., B. Dresen and J. Blömer (2020), *Modelling the distribution of tyre wear particles in Germany*. [122]

Gies, E. et al. (2018), "Retention of microplastics in a major secondary wastewater treatment plant in Vancouver, Canada", *Marine Pollution Bulletin*, pp. 133, 553-561, https://doi.org/10.1016/j.marpolbul.2018.06.006. [106]

Gündoğdu, S. et al. (2018), "Microplastics in municipal wastewater treatment plants in Turkey: a comparison of the influent and secondary effluent concentrations.", *Environmental Monitoring and Assessment*, Vol. 190/11, https://doi.org/10.1007/s10661-018-7010-y. [98]

Guppyfriend (2020), *Guppyfriend Washing Bag*, http://guppyfriend.com/ (accessed on 30 September 2020). [38]

Gustafsson, M. et al. (2009), "Factors influencing PM10 emissions from road pavement wear", *Atmospheric Environment*, Vol. 43/31, pp. 4699-4702, http://dx.doi.org/10.1016/J.ATMOSENV.2008.04.028. [71]

Hartline, N. et al. (2016), "Microfiber Masses Recovered from Conventional Machine Washing of New or Aged Garments", *Environ. Sci. Technol.*, Vol. 50, p. 11532−11538, https://doi.org/10.1021/acs.est.6b03045. [24]

Herweyers, L. et al. (2020), "Consumers' Perceptions and Attitudes toward Products Preventing Microfiber Pollution in Aquatic Environments as a Result of the Domestic Washing of Synthetic Clothes", *Sustainability*, Vol. 12/6, http://dx.doi.org/10.3390/su12062244. [35]

Hirsch, J. (2011), "Aluminium in innovative light-weight car design.", *Materials Transactions*, Vol. 52/5, pp. 818-824, https://doi.org/10.2320/matertrans.L-MZ201132. [65]

Hunter, R. et al. (2018), *Using natural wetlands for municipal effluent assimilation: a half-century of experience for the Mississippi River Delta and surrounding environs*, Springer, Cham., https://doi.org/10.1007/978-3-319-67416-2_2. [121]

Kelly, M. et al. (2019), "Importance of Water-Volume on the Release of Microplastic Fibers from Laundry", *Environmental Science & Technology*, doi: 10.1021/acs.est.9b03022, pp. 11735-11744, http://dx.doi.org/10.1021/acs.est.9b03022. [25]

Klüppel, M. (2014), *Wear and Abrasion of Tires*, Springer, https://doi.org/10.1007/978-3-642-36199-9_312-1. [56]

Koga, D. (2019), *Struvite Recovery from Digested Sewage Sludge*, https://doi.org/10.1007/978-981-10-8031-9_17. [105]

Kraftfahrtbundesamt (2019), *Fahrzeuguntersuchungen von Personenkraftwagen nach Mängelarten im Jahr 2019 gegenüber 2018.*, http://www.kba.de/DE/Statistik/Fahrzeuge/Fahrzeuguntersuchungen/fz_fu_fahrzeugunter_jahresbilanz/fz_fu_jahresbilanz_archiv/2019/2019_fu_jahresbilanz_gif2.html?nn=2601598 (accessed on 14 September 2020). [73]

Lant, N. et al. (2020), "Microfiber release from real soiled consumer laundry and the impact of fabric care products and washing conditions", *PLoS ONE*, Vol. 15/6, p. e0233332, https://doi.org/10.1371/journal.pone.0233332. [26]

Lares, M. et al. (2018), "Occurrence, identification and removal of microplastic particles and fibers in conventional activated sludge process and advanced MBR technology", *Water Research*, Vol. 133, pp. 236-246, http://dx.doi.org/10.1016/J.WATRES.2018.01.049. [95]

Lee, H. and Y. Kim (2018), "Treatment characteristics of microplastics at biological sewage treatment facilities in Korea", *Marine Pollution Bulletin*, Vol. 137, pp. 1-8, https://doi.org/10.1016/j.marpolbul.2018.09.050. [108]

Li, T. (2018), *Influencing Parameters on Tire–Pavement Interaction Noise: Review, Experiments and Design Considerations.*, p. 38, https://doi.org/10.3390/designs2040038. [57]

Liu, F. et al. (2019), "Microplastics in urban and highway stormwater retention ponds", *Science ofThe Total Environment* , Vol. 671, pp. 992-1000, https://doi.org/10.1016/j.scitotenv.2019.03.416. [114]

Liu, X. et al. (2019), "Transfer and fate of microplastics during the conventional activated sludge process in one wastewater treatment plant of China", *Chemical Engineering Journal*, Vol. 362, pp. 176-182, https://doi.org/10.1016/j.cej.2019.01.033. [118]

Li, Y. et al. (2011), "Analysis of impact factors of tire wear", *Journal of Vibration and Control*, doi: 10.1177/1077546311411756, pp. 833-840, http://dx.doi.org/10.1177/1077546311411756. [69]

Long, Z. et al. (2019), "Microplastic abundance, characteristics, and removal in wastewater treatment plants in a coastal city of China", *Water Research*, Vol. 155, pp. 255-265, https://doi.org/10.1016/j.watres.2019.02.028. [99]

Lv, X. et al. (2019), "Microplastics in a municipal wastewater treatment plant: Fate, dynamic distribution, removal efficiencies, and control strategies", *Science of The Total Environment*, Vol. 652, pp. 602-610, https://doi.org/10.1016/j.jclepro.2019.03.321. [85]

Magni, S. et al. (2019), "The fate of microplastics in an Italian Wastewater Treatment Plant", *Science of The Total Environment*, Vol. 652, pp. 602-610, https://doi.org/10.1016/j.scitotenv.2018.10.269. [107]

Magnusson, K. et al. (2016), *Swedish sources and pathways for microplastics to the marine environment A review of existing data. Revised in March 2017*, https://www.ivl.se/english/ivl/publications/publications/swedish-sources-and-pathways-for-microplastics-to-the-marine-environment.html. [78]

Mason, S. et al. (2016), "Microplastic pollution is widely detected in US municipal wastewater treatment plant effluent", *Environmental Pollution 218*, Vol. 218, pp. 1045-1054, https://doi.org/10.1016/j.envpol.2016.08.056. [94]

McIlwraith, H. et al. (2019), "Capturing microfibers – marketed technologies reduce microfiber emissions from washing machines", *Marine Pollution Bulletin*, Vol. 139, p. 40−45, https://doi.org/10.1016/j.marpolbul.2018.12.012. [37]

Meyer, D. et al. (2013), "Constructed Wetlands for Combined Sewer Overflow Treatment—Comparison of German, French and Italian Approaches", *Water*, Vol. 5/1, pp. 1-12, http://dx.doi.org/10.3390/w5010001. [123]

Murphy, F. et al. (2016), "Wastewater Treatment Works (WwTW) as a Source of Microplastics in the Aquatic Environment", *Environmental Science & Technology*, Vol. 50/11, pp. 5800-5808, https://doi.org/10.1021/acs.est.5b05416. [91]

Napper, I., A. Barrett and R. Thompson (2020), "The efficiency of devices intended to reduce microfibre release during clothes washing", *Science of the Total Environment*, Vol. 738/140412, https://doi.org/10.1016/j.scitotenv.2020.140412. [33]

Napper, I. and R. Thompson (2016), "Release of synthetic microplastic plastic fibres from domestic washing machines: Effects of fabric type and washing conditions", *Marine Pollution Bulletin*, http://dx.doi.org/10.1016/j.marpolbul.2016.09.025. [30]

Nayak, R. and R. Padhye (2016), "The use of laser in garment manufacturing: an overview", *Fashion and Textiles*, Vol. 3/5, https://doi.org/10.1186/s40691-016-0057-x. [12]

Niinimäki, K. et al. (2020), "The environmental price of fast fashion Kirsi", *Nature Reviews Earth & Environment*, Vol. 1, pp. 189-200, https://doi.org/10.1038/s43017-020-0039-9. [20]

Nikiema, J. et al. (2020), *Water pollution by plastics and microplastics: a review of technical solutions from source to sea*, United Nations Environment Programme, Nairobi, Kenya. [87]

Nikiema, J., J. Mateo-Sagasta and D. Saad (2019), *Solutions for water pollution by microplastic: a review of cost and effectiveness*. [84]

NIVA (2018), *Microplastics in road dust – characteristics, pathways and measures. Revised in 2020.*, Norwegian Institute for Water Research. [112]

OECD (2020), *Non-exhaust Particulate Emissions from Road Transport: An Ignored Environmental Policy Challenge*, OECD Publishing, Paris, https://dx.doi.org/10.1787/4a4dc6ca-en. [54]

OECD (2020), *Workshop on Microplastics from Synthetic Textiles: Knowledge, Mitigation, and Policy*. [100]

OECD (2019), *Accelerating Climate Action: Refocusing Policies through a Well-being Lens*, OECD Publishing, Paris, https://dx.doi.org/10.1787/2f4c8c9a-en. [75]

Özkan, İ. and S. Gündoğdu (2021), "Investigation on the microfiber release under controlled washings from the knitted fabrics produced by recycled and virgin polyester yarns", *The Journal of The Textile Institute*, Vol. 112/2, pp. 264-272, https://doi.org/10.1080/00405000.2020.1741760. [47]

Pant, P. and R. Harrison (2013), *Estimation of the contribution of road traffic emissions to particulate matter concentrations from field measurements: A review*, pp. 78-97, https://doi.org/10.1016/j.atmosenv.2013.04.028. [59]

Parker-Jurd, F. et al. (2019), *Investigating the sources and pathways of synthetic fibre and vehicle tyre wear contamination into the marine environment*, Report prepared for the Department for Environment Food and Rural Affairs (project code ME5435). [109]

Pena-Francesch, A. and M. Demirel (2019), "Squid-Inspired Tandem Repeat Proteins: Functional Fibers and Films", *Front. Chem.*, Vol. 7, p. 69, https://doi.org/10.3389/fchem.2019.00069. [17]

Pettinari, M., B. Lund-Jensen and B. Schmidt (2016), *Low rolling resistance pavements in Denmark*, E&E Congress 2016, 6th Eurasphalt & Eurobitume Congress, 1-3 June 2016, Prague, Czech Republic. [60]

Pirc, U. et al. (2016), "Emissions of microplastic fibers from microfiber fleece during domestic washing", *Environ Sci Pollut Res*, Vol. 23, pp. 22206–22211, https://doi.org/10.1007/s11356-016-7703-0. [10]

Piribauer, B. and A. Bartl (2019), "Textile recycling processes, state of the art and current developments: A mini review", *Waste Management & Research*, Vol. 37/2, pp. 112-119, https://doi.org/10.1177/0734242X18819277. [51]

PlanetCare (n.d.), *Independent Test Results*, http://www.planetcare.org/en/products/independent-tests-results (accessed on 30 September 2020). [41]

Pohrt, R. (2019), *Tire wear particle hot spots – Review of influencing factors*, pp. 17-27, https://doi.org/10.22190/FUME190104013P. [55]

Prata, J. (2018), "Microplastics in wastewater: State of the knowledge on sources, fate and solutions", *Marine Pollution Bulletin*, Vol. 129/1, pp. 262-265, https://doi.org/10.1016/j.marpolbul.2018.02.046. [110]

Raabe, D., C. Tasan and E. Olivetti (2019), *Strategies for improving the sustainability of structural metals*, pp. 64-74, https://doi.org/10.1038/s41586-019-1702-5. [66]

Roos, S., O. Levenstam Arturin and A. Hanning (2017), *Microplastics shedding from polyester fabrics*, Mistra Future Fashion: Stockholm, Sweden, http://mistrafuturefashion.com/wp-content/uploads/2017/06/MFF-Report-Microplastics.pdf. [11]

Ruan, Y. et al. (2019), "A preliminary screening of HBCD enantiomers transported by microplastics in wastewater treatment plants.", *Science of the Total Environment*, Vol. 674, pp. 171-178, https://doi.org/10.1016/j.scitotenv.2019.04.007. [90]

Salminen, H. (2014), *Parametrizing tyre wear using a brush tyre model.*, Royal Institute of Technology, Sweden. [67]

Serrenho, A., J. Norman and J. Allwood (2017), *The impact of reducing car weight on global emissions: The future fleet in Great Britain.*, p. 20160364, https://doi.org/10.1098/rsta.2016.0364. [64]

Shaker, K. et al. (2016), *Fabric manufacturing*, In: Textile Engineering. Berlin, Boston: De Gruyter Oldenbourg, pp. 47-82. [15]

Sillanpaa, M. and P. Sainio (2017), "Release of polyester and cotton fibres from textiles in machine washings", *Environ. Sci. Pollut. Res.*, Vol. 24, pp. 19313–19321, https://doi.org/10.1007/s11356-017-9621-1. [8]

Smithers, R. (2020), *Device to curb microplastic emissions wins James Dyson award*, http://www.theguardian.com/environment/2020/sep/17/device-to-curb-microplastic-emissions-wins-james-dyson-award (accessed on 17 September 2020). [113]

Soret, A., M. Guevara and J. Baldasano (2014), *The potential impacts of electric vehicles on air quality in the urban areas of Barcelona and Madrid (Spain)*, pp. 51-63, https://doi.org/10.1016/j.atmosenv.2014.09.048. [63]

Strassler, E. and K. Strellec (1999), *Preliminary Data Summary of Urban Storm Water Best Management Practices*, United States Environmental Protection Agency. [115]

Swedish EPA (2021), *Development projects for sustainable plastic use*, http://www.swedishepa.se/Guidance/Grants/sustainable-plastic-use/ (accessed on 19 April 2021). [124]

Swedish EPA (2018), *Filters for washing machines Mitigation of microplastic pollution*, Swedish Environmental Protection Agency, https://www.naturvardsverket.se/upload/miljoarbete-i-samhallet/miljoarbete-i-sverige/plast/1003-09-report-filters-for-washing-machines.pdf. [42]

Swedish EPA (2018), *Microplastics from industrial laundries (A laboratory study of laundry effluents)*, Brodin, M., Norin, H., Hanning, A., Persson, C., Okcabol, S. [103]

Talvitie, J. (2018), *Wastewater treatment plants as pathways of microlitter to the aquatic environment*. [83]

Talvitie, J. et al. (2017), "How well is micro litter purified from wastewater? - A detailed study on the stepwise removal of micro litter in a tertiary level wastewater treatment plant", *Water Research*, Vol. 109/1, pp. 164-172, https://doi.org/10.1016/j.watres.2016.11.046. [92]

Talvitie, J. et al. (2015), "Do wastewater treatment plants act as a potential point source of microplastics? Preliminary study in the coastal Gulf of Finland, Baltic Sea.", *Water Science and Technology*, Vol. 72/9, pp. 1495-1504, https://doi.org/10.2166/wst.2015.360. [97]

Talvitie, J. et al. (2017), "Solutions to microplastic pollution – Removal of microplastics from wastewater effluent with advanced wastewater treatment technologies", *Water Research*, Vol. 123, pp. 401-407, http://dx.doi.org/10.1016/j.watres.2017.07.005. [86]

The Fiber Year (2017), *World Survey on Textiles & Nonwovens.*, Editorial: Chemical Fibers. [14]

Timmers, V. and P. Achten (2016), "Non-exhaust PM emissions from electric vehicles", *Atmospheric Environment*, Vol. 134, pp. 10-17, http://dx.doi.org/10.1016/J.ATMOSENV.2016.03.017. [62]

Titos, G. et al. (2015), *Evaluation of the impact of transportation changes on air quality*, pp. 19-31, https://doi.org/10.1016/j.atmosenv.2015.05.027. [77]

Tumlin, S. and C. Bertholds (2020), *Distribution analysis of microplastics in the influent, effluent and within wastewater treatment plants*. [104]

UNEP (2020), *Sustainability and Circularity in the Textile Value Chain: global stocktaking*, https://wedocs.unep.org/20.500.11822/34184. [50]

Verschoor, A. and E. de Valk (2017), *Potential measures against microplastic emissions to water*, National Institute for Public Health and the Environment, The Netherlands. [72]

Wang, C. et al. (2016), "The influence of the contact features on the tyre wear in steady-state conditions", *Proceedings of the Institution of Mechanical Engineers, Part D: Journal of Automobile Engineering*, doi: 10.1177/0954407016671462, pp. 1326-1339, http://dx.doi.org/10.1177/0954407016671462. [68]

Wang, Y. and A. Boggio-Marzet (2018), *Evaluation of eco-driving training for fuel efficiency and emissions reduction according to road type*, p. 3891, https://doi.org/10.3390/su10113891. [74]

Weis, J. (2020), "Aquatic microplastic Research—A Critique and Suggestions for the Future.", *Water. Multidisciplinary Digital Publishing Institute*, Vol. 12, pp. 1475-1484. [88]

WHO (2019), *Microplastics in drinking water*, World Health Organisation. [93]

Xeros Technologies (2020), *Xeros Technologies - Technologies*, http://www.xerostech.com/technologies (accessed on 30 September 2020). [45]

Xu, X. et al. (2018), "Pollution characteristics and fate of microfibers in the wastewater from textile dyeing wastewater treatment plant", *Water Science & Technology*, Vol. 78/10, pp. 2046-2054, https://doi.org/10.2166/wst.2018.476. [21]

Yang, L. et al. (2019), "Microfiber release from different fabrics during washing", *Environmental Pollution*, Vol. 249, pp. 136-143, https://doi.org/10.1016/j.envpol.2019.03.011. [4]

Zambrano, M. et al. (2019), "Microfibers generated from the laundering of cotton, rayon and polyester based fabrics and their aquatic biodegradation", *Marine Pollution Bulletin*, Vol. 142, pp. 394-407, https://doi.org/10.1016/j.marpolbul.2019.02.062. [34]

Zhou, H., L. Zhou and K. Ma (2020), "Microfiber from textile dyeing and printing wastewater of a typical industrial park in China: Occurrence, removal and release.", *Science of the Total Environment*, Vol. 739/140329, https://doi.org/10.1016/j.scitotenv.2020.140329. [102]

Ziajahromi, S. et al. (2020), "Microplastic pollution in a stormwater floating treatment wetland: Detection of tyre particles in sediment.", *Science of the Total Environment*, Vol. 713/136356. [119]

Notes

1 The trend was observed in 100% polyester fabrics (Pirc et al., 2016[10]; Sillanpaa and Sainio, 2017[8]; De Falco et al., 2019[29]; Cai et al., 2020[28]; Napper and Thompson, 2016[30]; Carney Almroth et al., 2018[2]), in 100% acrylic fabrics (Cesa et al., 2020[18]; Napper and Thompson, 2016[30]), in 100% polyamide fabrics (Cesa et al., 2020[18]) and in blends of polyester/elastane and acrylic/polyamide (Belzagui et al., 2019[19]).

2 It has been suggested that the removal of microfibres could also be carried out using dry methods. Provided that the microfibres are disposed of in a safe way, dry methods could be most cost-effective than preliminary washing, as they enable the collection of microfibres before these are dispersed into sewage and/or air (Roos, Levenstam Arturin and Hanning, 2017[11]).

3 A relevant initiative is a project financed by the Swedish Environmental Protection Agency to identify, prevent, and reduce microplastics pollution from textile industries and wastewater treatment plants through pilot projects in coastal areas in China (Swedish EPA, 2021[124]).

4 According to the producers, parent companies Grundig AG - Arcelik A.Ş. have been working on developing a new washing machine with a built-in microplastic filter able to filter out 99.9% of microfibers released into water, although no further information is available on this product (Arcelik, 2018[125]).

5 Information gathered from conversation with experts held during the Workshop on Microplastics from Tyre Wear (17-20 May 2020) and during following meetings.

6 More recently, concerns have also emerged with regards to the potential for moulded granule surfaces in playing fields and other outdoor sport facilities to also release microplastics when not properly maintained, however this is still an emerging area of research.

7 The removal efficiency can be obtained on a percent mass basis (indicated by ^{m}) or on a percent number basis (^{n}). The latter is adopted throughout the section, except where otherwise specified.

8 The OECD defines tertiary treatment as treatment additional to secondary that removes nutrients such as phosphorus and nitrogen and practically all suspended and organic matter from waste water.

9 The range of contaminants typically targeted by WWT for industrial effluents from textile manufacturing/dyeing plants is exemplified in Table 3.12.

4 Emerging policy intervention and available policy tools to support microplastics mitigation

This chapter documents existing policy action addressing microplastics generated during the lifecycle of textiles and tyres. Secondly, it investigates emerging policy instruments that can be considered to support and advance mitigation action along the lifecycle of products: source-directed, use-oriented, end-of-pipe and end-of-life approaches.

4.1. Introduction

As scientific and public attention on microplastics pollution grows, policymakers are increasingly looking for policy options to better manage current and future environmental and human health risks associated with microplastics. This chapter looks at available policy tools to tackle the challenge of microplastics originating from textiles and tyres, in particular to encourage, incentivise, or mandate the uptake of the mitigation best practices and technologies outlined in the previous chapter. The current state of play on prevailing policy action and industry-led initiatives targeting microfibres and TRWP is outlined in Section 4.2. Then, the chapter discusses selected opportunities to broaden and/or deepen the scope of the existing policy coverage in OECD countries to comprehensively address the challenge at hand. Policy tools are categorised into: i) source-directed approaches (section 4.3.1), ii) use-oriented approaches (section 4.3.2) and iii) end-of-pipe and end-of-life approaches (section 4.3.3).

4.2. Review of existing policies and initiatives

Several OECD countries have formulated national or sub-national strategies that include measures to address microplastics pollution. Common denominators of existing action plans are, for instance:

- the *fostering of research* on microplastics releases and their potential environmental and human health impacts;
- mitigation action to tackle land-based and sea-based sources of *marine plastic litter*, e.g. waste management policies and single-use plastics policies; and
- the regulation of the placing on the market of products that lead to inevitable microplastics leakage, where technological solutions and natural alternatives exist. Notably, an increasing number of countries have *banned the use of microbeads* in PCCPs (Canada, 2017[1]; France, 2017[2]; GOV.UK, 2018[3]; United States, 2015[4]; Italy, 2017[5]). In the EU, ECHA has proposed wide-ranging restrictions on microplastics intentionally-added to products placed on the EU/EEA market. These are expected to prevent the release of more than 400 000 tonnes of microplastics over 20 years (ECHA, 2019[6]);

For textile-based microfibres and TRWP pollution, policy action has so far focused on providing the foundations for comprehensive and evidence-based mitigation frameworks. In general, existing and planned interventions tend to target several stages of the lifecycle of products. These include facilitating knowledge creation, fostering research, harmonising sampling and characterisation methods and establishing multi-stakeholder information-sharing and collaboration platforms, all of which aim to contribute to the work of identifying and assessing mitigation actions implementable at different stages of the lifecycle of products. More advanced (proposed or implemented) policies generally target mitigation entry points during the use phase, such as household, commercial and industrial laundering. Relevant *policy action* from governments is presented in Section 4.2.1 and *voluntary* industry-led initiatives in Section 4.2.2.

4.2.1. Policy action at the national and sub-national level

Several OECD countries have passed (or proposed) legislation primarily aimed at *accelerating research*, to close knowledge and data gaps on the mechanisms and magnitude of microfibre and TRWP emissions and to identify and assess mitigation measures. Further, as outlined in Chapter 3, the lack of harmonised test methods currently poses challenges for the aggregation and comparison of results on microplastics releases and the effectiveness of solutions. Thus, a number of governments have been mandating or encouraging *the development of standardised and harmonised microplastics definitions* and methods, including sampling and characterisation methods as well as test standards for tyre tread abrasion and microfibre shedding from products.

Although these measures do not directly contribute to microplastics mitigation, they are essential preconditions for the design, assessment and implementation of evidence-based regulatory, economic and voluntary policy interventions. An example of this is the ongoing work in the European Union to develop a standardised method to measure the tyre tread abrasion rate, based on state of the art available standards and regulations and the work carried out by industry (EU SAM, 2018[7]; EU, 2020[8]). As announced by the European Commission and approved by Regulation 2020/740, the long-term plan is to include the tyre tread abrasion rate into the existing EU Tyre Labelling Scheme, which has been in place since 2012 and currently provides consumers with essential information on the fuel efficiency, safety and noise of tyres placed on the market (EU, 2020[8]).

Existing *awareness-raising and consumer education initiatives* also contribute to addressing microfibre shedding and tyre wear and help promote "no-regret" mitigation interventions (see Chapter 5). In the case of textile use for instance, less frequent and shorter laundry cycles, low temperatures and the use of softeners can mitigate microfibre emissions, in addition to reducing households' energy and water consumption and improving the durability of garments. Consumer education and awareness-raising initiatives aim to influence consumer behaviour towards the uptake of best practices for the sustainable use of products. In addition, raising awareness can also lead to further public acceptability for policy action and increased civil society pressure on brands in the fashion and apparel sector to take industrial action.

The US State of Connecticut mandated via the "Act Concerning Clothing Fiber Pollution" the formation of a working group charged with formulating best consumer practices and with educating consumers on the topic of microfibre pollution. Consumer information messages may also be embedded in broader emerging initiatives aimed at fostering behavioural change towards environmentally beneficial practices for product use and maintenance. An example of this is the Swedish #Textilsmart# information campaign, which advises consumers on how to render their textile consumption more sustainable, including with information on microplastics shedding and prevention measures they can implement at home (Swedish EPA[9]).

Although less common, a few regulatory bodies have also introduced or considered *minimum standards* to mitigate microplastics releases into the environment. Notably, France recently approved an "anti-waste and circular economy" law which, among other things, requires all new washing machines sold from 2025 to have built-in filters to capture microfibres (France, 2020[10]).

Table 4.1 documents selected examples of relevant existing and proposed policies at the national and sub-national level across OECD countries.

Table 4.1. Selected examples of existing and planned policies targeting microfibres and TRWP

Description	Research	Methods	Awareness	Further action
Australia				
The National Plastics Plan 2021 announced that the Australian Government will work with industry to phase in microfibre filters on new residential and commercial washing machines by 1 July 2030 (DAWE, 2021[11])				(x)
Canada				
Under the Zero Plastic Waste strategy, Canada is implementing a comprehensive approach to reduce plastics pollution, which includes investing in science to close research gaps on macro and microplastics. The government provided funding to support research on microfibre release occurring during washing, to design dedicated test methods and to develop sampling methods for microfibres in laundry effluent and wastewaters.	x	x		

Description	Research	Methods	Awareness	Further action
European Union				
The Plastics Strategy (2018) called for an examination of policy options to reduce unintentional microplastics releases from tyres and textiles, including a development of methods to quantify emissions, targeted R&D funding, minimum design requirements and information requirements (EU SAM, 2018[7]). Both the European Green Deal (2019) and the new Circular Economy Action Plan (2020) reaffirm the priority to address microplastics releases (EU, 2020[12]). Regulation (EU) 2020/740 of May 2020 has mandated the European Commission with the development of a tyre tread abrasion test, with a view to include the degree of tyre abrasion into the EU tyre labelling scheme (EU, 2020[8]).	x	x		x
France				
As part of the 2020 anti-waste law for a circular economy, France introduced a mandatory requirement for all new professional and household washing machines to be equipped with a microfibre filter by 1st January 2025 (France, 2020[10]).				x
Netherlands				
The Dutch government has mandated research on mitigation measures for a range of use-based microplastics emissions, including microfibres and TRWP. On tyres, the government initiated a communication campaign on correct inflation pressure and suitable tyre types. In 2019, the campaign resulted in 250.000 extra cars with the right tire pressure (Dutch Government, 2020[13]).	x		x	
Norway				
The Norwegian Climate and Environment Ministry commissioned a review on microplastics pollution, which includes measures to target wear and tear of vehicle tires and textiles and losses from artificial turfs.	x			
Sweden				
In 2017, a first government assignment researched sources and releases of microplastics into the marine environment. In response to the findings, the Swedish EPA has financed research grants to deepen the knowledge base on microplastics pollution and on potential mitigation measures., set up initiatives to foster innovation and dialogues within the textile value chain and also set up a pre-procurement group for artificial sport pitches, with a focus on reducing releases of rubber granulate (Swedish EPA, n.d.[14]).	x			x
United Kingdom				
The UK government commissioned research projects to better understand the issue of microplastics losses from tyres and clothing. A Rapid Evidence Review has been commissioned to gather the evidence to progress approaches to more consistent definition, sampling and assessment methodologies for monitoring and reporting microplastics in water. Collaboration is also ongoing with the water industry to establish methods to detect, characterise and quantify microplastics in wastewaters and evaluate the removal efficiency of treatment processes.	x	x		
United States (national and sub-national level)				
Under the Trash Free Waters program, the US EPA is engaging with industry and commissioning research projects to identify and assess solutions to microfibre pollution. Several governmental agencies have sponsored research on the risks of microplastics in the environment. The US government has a multi-agency micro and nanoplastics information sharing group to share knowledge gathered via existing research projects.	x			
In 2018, Connecticut passed House Bill 5360 to target microfibres emitted during laundering. The bill mandated further research on microfibres, awareness-raising initiatives and the development of best consumer practices and industry efforts to prevent microfibre shedding. The bill also resulted in the formation of a dedicated Working Group, which published in January 2019 a draft report with recommendations to reduce microfibre pollution (Connecticut, 2018[15])	x		x	
New York State proposed Assembly Bill A01549 in 2018. This would require the following labelling for all products containing more than 50% synthetic material: "This garment sheds plastic microfibers when washed". The bill proposes recommending hand washing to reduce shedding (New York State Assembly, 2018[16])			(x)	
In 2018, California proposed Microfiber Bill AB 129, which would have required the State Water Resources Control Board to develop a standard methodology to evaluate the effectiveness of microfibre filtration systems and to identify best manufacturing practices for clothing. Additionally, public and private entities that use laundry systems would have been required to install suitable filtration systems (California Assembly, 2018[17]). In 2020, Bill AB 1952 was proposed. If approved, it would require the implementation of a pilot program to assess the efficacy of microfibre filtration systems and monitor the presence of microfibres in waste washwater (California Assembly, 2020[18]).	x	(x)		(x)

Note: Several other OECD countries have also funded research initiatives to assess sources and pathways of microplastics into aquatic environments and/or to investigate actions to monitor and curb microplastics pollution, including Belgium, Germany and Spain.
Source: Author's own elaboration

4.2.2. Voluntary initiatives

In parallel to government action, a number of voluntary industry initiatives have emerged to mitigate microfibre and TRWP pollution. Industry-led initiatives can have several benefits: they can facilitate information gathering, contribute to accelerating industrial R&D and foster the dissemination of information on the costs and benefits of mitigation solutions. In the context of microfibres and TRWP, industry stakeholders can use their technical knowledge and expertise to accelerate the understanding of the mechanisms and quantities of microplastics emissions and the identification of viable mitigation measures. Further, industry-led initiatives can support and promote policy action and contribute to reaching the objectives mandated or under consideration by governments. In particular, this can be achieved by:

- *Supporting and participating in research* carried out by academics and researchers;
- *Contributing to the harmonisation of test methods;*
- *Sharing information and collaborating in international platforms* to establish priorities for research and action; and
- *Sharing product information to consumers or along the value chain*, for instance via voluntary labelling schemes or environmental indicators.

In the textile and garment sector, several initiatives and research projects have emerged to close key knowledge and data gaps on microfibres. The Microfibre Consortium facilitates the development of practical solutions for the textile industry to minimise microfibre release to the environment from textile manufacturing and product life cycle (The Microfibre Consortium[19]). To date, the work carried out by the Microfibre Consortium has included the development of a standardised test method and research concerning the influence of various production parameters on shedding behaviours. In the European context, a number of industry associations (International Association for Soaps, Detergents and Maintenance Products, Comité International de la Rayonne et des Fibres Synthétiques, European Outdoor Group, Euratex and the Federation of the European Sporting Goods Industry), have formed a voluntary Cross Industry Agreement. The partnership aims to contribute to the development of international standardised test methods[1] to identify and quantify microfibres, share information on the progress of research, knowledge gaps, options and priorities and support and participate in industrial research for the development of feasible and effective solutions (Euratex, n.d.[20]). Further, certain fashion brands have partnered with research organisations to conduct research on microfibre pollution of marine environments and the mechanisms of shedding occurring during laundering (Patagonia, n.d.[21]).

In the tyre manufacturing sector, several companies and industrial associations have also been looking at the issue of TRWP pollution, in particular with regards to opportunities for international cooperation, knowledge sharing and the development of harmonised definitions and measurement standards. The Tire Industry Project (TIP) was established in 2005 by 11 major tyre manufacturing companies, under the umbrella of the World Business Council of Sustainable Development (WBCSD). The TIP aims to identify and implement feasible measures in order to reduce the impact of the life cycle of tyres on the environment, also in the context of microplastics pollution. The European Tyre and Rubber Manufacturers Association (ETRMA) initiated the European Tyre and Road Wear Particle Platform in July 2018. This international multi-stakeholder platform aimed to facilitate research, encourage stakeholder cooperation and knowledge-sharing and explore mitigation options to reduce TRWP pollution. In the European context, the European Tyre and Rime Technical Organization (ETRTO) is working on assessing the feasibility and accuracy of a standard test method for the tyre abrasion rate to propose to the European Commission.

Box 4.1. Mitigation measures and priorities identified by the European TRWP Platform

Multi-stakeholder meetings held in the context of the European TRWP Platform identified more than 30 potential mitigation solutions for TRWP pollution. These included interventions to reduce the generation of TRWP (e.g. harmonisation of standard test methods for tyre tread abrasion, research on road abrasion, tyre and road material innovation, awareness campaigns for drivers), as well as options to capture TRWP before these enter the environment (e.g. identifying hotspots for mitigation action, improved road cleaning, implementation of end-of-pipe stormwater management solutions).

Among these, the platform identified a number of measures, which can be prioritised in the short-term:

- working on methodologies to develop a test method for the tyre tread abrasion rate as well as analytical methods for TRWP in the environment;
- closing knowledge gaps, such as on the composition, occurrence and fate of TRWP in the environment, as well as on the impact of influence factors (e.g. road characteristics) on TRWP generation;
- developing permanent platforms to share and disseminate knowledge and create synergies among different research projects;
- creating incentives towards eco-driving practices, for instance through awareness raising campaigns; and
- identifying hotspots to facilitate the launch of regional pilots and test the relative effectiveness of mitigation solutions.

Source: (ETRMA, 2018[22])

4.3. Opportunities for further policy intervention

4.3.1. Source-directed approaches

Source-directed policy approaches aim to impose or incentivise measures which prevent the release of pollutants to aquatic, terrestrial and aerial environments and reduce the potential risks for ecosystems and human health. Source-directed action has the advantage of preventing emissions, thus reducing the need for end-of-pipe capture solutions further downstream. In the case of tyres and textiles, source-directed action mainly relates to the implementation of mitigation measures aimed at mandating or incentivising the manufacturing of products containing less toxic components (e.g. non-hazardous dyes employed in textile manufacturing) and with a lower tendency to generate microplastics emissions. Actions aimed at limiting industrial emissions of synthetic polymers and fibres (and the associated chemical substances) also fall in this category.

Table 4.2 summarises various regulatory, economic and voluntary policy tools that can be considered to target the design and manufacturing stage of microplastics emissions originating from tyres and textiles. These are primarily targeted at industry stakeholders along the value chain: textile and apparel manufacturing industries and tyre manufacturing companies. Additionally, regulatory bodies, textile and tyre manufacturing industry associations and other relevant industrial representatives along the apparel and vehicle manufacturing value chain may also contribute to the creation of incentives to minimise industrial emissions and/or to support the development of products leading to lower microplastics emissions.

The following sections describe selected source-directed policy tools in more details and provide a discussion of the relative benefits and barriers to implementation.

Table 4.2. Summary of relevant source-directed policy instruments for microplastics mitigation

Type	Policy instrument	Description
Regulatory	Standardisation of definitions and terminology	Development of harmonised and standardised vocabulary and definitions for microplastics.
	Standardisation of test methods	Development of harmonised and standardised methods for the measurement and analysis of microfibre shedding from garments and tyre tread abrasion.
	Minimum standards	Product eco-design standards imposing minimum requirements for the resistance of products to microplastics shedding for these to be placed on the market. These can target the microfibre shedding rate or the tyre tread abrasion rate, but potentially also complementary products (e.g. road surfaces). Technological standards imposing (or banning) the use of manufacturing processes associated with a lower (or higher) propensity of the final product to shed microplastics. For instance, a requirement that clothing manufacturers / importers must carry out preliminary washing of textiles under controlled conditions before they are sent to retailers or sold to consumers.
	Substance bans	Prohibition or limitation of use of hazardous substances in the manufacturing of products.
	Certification schemes	Certification schemes can be employed to set the criteria against which products are judged and to provide the basis for compliance with minimum performance standards or for information provision via mandatory or voluntary labelling schemes (detailed below). For instance, business could certify (usually via third-party testing) the tendency of intermediary or final products to shed microfibres or to undergo tyre tread abrasion.
	Labelling and information systems	Labelling schemes can be implemented to share information related to the tendency of intermediary or final products to release microplastics along the value chain (business-to-business) or to consumers (business-to-consumers)
	Best available techniques	Best Available Techniques (BAT) are state-of-the-art techniques for the prevention and control of industrial emissions. These can provide the basis for legally-binding microplastics emission limit values and/or the uptake of best practices in manufacturing processes.
	Green public procurement	By taking advantage of their purchasing power, public authorities can play an important role in steering production towards a more sustainable direction. Microplastics leakage avoidance could be included in the criteria for sustainable public procurement of textiles, tyres and associated services (e.g. laundering equipment and services). Pre-procurement purchasing groups can also be set up to drive innovation and R&D from the demand side for a range of products associated with microplastics release.
Economic	Subsidies	Subsidies or tax incentives from governments to incentivise the uptake of eco-design practices and/or mitigation technologies for tyres, textiles and complementary products Financial support to encourage the prevention and/or minimisation of industrial emissions.
	Taxes and mandatory charges	Taxes or charges to industry for placing on the market products with a high tendency to shed microplastics. Weight-based charges to favour light-weighting of vehicles (e.g. vehicle registration fees or annual taxes partially based on vehicle weight). Taxes or charges to manufacturing plants for discharging microplastics and/or the associated toxic substances into water bodies.
Voluntary	Information campaigns	A lack of awareness over the magnitude of the issue and the available solutions may also pose a barrier to the uptake of best design and manufacturing practices. The transfer of knowledge from researchers to consumers and industry on why and how to reduce microplastics pollution can contribute to accelerating R&D efforts and the uptake of available mitigation measures.
	International and cross-industry information and data sharing and cooperation	Collaboration across the private sector and between industry and other stakeholders (e.g. public sector, research institutes) to foster research and implement strategies to prevent and mitigate microplastics pollution. Promotion of higher transparency standards along the value chain to facilitate the identification and evaluation of mitigation measures implementable at the production stage
	Voluntary eco-design initiatives	Introduction of microplastics mitigation best practices into industry-led sustainability initiatives. This may include the uptake of best manufacturing practices and technologies and/or the selection of manufacturing materials which are intrinsically less toxic (e.g. selection of non-hazardous dyes in textiles).
	Due Diligence for the Garment and Footwear Sector	Due Diligence approaches for the Garment and Footwear Sector can help companies understand their exposure to microplastics harm in their value chain and take action to cease, prevent, mitigate the impact, as well as to monitor and report on this process. Although this is a voluntary approach, the 50 governments who have adhered to the OECD instruments have committed to promoting and disseminating this guidance.

Type	Policy instrument	Description
	Voluntary commitments to limit industrial emissions	Voluntary agreements exist to tackle certain sources of unintentional microplastics leakage, notably the accidental loss of plastic pellets occurring along the plastics value chain (PlasticsEurope, 2017[23]). Similar voluntary schemes could be developed to identify, share and implement best practices and technologies to prevent industrial emissions of microplastics occurring at manufacturing plants, for instance via the use of air filters to capture airborne microfibres.

Note: Policy instruments marked in bold are further discussed in the following sections
Source: Author's own elaboration

Minimum standards, certification systems and labelling and information schemes

Insufficient or inadequate information supply, identified as a barrier to more sustainable production and consumption practices (Laubinger and Börkey, forthcoming[24]), also undermines opportunities to reduce microplastics emissions. The lack of information provision on the shedding propensity of tyres and garments available on the market limits consumers' ability to make informed purchasing decisions. Also, a lack of information sharing along the value chain may restrict manufacturers' ability to manage environmental risks associated with a product's design and production, including those related to microplastics shedding. In the case of textiles, the set of practices which a product has undergone during manufacturing, from fibre production to finishing treatments, will influence its propensity to shed microfibres. However, inadequate information on the product history and content may inhibit manufacturers' capability to assess the quality of products and the potential to implement eco-design practices.

Once measurement standards for microfibre shedding and tyre tread abrasion are available, it should become possible to differentiate products based on their tendency to emit microplastics. This can allow for the development of standards, certification schemes and labelling and information schemes, a set of interdependent policy tools which could be employed to incentivise eco-design and to help overcome the existing barriers related to the paucity of reliable and effective information supply.

- *Minimum standards* can be considered to restrict the worst performing textile products and tyres from being sold on the market, in order to minimise the contribution of the products with the largest emissions and incentivise producers to implement eco-design manufacturing practices and technologies (Eunomia, 2018[25]). In addition to textiles and tyres, minimum standard requirements could also be conceived for complementary products, as discussed in Section 4.3.2 for washing machines. These could be designed in two ways: a) *technology standards* mandating the adoption of certain identified eco-design practices or banning the use of harmful manufacturing processes, or b) *performance standards* setting a maximum threshold for microfibre shedding or tyre tread abrasion. Distinctive benefits would need to be considered, typically as regards to incentives for innovation. In general, performance standards are preferable as these allow for greater flexibility to search for the cheapest options to reach the set pollution reduction goals. In turn, where specific design characteristics and manufacturing processes have been identified as particularly harmful to microplastics mitigation, technology standards can provide a low-cost option to abate emissions.
- *Certification schemes* may be introduced to establish the set of criteria (standards) against which the product is being judged. For instance, business could certify (either autonomously or via third-party testing) the tendency of intermediary or final products to shed microfibres (for garments) or to undergo tread abrasion (for tyres). These could provide the basis for compliance with minimum performance standards or for information provision via mandatory or voluntary labelling schemes detailed below.
- *Environmental Labels and Information Schemes* are policies and initiatives that aim to provide information to external users about one or more aspects of the environmental performance of a product or service (Gruère, 2013[26]). These can be employed to provide aggregated and simplified information to consumers on the microplastics shedding propensity of products placed on the

market via consumer-oriented labels (B2C), or to facilitate the information flow between businesses via business-to-business (B2B) information systems to enable the uptake of eco-design practices (Laubinger and Börkey, forthcoming[24]).

Minimum standards, certification schemes, labels and information systems can be deployed in conjunction to facilitate the flow of information relating to the environmental performance of tyres and textile products, incentivise the uptake of mitigation options at the production stage and stimulate market development and innovation. A more detailed assessment of relevant considerations in the design and implementation of these policy tools is presented in Annex 4.A. In particular, two options are discussed: a) B2B information systems to facilitate the information flow on the characteristics, content and microfibre shedding propensity of intermediary and final products along the textile and apparel supply chain, and b) minimum standards and B2C certification and labelling schemes for both vehicle tyres and textile products.

Best Available Techniques

Best Available Techniques (BAT) are state-of-the-art techniques for the prevention and control of industrial emissions, developed at a scale that enables them to be implemented under economically and technically viable conditions. A growing number of governments use BAT to set legally binding emission levels and other conditions in environmental permits for industrial installations.[2] The permit conditions are usually established based on a range of legally binding BAT-associated environmental performance levels.[3] In the EU, these are set out in BAT reference documents (BREFs).

In the context of microplastics pollution originating from tyres and textiles, BAT could be employed to minimise releases occurring during industrial processes. Potentially, there might also be value in exploring the opportunities for taking a value chain approach when introducing BAT in industrial operations, to encourage the uptake of manufacturing practices that optimise textile products and tyres for lower microplastics release during use. For instance, the removal of microfibres (e.g. via industrial pre-washing under controlled conditions) is an example of a practice which can reduce industrial emissions as well as emissions during the first washes done by the consumer. A more detailed assessment of the potential benefits and relevant implementation considerations for taking a BAT-based approach to microplastics leakage is outlined in Annex 4.A.

Due Diligence in the Garment and Footwear Sector

Due Diligence can facilitate the implementation of sustainable production practices and improve data flows and transparency. The OECD Due Diligence Guidance for Responsible Supply Chains in the Garment and Footwear Sector (i.e. "the Guidance") helps enterprises implement the due diligence recommendations contained in the OECD Guidelines for Multinational Enterprises along the garment and footwear supply chain in order to prevent and address the potential and actual negative human and labour rights, environmental and integrity impacts of their activities. It supports the aims of the OECD Guidelines to ensure that the operations of enterprises in the garment and footwear sector are in harmony with government policies to strengthen the basis of mutual confidence between enterprises and the societies in which they operate. The Guidance promotes a set of non-binding, practically-oriented principles on how companies should carry out risk-based due diligence with an emphasis on constructive collaborative approaches to complex challenges.

Water pollution is considered a prevalent sector risk in the garment and footwear sector. The Guidance contains a section on water pollution, which outlines steps to be implemented to identify potential and actual harms and to cease, prevent, or mitigate risks related to water pollution. In general, companies are expected to conduct ongoing, proactive and reactive risk-based due diligence, including to pick up on emerging environmental risks. The Guidance also encourages companies to collaborate at a sector level to pool knowledge, share information and scale up effective measures, although cross-industry collaboration does not alter the responsibility of the individual enterprise to identify, prevent or mitigate harm.

While microfibre pollution is not specifically targeted in the existing Guidance, Due Diligence approaches can help companies understand their exposure to microplastics harm in their value chain, take action to cease, prevent and mitigate the impact, as well as to monitor and report on this process. In considering the environmental impacts of a product across its full life cycle, it may be necessary for a company to also take action to prevent, cease and mitigate harm downstream in the value chain, for example by providing washing instructions to end consumers to reduce the water impacts, or by taking preventative action to reduce microplastics shedding and pollution (OECD, forthcoming[27]).

Environmental taxes and mandatory charges

Market-based instruments,[4] such as environmental taxes and mandatory charges, could also be considered to incentivise the development and uptake of best manufacturing practices in line with reduced microplastics leakage. In general, market-based instruments allow for flexibility in the way production processes are adapted in response to price signals and thus can deliver environmental improvements at a lower cost than regulatory interventions. Further, taxes could be earmarked to cover the costs of mitigation and pollution prevention, such as support for further research and R&D initiatives, for the costs of improved wastewater and stormwater treatment or for the implementation of use-phase mitigation technologies (e.g. microfibre filters for washing machines).

The implementation of market-based policies would require a careful consideration of several policy design aspects, particularly the setting of policy targets and the price signals. Two main alternatives exist in this sense, each entailing different advantages and disadvantages:

- Taxes or charges based on the *propensity of tyres and textiles to shed microplastics* are likely to be effective at incentivising the uptake of mitigation measures in line with the eco-design of products, as well as at encouraging research and development in material and product design to minimise shedding. These could apply either to producers and importers or to consumers. The main drawbacks of implementing price signals on final products are the extensive information requirements to assess the tendency of products to shed microplastics and the high monitoring costs that would be necessary for the intervention to be effective.
- Alternatively, market-based measures could be designed to target microfibre pollution indirectly, via taxes or charges on the *synthetic content of textiles and garments*. These could target either intermediate materials, i.e. the plastics input during manufacturing or the manufactured good, i.e. the synthetic content of the final product. Relying on a proxy for microfibre shedding may facilitate implementation and simplify compliance checks, as information on product content is readily measurable and usually already available (e.g. fibre content in existing product labels for textile products). However, this may come at the cost of a significant loss of policy efficiency. Most importantly, taxes targeting the synthetic content would not discern between different plastic materials and their propensity to emit microplastics and thus would not necessarily incentivise the development of eco-design solutions for synthetic-based textiles. In addition, they could also create incentives to shift to natural alternatives with higher environmental footprints.

Overall, given the potentially high monitoring requirements and implementation costs and the paucity of data to measure microplastics emissions and the associated risks, it remains to be seen whether market-based policies are feasible and adequate policy tools to incentivise eco-design practices in line with microplastics mitigation. These may become more viable as an effective policy tool in conjunction with regulatory efforts (e.g. minimum standards, or mandatory certification) and once the knowledge on hazards and the effectiveness of mitigation options improves. As the lifecycles of vehicle tyres and textile products also bear several environmental consequences other than the emission of microplastics, the risks of potential burden-shifting would need to be carefully assessed in the design of market-based policies.

4.3.2. Use-oriented approaches

Use-oriented policy approaches aim to impose or encourage the prevention or reduction of microplastics emissions occurring during product use and their release into the environment. These include measures aimed at preventing the abrasion of products containing synthetic polymers, as well as options to prevent the leakage of the emitted microplastics into the environment. Although use-oriented policy approaches have not yet been comprehensively included in policy frameworks targeting microplastics pollution, some have been considered by countries looking to reduce emissions of use-based secondary microplastics.

The use phase is perceived as a particularly relevant point for mitigation action for several reasons. Firstly, several mitigation options implementable at the use stage have the advantage of being already available and relatively easy to implement, in comparison to relevant source-directed and end-of-pipe options. This is the case for instance of microfibre filtering devices for washing machines, when compared to changes in textile design or to potentially-costly upgrades in wastewater treatment plants. Secondly, certain measures which can prevent the emissions of microfibres and TRWP, i.e. best laundering practices and eco-driving practices, can usually be implemented at low costs and also lead to additional environmental benefits (i.e. lower fuel consumption during driving, lower water and energy consumption for laundering).

Table 4.3 summarises various use-oriented policy instruments, most of which are aimed at the general public, industrial laundering facilities and washing machine manufacturers. The following paragraphs describe some of these policy instruments relevant to either foster the uptake of best use practices or the implementation of mitigation technologies.

Table 4.3. Summary of relevant use-directed policy instruments for microplastics mitigation

Type	Policy instrument	Description
Regulatory	**Minimum standards**	Mandatory performance standards for products and appliances sold on the market which influence the use phase of textiles and tyres (e.g. washing machines, laundry detergents, vehicles, roads). For instance, these could target the adoption of filtering technologies for domestic, commercial, or industrial washing machines, the uptake of tyre pressure monitoring systems for new vehicles, or the provision of real-time information on driving behaviour.
	Restrictions on product use	Restrictions on non-essential use of products with lead to significant microplastics releases. This applies for instance to the use of winter tyres, associated with a higher tyre tread abrasion rate, during the summer months. Restrictions on road transport activity, for instance to mandate stricter regulations on product maintenance (e.g. controls on tyre pressure or wheel alignment) or to mandate the uptake of use practices aligned with higher safety requirements or lower emissions of GHG and air pollutants, such as (stricter) speed limits or broader strategies to reduce overall transport volumes.
Economic	Market-based instruments	Financial support for the uptake of mitigation technologies implementable during the use phase, such as add-on filtering devices for washing machines. Market-based disincentives (e.g. vehicle purchase taxes, registration fees, annual taxes, congestion pricing, parking pricing) to incentivise consumers to reduce or change consumption behaviour.
Voluntary	**Public information campaigns**	Information provision and consumer education initiatives to influence households' and drivers' behaviour. Awareness-raising campaigns can also improve public acceptance for further policy measures
	Consumer-oriented labelling and information schemes	Consumer labels and product information can help inform consumers about best practices for maintenance and use of purchased products.
	Voluntary commitments to limit emissions	Voluntary schemes could be developed to identify, share and implement best practices and technologies to prevent industrial emissions of microplastics occurring during product handling, for instance via the uptake of additional filters in industrial and commercial laundering facilities.

Note: Policy instruments marked in bold are further discussed in the following sections
Source: Author's own elaboration

Minimum standards

Existing incentives may be insufficient to promote the development and implementation of mitigation technologies identified in Chapter 3. Adoption rates remain low, also due to a lack of independent testing carried out to assess and compare the effectiveness of different options in real-life conditions. In this sense, the introduction of regulatory or financial incentives can accelerate the development, testing and uptake of technological solutions.

Minimum standards could be introduced to set eco-design requirements for complementary products that influence microplastics release during the use phase of textiles and tyres. To date, minimum standards have been considered in particular to mandate the adoption of filtering technologies for microfibres in washing machines (Swedish EPA, 2019[28]). For instance, the European Parliament has called on the Commission to include assessments on the release of microplastics into the aquatic environment in eco-design measures, where appropriate and to introduce mandatory requirements for microplastic filters in the next review of the Ecodesign Directive for household washing machines and washer dryers (EP, 2018[29])

Microfibre capturing and filtering devices

The analysis outlined in Chapter 3 suggests that there are several elements which need to be taken into consideration in the design of policies mandating the adoption of filtering technologies for washing machines:

- *Scientifically sound evidence* should inform the setting of the standards criteria for filters, for instance the mesh size of filters and the acceptable effectiveness rate. Standardised definitions and clear requirements for filters are needed to enable the development of technological solutions.
- Options that *minimise the additional financial and maintenance costs for consumers* are expected to be more feasible to implement. This includes built-in filters as well as low-cost and low-maintenance add-on filters and consumer products. Furthermore, since the effectiveness of the use of filters is highly dependent on how these are maintained and operated (see Section 3.2.2), it will be crucial that their introduction is accompanied by the *provision of consumer information* on adequate maintenance and disposal.
- *Potential conflicts with other relevant environmental and climate targets* (e.g. energy use, water use) should be assessed and prevented. In this sense, *industry cross-collaboration* between filter and washing machine producers, as well as with research organisations, is essential to ensure that built-in or add-on devices are compatible with household (or industrial) appliances and that they adequately respond to user needs.

The cost-effectiveness of implementing filters is likely to be dependent on the specific mitigation entry points (e.g. household-level or commercial/industrial level), the characteristics of the technology (e.g. type of filtering device, effectiveness, costs of implementation) and the end-of-pipe capture infrastructure in place (e.g. the presence of on-site pre-treatment of industrial effluents, type of urban wastewater treatment technologies employed, likelihood of CSOs, method of sludge disposal). In general, context-specific assessments will need to be carried out in order to identify potential pollution hotspots for microfibres and assess whether the implementation of ad-hoc filtering technologies is cost-effective.

Public information campaigns and consumer-oriented labelling schemes

As discussed in Chapter 3, the way products are handled and used can greatly affect the degree of microplastics shedding occurring from products. Since insufficient information and consumer awareness is one of the key barriers to the adoption of use-oriented mitigation solutions for microfibres and TRWP, consumer education and awareness-raising campaigns may play a major role in encouraging behavioural change. Information provision can increase the environmental awareness of the public, the adoption of use-oriented mitigation measures, public acceptance for policy measures requiring behavioural change, as well as the attention of businesses to emerging environmental issues.

Information initiatives can take multiple forms, from public information campaigns and publications for targeted groups to mandatory or voluntary product labels. Selected examples are outlined below:

- *Communication campaigns* on microfibre shedding and tyre tread abrasion can be included into existing public awareness schemes on plastic pollution, sustainable consumption of textiles, or sustainable transport practices. For instance, information on TRWP emissions for different transportation modes could be included into existing awareness-raising campaigns to promote more sustainable transport habits. Information campaigns can also be designed to target specific microplastics mitigation options. An example of this is the communication campaign launched by the Dutch government to educate drivers on correct tyre pressure and suitable tyre types. The campaign resulted in 250 000 extra cars with the right tyre pressure in 2019, which prevented an estimated 5-10 tonnes of microplastic releases into water bodies (Dutch Government, 2020[13]).
- *Consumer best use and maintenance guidelines* could also be incorporated into *existing labels or information provision tools*. In the textile sector, standardised textile care labels already exist and are mandatory in several countries (ISO, 2012[30]). These sewn-in labels provide consumers and laundry professionals with information on the adequate product washing and care practices. It has been suggested that washing guidelines in line with best practices to mitigate microfibre shedding could be included into existing sewn-in labels (Eunomia, 2018[25]). Similar initiatives already exist: for instance, the clevercare logo is a voluntary initiative which uses sewn-in labels to direct consumers to best eco-care practices to extend garment lifetimes and minimise water and energy consumption (GINETEX, n.d.[31]).
- The *provision of salient information during the use of products* can foster the uptake of best use and maintenance practices. For instance, in the case of road transport, the provision of real-time information on fuel consumption on passenger vehicles can encourage the adoption of eco-driving practices and contribute to TRWP mitigation, in addition to reducing GHG emissions and air pollution. As an example, the ongoing uCARe project aims to investigate strategies to reduce the overall pollutant emissions of the existing combustion engine vehicle fleet via the provision of simple and effective tools to decrease individual emissions to drivers (uCARe[32]).

4.3.3. End-of-pipe and end-of-life approaches

End-of-pipe solutions include water treatment processes that aim to preserve water quality by removing contaminants from used water resources before these are reintroduced into the environment. As outlined in Chapter 3, end-of-pipe measures relevant for microplastics pollution are mainly wastewater treatment, proper disposal of wastewater sludge and the collection and management of stormwater and road runoff.

Although improvements in product design and the implementation of mitigation best practices and technologies during product use could substantially reduce emissions, mitigation upstream cannot entirely prevent microfibre shedding and tyre tread and alleviate pollution. Thus, while end-of-pipe measures alone cannot suffice to solve the problem of microplastics and other micropollutants in water (for instance, because end-of-pipe capture has difficulty in retaining smaller particles and because some microplastics are emitted into air), they may constitute necessary complements to action at source to reduce the overall risks associated with microplastics pollution.

End-of-life measures may also be relevant for microplastics pollution mitigation. As the mismanagement of plastic waste contributes to microplastics emissions, it is likely that the mismanagement of waste textiles and tyres (for instance via illegal incineration, dispersal in the environment, or landfilling) also contributes to the release of microplastics into air, water and soil. In this sense, policies aimed at preventing the mismanagement of waste textiles and tyres could also contribute to reducing microplastics generation and leakage. Relevant policy instruments include the setting of more stringent requirements for the collection and management of used textiles and tyres to improve reuse and recycling, as well as policy interventions which target microplastics emissions from artificial sport turfs (see also pre-procurement purchasing groups detailed in Table 4.2).

Table 4.4 summarises various end-of-pipe policy instruments for microplastics mitigation, as well as selected policy tools relevant for the end-of-life management of textiles and tyres.

Table 4.4. Summary of relevant end-of-pipe policy instruments for microplastics mitigation

Type	Policy instrument	Description
Regulatory	Environmental quality standards (EQS)	Quality standards set requirements, specifications, or guidelines that must be complied with in order to achieve specific environmental quality objectives in the long term. For instance, these can define concentration thresholds for pollutants which should not be exceeded in the aquatic or aerial environment.
	Best available techniques	Definition of best technology options for improved wastewater treatment
	Wastewater treatment standards	Definition of performance standards for wastewater treatment, without requiring a specific technology upgrade. The main barrier to the implementation of wastewater treatment standards (or EQS) is the lack of microplastics monitoring and of data on ecotoxicological effects to demonstrate risks above certain concentration thresholds.
	Green public procurement	Specific criteria can be developed for green public procurement of wastewater infrastructure in order to reduce releases of microplastics and other contaminants of emerging concern.
	More stringent rules for the separate collection and management of used tyres and textiles	Clothing and tyres contribute in a significant way to waste volumes. At the same time, these waste streams hold substantial potential for product reuse and recycling of non-reusable items. Separate collection for textile waste (either via door-to-door pick-up, street containers or take-back schemes) and for used tyres (e.g. via tyre vendors and intermediaries) can enable higher rates of reuse and recycling.
Economic	**Extended Producer Responsibility (EPR)**	Producer's responsibility for a product is extended to the post-consumer stage of a product's life cycle. This may entail the end-of-life stage of products (e.g. costs of waste collection and management) or potentially also the end-of-pipe capture of pollutants (e.g. costs of improved wastewater treatment).
	Wastewater tariffs or taxes for improvements in wastewater	Tariffs or taxes designed to signal the cost of wastewater treatment to remove microplastics to the public and consumers Tariffs or taxes designed to signal the cost of stormwater management and treatment to the public and consumers
	Subsidies for improved stormwater management and/or road dust collection	Financial support from governments to incentivise investments in improved stormwater management infrastructure, or to promote research on microplastics retention during stormwater treatment. Financial support could also be envisioned for road dust collection measures (e.g. street sweeping).
	Subsidies for improved wastewater treatment	Subsidies from governments to incentivise operators to invest in advanced wastewater treatment and/or to promote research on technologies adapted to microplastics removal
	Payments for Ecosystem Services (PES)	Stormwater runoff provides several ecosystem services, including soil moisture, groundwater recharge and filtration of water through the environment. Payments for Ecosystem Services can be explored to internalise water pollution and other environmental externalities and fund the restoration of selected green infrastructure, such as wetlands, for stormwater treatment and flood management.
Voluntary	Waste collection / take-back initiatives	Voluntary schemes to collect used garments and tyres
	Consumer awareness initiatives to reduce textile waste generation	Dedicated consumer-oriented awareness campaigns to promote responsible and sustainable use and disposal choices in the garment and apparel sector and guide consumers towards extended use, second-hand markets and reuse and separate collection schemes.

Note: Policy instruments marked in bold are further discussed in the following sections
Source: Author's own elaboration

The availability of funding to finance investments in end-of-pipe infrastructure or to adapt to updated water quality regulation is a crucial concern for water utilities. The costs of upgrading wastewater treatment technologies to comply with future stricter requirements for wastewater and drinking water treatment could amount to several billions euros per year in investment in advanced water treatment technologies and additional operational costs (EurEau, 2019[33]).

Several options exist to finance WWTP upgrades, including: public taxes, wastewater tariffs, charges passed onto the manufacturing industries, or a combination thereof (OECD, 2019[34]). For instance, Switzerland has implemented a wastewater tax to partially fund the upgrade of approximately 120 WWTPs to remove 80% of contaminants of emerging concern (mainly pharmaceutical residues) from wastewaters by 2040 (OECD, 2019[34]). Taxes on inputs, such as product charges and other proxies for pollution, could also be used to raise funds for investments in water quality infrastructure and management.

Funding mechanisms should also be considered to finance improvements in stormwater management infrastructure. For instance, stormwater charges for stormwater pollution from impervious surface runoff in urban areas can incentivise reductions in stormwater runoff and finance a greater proportion of urban land to be connected to a drainage system with stormwater treatment. Payments for Ecosystem Services can be explored to fund the restoration of selected green infrastructure, such as wetlands, for stormwater treatment and flood management.

Extended producer responsibility (EPR) may be a relevant option for facilitating and financing microplastics pollution prevention at several levels of the product lifecycle, from production to end-of-life and end-of-pipe capture. This is discussed in the next section.

Extended Producer Responsibility

Extended Producer Responsibility (EPR) is an environmental policy approach in which a producer's responsibility for a product is extended to the post-consumer stage of a product's life cycle. More than 400 EPR systems are currently in place in OECD countries and beyond, mainly with the policy objective of increasing waste recovery and recycling (OECD, 2016[35]). EPR schemes allow producers to exercise their responsibility for end-of-life products, either by providing the financial resources required and/or by taking over the operational and organisational aspects of the process from municipalities.

EPR policy is consistent with the Polluter-Pays Principle in so far as financial responsibility for treating end-of-life products is shifted from taxpayers and municipalities to producers and, ultimately, consumers. Where implemented, it generates financial resources to deal with the end-of-life costs of products. Additionally, EPR schemes may also create economic incentives for producers to minimise the environmental impact of products. This may include redesigning products to facilitate their end-of-life handling or avoiding using materials that may pose risks to human health or the environment, to improve recyclability and minimise environmental hazards. In some cases, EPR schemes have been designed to provide a framework where industry stakeholders can collaborate and share information, which can facilitate the identification of ways to minimise the costs of pollution mitigation overall.

EPR schemes hold some potential for microplastics mitigation (EurEau, 2019[33]). First, EPR fees could be employed to finance improvements and upgrades of both wastewater and stormwater management, including expanding WWT capacity and upgrading existing plants, improving street and roadside cleaning, and implementing infrastructure for the treatment of stormwater and road runoff. Second, EPR schemes with advanced fee modulation (Laubinger et al., forthcoming[36]) could potentially provide incentives to producers to improve textile and tyre eco-design, for instance by employing less hazardous materials during manufacturing and investing in R&D to develop products which are less prone to microplastics shedding.

Although EPR schemes generally bear significant implementation costs, these could be particularly attractive policy tools for microplastics pollution mitigation where EPR schemes for the management of end-of-life management of tyres and textile products already exist. Several OECD countries have EPR schemes and other end-of-life management schemes (e.g. take-back obligations) in place to facilitate the separate collection and environmentally sound handling of used tyres (see Chapter 2). In France, an EPR schemes for textiles which puts the responsibility on companies to manage textile waste has also been in place since 2008.

References

California Assembly (2020), *A.B. 1952.* [18]

California Assembly (2018), *A.B. 129.* [17]

Canada (2017), *Microbeads in Toiletries Regulations (SOR/2017-111), 2 June 2017*, Government of Canada, http://www.canada.ca/en/health-canada/services/chemical-substances/other-chemical-substances-interest/microbeads.html (accessed on 1 August 2018). [1]

Connecticut, S. (2018), *Substitute House Bill No. 5360*, http://www.cga.ct.gov/2018/ACT/pa/2018PA-00181-R00HB-05360-PA.htm. [15]

DAWE (2021), *National Plastics Plan 2021.* [11]

Dutch Government (2020), "Towards Osaka Blue Ocean Vision: G20 Implementation Framework for Actions on Marine Plastic LItter", *the Netherlands - Actions and Progress on Marine Plastic LItter*, https://g20mpl.org/partners/netherlands (accessed on 3 August 2020). [13]

EC (2018), *Kick-off meeting for the review of the Best Available Techniques (BAT) Reference Document for the textiles industry, Seville, 12-15 June 2018, Meeting Report*, https://eippcb.jrc.ec.europa.eu/reference/BREF/TXT/TXT_KoM_meeting_report_Sept18.pdf. [43]

ECHA (2019), *ANNEX XV Restriction Report. Proposal for a restriction - intentionally added microplastics.* [6]

EP (2018), *Implementation of the Ecodesign Directive. European Parliament resolution of 31 May 2018 on the implementation of the Ecodesign Directive (2009/125/EC) (2017/2087(INI)).* [29]

ETRMA (2018), *Way Forward Report.* [22]

EU (2020), *Circular Economy Action Plan*, https://ec.europa.eu/commission/presscorner/detail/en/fs_20_437. [12]

EU (2020), *Regulation (EU) 2020/740 of the European Parliament and of the Council of 25 May 2020 on the labelling of tyres with respect to fuel efficiency and other parameters, amending Regulation (EU) 2017/1369 and repealing Regulation (EC) No 1222/2009.* [8]

EU (2017), *Regulation 2017/1369 of the European Parliament and of the Council of 4 July 2017 setting a framework for energy labelling and repealing Directive 2010/30/EU.* [39]

EU (2010), *Directive 2010/75/EU of the European Parliament and of the Council of 24*, https://eur-lex.europa.eu/legal-content/EN/TXT/PDF/?uri=CELEX:32010L0075&from=EN. [42]

EU SAM (2018), *Microplastic Pollution: The Policy Context*, https://op.europa.eu/s/plSs. [7]

Eunomia (2018), "Investigating options for reducing releases in the aquatic environment of microplastics emitted by (but not intentionally added in) products - Interim Report", *Report for DG Environment of the European Commission*, p. 335, http://dx.doi.org/10.1002/lsm.22016. [25]

Euratex (n.d.), *Euratex: The European Apparel and Textile Confederation*, https://euratex.eu/cia (accessed on 26 September 2020). [20]

EurEau (2019), *Study on the feasibility of applying Extended Producer Responsibility to micropollutants and microplastics emitted in the aquatic environment from products during their lifecycle*. [33]

France (2020), *LOI n° 2020-105 du 10 février 2020 relative à la lutte contre le gaspillage et à l'économie circulaire*, http://www.legifrance.gouv.fr/eli/loi/2020/2/10/TREP1902395L/jo/texte. [10]

France (2017), *Décret n° 2017-291 du 6 mars 2017 relatif aux conditions de mise en œuvre de l'interdiction de mise sur le marché des produits cosmétiques rincés à usage d'exfoliation ou de nettoyage comportant des particules plastiques solides et des bâtonnets ouatés à usage domestique dont la tige est en plastique*. [2]

GINETEX (n.d.), *clevercare.info*, http://www.clevercare.info/ (accessed on 21 January 2021). [31]

GOV.UK (2018), *World-leading microbeads ban takes effect*, http://www.gov.uk/government/news/world-leading-microbeads-ban-takes-effect (accessed on 22 August 2019). [3]

Gruère, G. (2013), "A Characterisation of Environmental Labelling and Information Schemes", *OECD Environment Working Papers*, No. 62, OECD Publishing, Paris, http://dx.doi.org/10.1787/5k3z11hpdgq2-en. [26]

ISO (2012), *ISO 3758:2012 Textiles – Care labeling code using symbols*. [30]

Italy (2017), *Legge n 205 del 27 dicembre 2017. Bilancio di previsione dello Stato per l'anno finanziario 2018 e bilancio pluriennale per il triennio 2018-2020.*. [5]

JATMA (2009), *Guideline for tyre labeling to promote the use of fuel efficient tyres (labeling system)*. [40]

Laubinger, F. and P. Börkey (forthcoming), *Labelling and Information Schemes for the Circular Economy*. [24]

Laubinger, F. et al. (forthcoming), "Modulated fees for extended producer responsibility schemes (EPR)", *OECD Environment Working Papers*. [36]

Legal Information Institute (n.d.), *49 CFR 575.104 Uniform Tire Quality Grading Standards*. [41]

New York State Assembly (2018), *Bill No. A01549*. [16]

OECD (2019), "Best Available Techniques (BAT) for Preventing and Controlling Industrial Pollution, Activity 3: Measuring the Effectiveness of BAT Policies", *Environment, Health and Safety, Environment Directorate*, http://www.oecd.org/chemicalsafety/risk-management/measuring-the-effectiveness-of-best-available-techniques-policies.pdf. [44]

OECD (2019), *Pharmaceutical Residues in Freshwater: Hazards and Policy Responses*, OECD Studies on Water, OECD Publishing, Paris, https://dx.doi.org/10.1787/c936f42d-en. [34]

OECD (2018), "Best Available Techniques for Preventing and Controlling Industrial Pollution: Activity 2, Approaches to Establishing Best Available Techniques (BAT) Around the World", *Environment, Health and Safety, Environment Directorate, OECD*. [46]

OECD (2017), *Report on OECD Project on Best Available Techniques for Preventing and Controlling Industrial Chemical Pollution - Activity I: Policies on BAT or Similar Concepts Across the World*, OECD Publishing, Paris, http://www.oecd.org/chemicalsafety/risk-management/policies-on-best-available-techniques-or-similar-concepts-around-the-world.pdf. [45]

OECD (2016), *Extended Producer Responsibility: Updated Guidance for Efficient Waste Management*, OECD Publishing, Paris, https://dx.doi.org/10.1787/9789264256385-en. [35]

OECD (forthcoming), *Responsible Business Conduct tools and instruments to address environmental challenges*. [27]

Oeko-Tex (2019), *OEKO-TEX® | Global importance*, http://www.oeko-tex.com/kr/about_oeko_tex/oeko_tex_success_story/oeko_tex_success_story.xhtml (accessed on 30 July 2019). [37]

Patagonia (n.d.), *Teaming Up to Get to the Bottom of Microfiber Pollution*, https://eu.patagonia.com/fr/en/stories/teaming-up-to-get-to-the-bottom-of-microfiber-pollution/story-71999.html (accessed on March 26 2021). [21]

PlasticsEurope (2017), *PlasticsEurope Operation Clean Sweep*, http://www.opcleansweep.eu/wp-content/uploads/2017/09/OCS_Report2017.pdf. [23]

Sustainable Apparel Coalition (2019), *Higg Brand Tool – Sustainable Apparel Coalition*, https://apparelcoalition.org/higg-brand-tool/ (accessed on 25 February 2019). [38]

Swedish EPA (2021), *Textilsmart - Naturvårdsverket*, http://www.naturvardsverket.se/Miljoarbete-i-samhallet/Miljoarbete-i-Sverige/Uppdelat-efter-omrade/Konsumtion-och-produktion/Hallbara-textilier/Textilsmart/ (accessed on 28 January 2021). [9]

Swedish EPA (2019), *The Eco-Design Directive as a driver for less microplastic from household laundry*. [28]

Swedish EPA (n.d.), *Mikroplast - Naturvårdsverket*, http://www.naturvardsverket.se/Miljoarbete-i-samhallet/Miljoarbete-i-Sverige/Uppdelat-efter-omrade/Plast/Mikroplast/ (accessed on 21 January 2021). [14]

The Microfibre Consortium (n.d.), *TMC Strategic Workplan*, http://www.microfibreconsortium.com/ (accessed on 18 January 2021). [19]

uCARe (n.d.), *uCARe*, http://www.project-ucare.eu/ (accessed on 9 October 2020). [32]

United States (2015), *Microbead-Free Waters Act of 2015*. [4]

Annex 4.A. Assessment of selected source-directed policy approaches

Minimum standards, certification schemes and labelling and information systems

Business-to-business information sharing along textile and apparel value chains

Transparency on the composition and characteristics of input materials and products is important for companies downstream to manage environmental risks associated with the products they manufacture and place on the market. Textile and apparel value chains are complex and globally dispersed, which makes it difficult to keep track of individual manufacturing processes a product has undergone and to identify environmental hotspots. As a result, clothing manufactures, fashion brands and other stakeholders downstream often have incomplete or inadequate information on the content and characteristics of intermediary and/or final products.

In the context of microfibre mitigation, paucity of information for different actors along the value chain leads to a number of market inefficiencies:

- Manufacturing companies may be exposed to information deficiencies on the content and characteristics of intermediary products and the manufacturing practices employed at previous stages of the value chain. This may constrain the potential to quantify the shedding propensity of the final product and provide accurate information to consumers.
- Poor information on the materials and chemical substances employed at earlier stages may also pose a barrier to the implementation of best manufacturing practices. For instance, whereas preliminary washing has been identified as a potential mitigation measure for microfibres, lack of information on the history of the product and the substances it may release during washing, may hinder adequate handling.
- Information asymmetries may also be detrimental to progress in research and development, in particular with regards to the identification and assessment of mitigation solutions implementable during design and manufacturing. Research efforts may be constrained by poor traceability of products available on the market and limited transparency over the material and chemical content and the manufacturing practices these have undergone.

Business-to-business (B2B) information systems can be useful tools to improve the transparency of products and to address information asymmetries along the supply chain on the quality of intermediary products. A variety of B2B information systems and metrics that address other sustainability aspects have been developed in the textile sector, such as the manufacturing restricted substances list (MRSL) to facilitate chemicals management (detailed in Box 2.1) and the Oeko-Tex Standards, which allow brands, retail companies and manufacturers to monitor and communicate environmental sustainability achievements across the supply chain (Oeko-Tex, 2019[37]).

Information schemes could be developed to share information relevant to assess the microfibre shedding propensity of final garments along value chain actors. Ideally, quality controls for microfibre shedding would apply to textile products at all processing stages. Where this is difficult or costly to implement, for instance because fibre and textile production occurs in small enterprises in emerging economies, third-party testing can be employed further downstream to certify the performance of imported products. As legislation (e.g. the EU REACH regulation) generally puts the responsibility for managing the environmental footprint of products on brands downstream, the introduction of voluntary or mandatory certification schemes of B2B information systems can also enable the development of regulatory policy and facilitate compliance by fashion brands downstream (Laubinger and Börkey, forthcoming[24]).

As microfibre pollution is only one of the environmental issues associated with textile production and use, it may be preferable to include microfibre information into existing schemes which take a holistic, lifecycle approach to environmental impacts. An example of such a B2B information scheme is the Higg Index, a suite of assessment tools which allows brands, retailers and manufacturers in the apparel and footwear industry to measure environmental, social and labour impacts across the lifecycle of products. The Higg Materials Sustainability Index (MSI) is used as a B2B tool to measure the environmental footprint of apparel products based on metrics on hazardous chemicals, water use, energy and deforestation (Sustainable Apparel Coalition, 2019[38]). Microplastics are recognised as an important environmental impact aspect to be included into LCA methods such as the Higg MSI, however its incorporation will only become possible once standardised methodologies for microfibre shedding are available.[5]

Business-to-consumer information schemes and product standards

Absence of information on the shedding propensity of tyres and garments available on the market limits consumers' ability to discern products based on their environmental performance. The provision of consumer-oriented information on microfibre shedding propensity of textiles and on the rate of tyre tread abrasion can help address several existing market inefficiencies and environmental externalities associated with microplastics leakage. Although several other criteria also influence consumers' purchasing decisions, the provision of this information is expected to steer consumption towards products with a higher resistance to microplastics shedding (Eunomia, 2018[25]). [6]In turn, the implementation of B2C information and labelling schemes is also expected to trigger a shift at the production stage towards tyres and textile products with a lower propensity to release microplastics.

The design and implementation of information systems for microfibre shedding and tyre tread abrasion would differ depending on the context and specific objectives to be targeted. Labelling schemes could be designed to map the resistance of products to microplastics shedding on a scale. Examples of this are the EU's energy labelling and eco-design regulations (A***-E, previously A-G), the Japanese Tyre Labelling Scheme (AAA-D) and the US Uniform Tire Labelling Grading (AA-C)[7] (EU, 2017[39]; JATMA, 2009[40]; Legal Information Institute, n.d.[41]). Alternatively, B2C certification labels can be employed to indicate that a product meets certain predetermined environmental criteria (e.g. European Union Eco-Label, Nordic Swan Ecolabel). In addition to labelling schemes, information on the shedding propensity of products could also be included via other information provision tools, such as product packaging and additional garment tags or stickers.

Integrating microplastics information into existing information schemes may be the most cost-effective option. Given the low weight of microfibre and TRWP pollution relative to other selection criteria for textiles and tyres (environmental, quality, or safety concerns), the issue may not justify creating an additional labelling scheme. Also, information on microfibre shedding or tyre tread abrasion may be most salient to the consumer if provided in conjunction with other relevant information on the overall environmental footprint of the product. Even where microfibre information cannot be easily provided as part of existing certification and labelling schemes, options that take a holistic perspective on the environmental footprint of the lifecycle of products should be preferred.

In parallel to labelling schemes, product standards could be introduced to set eco-design requirements for textiles and tyres placed on the market. These could be designed in two ways: a) *technology standards* mandating the adoption of certain identified eco-design practices or banning the use of harmful manufacturing processes, and b) *performance standards* setting maximum thresholds for microfibre shedding or tyre tread abrasion.

Technology and performance standards are not mutually exclusive and could also be implemented in conjunction, depending on the context and identified mitigation solutions. Performance standards allow for greater flexibility to search for the cheapest options to reach the set pollution reduction goals. In turn, where certain manufacturing processes have been identified as particularly harmful to microplastics mitigation, technology standards can provide a low-cost option to abate emissions. An important aspect in the design of minimum standards is that these must be dynamic in nature in order to allow and incentivise innovation and eco-design. For instance, where performance standards are introduced in conjunction with labelling schemes mapping the microfibre shedding propensity or tyre tread abrasion rate on a alphanumerical scale, this can be used to set and regularly update the threshold for the acceptable performance of products.

Several options exist to establish the certification criteria against which products should be judged to determine whether it complies with minimum standards or to grant it a labelling classification. The most cost-effective option is likely to be the use of self-certifications to attest the expected performance of products based on standardised testing (Eunomia, 2018[25]). For instance, under the EU Tyre Labelling Regulation, the performance of tyres is self-certified in accordance with EU standardised tests.

Best Available Techniques

The OECD is not familiar with any jurisdictions that, to date, have published BAT and BAT-associated environmental performance levels (BAT-AEPLs) concerning the release of microplastics. In the European Union, industrial emissions of microplastics (specifically synthetic fibres and releases plastic pellets along the industrial supply/production chain) are within the scope of the Industrial Emissions Directive (IED), the EU BAT legislation (EU, 2010[42]; EU SAM, 2018[7]). No relevant BAT and BAT-AEPLs have been defined on this parameter, also due a lack of data, harmonised measurements and monitoring on industrial microplastics releases. However, the Technical Working Group in charge of regularly reviewing the BREF for the Textile Industry has recently decided to collect information on microplastic from various studies to be included in the relevant BREF, possibly preparing for the determination of BAT on microplastic in future revisions (EC, 2018[43]).

Benefits of a BAT-based approach

A BAT-based approach to microplastics emissions could bring several benefits:

- *Evidence-based standards:* The process to determine BAT is based on a comprehensive collection and exchange of information on existing pollution prevention and control techniques and other relevant data, such as emissions data. The information collection is followed by a thorough assessment of the technical, environmental and economic aspects of existing techniques. As a result, the process to determine BAT and the associated emission levels is rooted in evidence as well as expert judgement. Consequently, BAT-based emission limit values are more likely to result in emissions reduction than those solely based on other benchmarks such as environmental quality standards.
- *A holistic approach to environmental protection*: studies show that the implementation of BAT can ensure considerable reductions in industrial emissions and thus important savings to society and industry, as a result of improved environmental management of industrial operations. Furthermore, all OECD member countries are recommended to implement an integrated pollution prevention and control (IPPC) approach (OECD, 1991), i.e. covering emissions to air, water and soil alike. BAT can contribute to the implementation of such an approach, to ensure that pollutants are mitigated rather than shifted between different environmental media.
- *Multi-stakeholder dialogue:* In order to determine BAT and associated emission levels, countries or regions usually set up sector-specific Technical Working Groups, typically consisting of experts

from industry, government and environmental NGOs. This allows stakeholders to build a mutual understanding of industrial operators' key environmental challenges and of the means to address these. Thanks to the multi-stakeholder dialogue, BAT-based permit conditions reflect a balance of interests. This approach also tends to increase the acceptability of permit conditions across stakeholders involved, including industry operators.

- *Level playing field*: by aligning environmental performance requirements across industrial installations in each country or region, BAT-based permitting creates a level playing field for industry.
- *Cost-effective upgrade of industry*: when determining BAT, the Technical Working Groups usually consider the costs and advantages of candidate techniques, in order to identify those that reduce the environmental impacts of industrial operations in a cost-effective manner without hampering other aspects of the operations. Moreover, while there may be a cost associated with the implementation of BAT for industrial operators, the introduction of BAT enables an upgrade of industrial operations, making installations greener and potentially also more resource-efficient.
- *Flexibility at the implementation stage:* Although the emission levels associated with BAT are legally binding, the BAT per se are usually not prescriptive. This implies that industrial operators are free to choose whatever technique they find suitable to prevent or control emissions, provided that they reach compliance with the emission limit values set by environmental permits.

Possible steps forwards

In order to ensure the introduction of BAT for the prevention and control of microplastic releases during industrial operations or further down in the lifecycle of products, governments would have to establish relevant BAT and BAT-AEPLs in BREFs and set legally binding permit conditions for industrial installations on that basis. These could be implemented through the following steps:

- Identify microplastic releases as a key environmental issue to be considered during the drawing up or review of BREFs pertaining to relevant industrial activities, such as textile production;
- for the selected sectors, collect data on 1) available techniques for prevention and control of microplastic releases occurring during manufacturing, as well as on reported industrial releases, and/or 2) best available manufacturing techniques for the prevention of MP release during product use;
- following the information collection, determine BAT for prevention and control of microplastic releases based on a comprehensive evaluation of the environmental, economic and technical aspects of available techniques, conducted by sector-specific Technical Working Groups consisting of experts from government, industry and NGOs;
- derive ranges of legally binding BAT-associated emission levels and other associated environmental performance levels (BAT-AEPLs), e.g. related to the release of pre-production plastic emissions, tyre abrasion under standard use; and
- in compliance with the ranges of BAT-AEPLs, determine permit conditions pertaining to microplastic releases for industrial installations at local/national permitting authorities.

Notes

[1] The CIA-produced test method for microfibre shedding has been submitted for approval to the CEN Working on Microplastics, an entity charged with setting standardized test methods for the determination of the release, identification and evaluation of microplastics from textile sources, during manufacture and use.

[2] The OECD's BAT reports (OECD, 2017[45]; OECD, 2018[46]; OECD, 2019[44]) provide information on policies based on BAT or similar concepts in the European Union, Chile, Israel, Korea, New Zealand, the United States, the People's Republic of China, India, the Russian Federation and EECCA countries.

[3] BAT-associated environmental performance levels (BAT-AEPLs) encompass BAT-associated emission levels (BAT-AELs) as well as other performance levels, such as those related to consumption of material, water or energy, the generation of waste, abatement efficiency on pollutants and duration of visible emissions.

[4] Extended Producer Responsibility could also hold some potential for the mitigation of microplastics shedding from products, as discussed in 4.3.3. The implementation of EPR with advanced fee modulation would likely face the same information challenges than market-based instruments such as environmental taxes.

[5] According to the OECD Due Diligence Guidance for the Garment and Footwear Sector, companies have a responsibility to take action to identify, prevent, and mitigate risks to water quality, regardless of whether specific environmental harms are incorporated into existing voluntary initiatives.

[6] A recent survey carried out in the European Union found that there is strong consumer demand for information about tyre tread abrasion rates (Eunomia, 2018[25]).

[7] The US Uniform Tire Labelling Grading already includes a numerical index for tyre wear. However, since the reference tyre on which tread wear is measured differs for each brand, this measure cannot be used to compare tyres of different brands placed on the market.

5 Elements to guide policy action

Drawing from previous sections and chapters, this concluding chapter presents a set of elements that can guide central government and other stakeholders towards appropriate prevention and management measures for microplastics originating from tyres and textiles.

5.1. Towards life-cycle, strategic and holistic approaches for microfibre and TRWP mitigation

Microplastics are pervasive in the environment. As our human population and dependence on plastics continue to grow at current rates, it is expected that microplastics concentrations in aquatic environments and the associated risks will steadily increase. According to the *precautionary principle*, precautionary measures should be considered when the environmental and human health risks are uncertain and the potential consequences of inaction are high. In the case of microplastics, effective preventive action is recommended in order to halt the accumulation of microplastics in the environment and prevent widespread health risks to ecosystems and human health.

The generation of microplastics from textile products and vehicle tyres is a complex phenomenon, for which no single effective technological or policy fix exists. Microplastics emitted at different points of the lifecycle of products differ in their characteristics, entry pathways into the environment and inherent potential to cause harm. This underlines the complexity of designing policy solutions to comprehensively target textile- and tyre- based microplastics in marine and freshwaters.

Key elements to take into consideration when evaluating different mitigation entry points are outlined in Table 5.1. Measures aimed at preventing the emission of microplastics at source are likely to have the largest mitigation potential. Especially for diffuse sources of pollution (i.e. Tyre and Road Wear Particles, microfibres emitted into air during wearing and drying), the Principle of Pollution Prevention reflects that pollution prevention is often more cost effective than treatment/restoration options downstream (OECD, 2017[11]). Yet, given the diffuse nature of emissions and the variety of entry pathways, measures upstream cannot entirely alleviate the risk of microplastics pollution for the water cycle. Measures upstream will need to be complemented by effective end-of-pipe capture solutions to impose, incentivise, or encourage improved end-of-pipe capture.

The most cost-effective way of tackling the issue is likely to consist in the implementation of a mix of policy tools targeting different mitigation entry points along the lifecycle of products. Lifecycle approaches are also likely to benefit from higher levels of stakeholder acceptance and easier implementation overall, as they aim to target several relevant actors and share responsibility for pollution prevention and management.

Table 5.1. Comparing mitigation entry points along the lifecycle of products

Lifecycle stage	Advantages	Disadvantages / Barriers to implementation
Design and manufacturing	• High mitigation potential • Certain best practices are already available for implementation	• Need of further research to evaluate the impact of certain manufacturing parameters • Identification and development of eco-design options may take time • Trade-offs between microplastics mitigation and other policy objectives should be carefully considered to avoid burden-shifting (e.g. energy and water consumption and chemicals use for textile production, safety for tyres) • Potentially-high implementation barriers and costs for manufacturing facilities in non-OECD countries
Use	• High mitigation potential • Low-cost options already available (best practices and technological solutions) • Large opportunities for co-benefits: e.g. best maintenance and care for textiles, lower GHG emissions and air pollution from road traffic	• Lack of public awareness over the issue and the low-cost mitigation options available to consumers • Lack of financial or regulatory incentives to implement mitigation solutions

Lifecycle stage	Advantages	Disadvantages / Barriers to implementation
End-of-life	• Opportunity to prevent textile and tyre waste mismanagement overall • Opportunity to improve material resource productivity via reuse or recycling practices	• Uncertain relationship between microfibre shedding and reuse/recycling practices for clothing. • Weak markets for second-hand garments or recycled fibres
End-of-pipe	• Several opportunities to exploit synergies with other pollutants • Prevention of diffuse pollution and CSOs to preserve freshwater and marine water quality • Improved wastewater management and treatment offers co-benefits for the capture of all microplastics and other relevant micropollutants • Low-cost mitigation measures (e.g. for road dust particle collection)	• Generally high costs for WWTP upgrades • Higher contamination levels of sewage sludge poses environmental impacts elsewhere (if landspreaded) • Lack of reliable data on the cost-effectiveness of different stormwater treatment options for microplastics retention

Source: Author's own elaboration

At the same time, current scientific evidence on the hazards associated with textile microfibres and TRWP may not yet be sufficient to justify resource-intensive policy efforts. Researchers and industry have identified several mitigation best practices and technologies that can be implemented during the lifecycle of textiles and tyres to prevent or reduce emissions. Yet, often further research is required to evaluate their relative cost-effectiveness, implementation feasibility and the potential trade-offs with other relevant environmental benefits. Certain end-of-pipe mitigation options, such as advanced wastewater treatment or nature-based solutions, primary designed to mitigate other pollutants, can generate significant co-benefits for microplastic mitigation, although microplastics pollution alone is unlikely to justify the additional capital and operation & maintenance costs.

In general, current scientific evidence alone may not be sufficient to drive costly investment decisions or to justify trade-offs with other relevant environmental consequences. Furthermore, further knowledge and data is still required in several areas (e.g. mitigation effectiveness, including the need for standardised test methods to measure it, the magnitude of current emissions, information about the full life-cycle impacts of interventions), in order to evaluate the cost-effectiveness of different mitigation measures. Based on these considerations, the next sections present key recommendations to guide governments and other stakeholders towards improved control of microfibre and TRWP mitigation. These are organised around two priorities:

- *Advancing knowledge* to strengthen the evidence base and inform policymaking via the fostering of research, the promotion of international and cross industry collaboration, the development of harmonised test methods; and
- *Seeking out and valuing co-benefits* with other environmental policy areas (e.g. circular practices in the textile and apparel sector, sustainable transport policy, water quality policies, guidelines and strategies for plastics) and *exploiting low-cost "no regret" mitigation measures.*

Additionally, when information on the effectiveness of mitigation measures has improved, *additional and more specific policy measures* will be needed to mandate, incentivise or encourage the uptake of mitigation technologies and best practices. As outlined in Chapter 4, some of these policy measures, such as requirements to add microfibre filters to washing machines and consumer-awareness initiatives, are already being explored by governments.

Preventive mitigation action should be in line with wider objectives of environmental and health protection. Measures taken should be proportional, consistent with existing policy frameworks, based on adequate cost-benefit analysis considerations and sufficiently flexible to encourage scientific research and allow for innovation in mitigation solutions. In particular, it will be crucial to consider holistic system-wide impacts of proposed measures, to ensure that these do not cause unintended adverse consequences, such as burden-shifting towards other environmental policy areas. This could be the case for instance of higher resource use associated with the use of alternative materials during product manufacturing, or increased terrestrial microplastics pollution as a consequence of sludge application and improved wastewater treatment technologies. Evidence-based impact assessments of proposed measures will need to be carried out in order to ensure that policy measures are cost-effective and ensure net environmental benefits.

There may be a case for prioritising the implementation of mitigation technologies at pollution hotspots, to achieve a higher cost-effectiveness of the mitigation measures. For instance, prioritising the implementation of microfibre filters at commercial (e.g. restaurants, hospitals, etc.) and industrial laundering facilities could potentially enable the capture of microfibres from highly polluted wastewaters as close to the source of emission as possible and before these diluted into sewage. Similarly, the allocation of improved wastewater and stormwater technologies can be optimised to prioritise the treatment of highly polluted wastewaters or road runoff. On-site treatment generally tends to be less cost-effective than upgrading centralised WWT technologies, however this may not be the case for low-cost improvements in stormwater management and treatment. As outlined in Chapter 3, there may be large pollution prevention gains to be made by directing the implementation of low-cost stormwater treatment technologies at TRWP pollution hotspots, i.e. locations with high potential for the generation of TRWP and/or direct transportation into the environment. Country-specific hotspot analyses will be required in order to identify potential pollution hotspots for microfibres and TRWP and assess whether the implementation of ad-hoc treatment and filtering technologies is more cost-effective compared to large-scale installations.

5.2. International collaboration and data-sharing to advance knowledge and reduce uncertainty

Sound scientific evidence will need to play a key role in the determination and implementation of policy measures. Opportunities to extend and deepen the evidence base for intervention include:

- Better data quality and gathering on the quantities and concentrations of microplastics in the environment, including broadening the scope to all relevant loci of concern (e.g. marine and freshwaters, air, soil, sediments, aquatic and marine species and the human body);
- Improved understanding of the concentration levels at which adverse health effects occur;
- Development of risk assessments and forecasting on the hazards posed to humans and ecosystems. Further research is particularly required to assess risks in realistic environmental concentrations, as well as to close existing knowledge gaps with regards to the fragmentation of plastics and the hazards posed by smaller microplastics and nanoplastics;
- Improved understanding of the quantities and release mechanisms for textile- and tyre-based microplastics release, also including industrial emissions, end-of-life leakage and other relevant stages of the use phase (e.g. wearing and drying of garments)
- Research and development of mitigation technologies and best practices implementable at different stages of the product lifecycle, from manufacturing to end-of-pipe measures for stormwater and wastewater; and
- Improved evaluation of the relative cost-effectiveness of the mitigation measures available along the lifecycle of products.

There is also a need to support to the identification, development and assessment of mitigation technologies and best practices along the lifecycle of products. At the manufacturing stage, further efforts are required to develop innovative textiles and vehicle tyres that undergo lower abrasion, without compromising on other relevant characteristics. Further research is also required to develop best practices and technologies for the design and manufacturing of complementary products (e.g. washing machines and laundry detergents) and infrastructure (e.g. roads and roads) which cause lower product abrasion and mitigate MP generation. At the use stage, further research is required to assess the mitigation potential best practices and technological solutions that have been identified as well as of the possible entry points for their implementation (e.g. household vs commercial or industrial washing machines). At the end-of-pipe stage, further research is required to assess the effectiveness of available options to reduce microplastics in stormwater and wastewaters. Overall, there is a need to perform evaluations of the relative cost-effectiveness of mitigation measures available to inform intervention action.

In order to accelerate research and perform robust risk assessments, it will be crucial to agree on common definitions, standardise and harmonise data types and share existing information. Currently, the use of different methodologies and definitions makes it difficult to compare and aggregate findings and constitutes a vast bottleneck in several fields of action. International and interdisciplinary cooperation and information sharing will be key enablers the advancement of research and to the standardisation and harmonisation of test methods. Further, the development of common databases to establish cross-border access to harmonised data can reduce time and costs associated with documenting robust policy decisions at national and international levels.

In particular, the following list of recommendations can facilitate methods harmonisation and international collaboration:

- *Agreeing on common definitions and methods* to sample and analyse microplastics in the environment and to report results on adverse health effects on ecosystem and human health.
- *Defining common and harmonised standards for microfibre shedding and tyre tread abrasion.* Currently, the lack of standardised test methods to measure microplastics shedding poses a key barrier to research and mitigation. As outlined in Chapter 4, ongoing efforts and stakeholder collaboration to establish standardised and harmonised test methods for microfibre shedding and tyre tread abrasion will be crucial to accelerate research and enable the implementation of mitigation measures such as minimum standards and labelling and information schemes.
- *Defining uniform protocols to measure and evaluate the effectiveness of mitigation technologies,* including standardised criteria to assess the effectiveness of different stormwater treatment infrastructure to retain TRWP.
- *Developing standardised measurement procedures for the sampling and analysis of microplastics* in different environmental media (e.g. TRWP, MP in wastewaters and stormwater)
- *Establishing international databases and information exchange platforms* to improve accessibility to available knowledge, exploit synergies across different projects and accelerate research.
- *Improving accessibility on best manufacturing practices and technologies* to prevent information asymmetries and enable industry to develop and implement mitigation measures
- *Promoting international and interdisciplinary collaboration.* The promotion of international and interdisciplinary collaboration will be a key enabler for the objectives outlined above, in particular to accelerate research, establish cross-border access to standardised data and inform policy responses. Existing voluntary initiatives to establish stakeholder platforms should be sustained to facilitate the dissemination of knowledge in the long-term.

5.3. Opportunities to exploit synergies with other environmental policy objectives

Given the significant trade-offs and often high costs involved, it is unlikely that microplastics pollution alone will drive policy decisions. As outlined in earlier parts of the report, a strategic way of addressing the issue of microfibres and tyre-based microplastics could consist of seeking out and valuing co-benefits with other environmental, climate, human health, or safety policy areas while not compromising progress on microplastics mitigation. Where other policy objectives drive investment and policy decisions, there may be scope for integrating microplastics into existing frameworks to achieve pollution reduction at a low-cost. There are also several cases of "no-regret" policy opportunities, where mitigation action for microplastics pollution either comes as a co-benefit of measures in other policy areas, such as in the case of the reduction of total transport volumes, or bears low costs and low risk for unintended consequences, which could be the case of new technological innovations in the production of textiles, tyres and complementary products. Drawing from the analysis of Chapters 2-4, the following paragraphs outline key opportunities to prioritise synergistic and/or low-cost microplastics mitigation interventions along the lifecycle of textiles (Section 5.3.1) and tyres (Section 5.3.2) and at the end-of-pipe stage (Section 5.3.3).

5.3.1. Textile and apparel sector

Several potential synergies exist between actions to mitigate microplastics pollution from textiles and actions aimed at prompting a transition towards a more circular textile sector. Crucially, fibre shedding reduces the serviceability of garments, so practices aimed at reducing fibre release generally also contribute to enhancing the durability of textile products. Given the high environmental impacts associated with the lifecycle of garments and the current linear nature of textile value chains, there is a strong case for embedding microfibre mitigation measures into sector-specific policymaking for the textile and apparel sector.

In general, a holistic approach to the mitigation of textile microfibres is required in order to also take into consideration potential trade-offs with other environmental impacts (e.g. climate impacts, land use, chemicals use and water pollution, resource use) and risks for potential burden-shifting. Notably, as discussed in Chapter 2, there is a strong case for focusing interventions which reduce shedding rather than substituting away from synthetic fibres in textile and apparel manufacturing, given that the production of cellulose-based fibres can bear significant environmental and climate impacts and that cellulose-based microfibres are abundantly present in the environment.

In particular, the following strategic measures are proposed and detailed in Table 5.2:

- Promoting *cross-industry collaboration* and dialogue between the textile sector and other stakeholders, in particular to gain a clear understanding of where and how releases occur and share best practices for microfibre mitigation to inform intervention.
- *Curbing fast fashion trends, in particular promoting higher quality and longer lasting textiles/clothing and the higher uptake of circular business models,* via consumer education, awareness-raising initiatives, incentives for eco-design and voluntary action.
- Mandating *minimum eco-design standard requirements* in line with the sustainable production and consumption of textiles. Further regulation targeting the microfibre shedding tendency of products can be considered once measurement standards are agreed upon.
- Requiring or encouraging greater transparency from brands over the products they manufacture or sell, for instance via mandatory or voluntary standardised *eco-labelling schemes* including the microfibre shedding rate along with a number of relevant environmental and climate parameters.
- Sharing responsibility for microfibre mitigation across all relevant stakeholders and mitigation entry points, for instance by including parameters relevant for microfibre pollution into *minimum performance standards* for household, commercial, or industrial washing machines.
- *Promoting international-level voluntary initiatives and targets along the textile and apparel supply chain* to promote sustainable production and consumption practices in the sector. Although microfibre mitigation options are not yet envisioned in existing best practices and guidelines for industry action, Responsible Business Conduct and Due Diligence initiatives (see Section 4.3.1) can also contribute to improving sustainability during production, preventing industrial emissions and fostering stakeholder dialogue and engagement.

- *Promoting research and innovation* to develop fibres and fabrics with a lower tendency to shed microfibres and a lower environmental impact overall. Once standardised measurement standards are available, it is recommended to incorporate the issue of microfibre shedding into life-cycle assessments for textiles (Sandin, Roos and Johansson, 2019[2]).

Table 5.2. Selected mitigation measures for the reduction of microplastics pollution from textiles

	Relevant stakeholders	Mitigation measure [key co-benefits with other policy objectives]	Possible policy instruments
Cross-cutting	Governments, industry, research organisations	Strengthen knowledge of the factors which influence microplastics release, identify hotspots, identify and assess mitigation best practices and technologies	Necessary interventions for the introduction of subsequent policy measures
		Support the development of standardised and harmonised test methods for microfibre shedding	
		Promote international and interdisciplinary cooperation	
Design and manufacturing	Industry, government	Eco-design of fibres and textiles • Research and innovation on fibres, with assessment of fibres over their full life cycle for unintended consequences • Elimination of harmful substances [lower toxicity overall] • Adoption of available best design and manufacturing practices • Adoption of best practices to mitigate industrial emissions Eco-design of complementary products (laundry detergents, washing machines) • Research and innovation to minimise emissions of microplastics	• Minimum standards, certification systems and labelling schemes • Inclusion of additional requirements into industrial licences, e.g. via BAT-based approaches • Regulatory instruments to prevent the emission of intentionally-added microplastics (e.g. in laundry detergents)
Use	Consumers, Textile and Apparel industry, Government	• Reductions in textile (production and) consumption • Adoption of best practices for maintenance and care [higher durability of garments, lower waste generation] • Identification of hotspots for microfibre emissions • Development and assessment of the cost-effectiveness of mitigation technologies	• Consumer awareness campaigns • Provision of consumer-oriented information (e.g. via labelling schemes) • Research initiatives to inform the assessment of different mitigation entry points for filtration devices (i.e. household vs commercial and industrial level).
End-of-life	Industry, solid waste utilities, municipalities and government	• Reductions in textile waste generation • Separate collection of used garments [opportunities for reuse and recycling] • Identification of best practices for the recycling/reuse of garments without a higher burden on MP pollution	• Larger adoption of separate collection schemes for used textiles • Requiring brands/industry to take responsibility for their products at end-of-life, e.g. via targets, taxes, or EPR schemes

Note: End-of-pipe mitigation measures are presented separately in Section 5.3.3
Source: Author's own elaboration

5.3.2. Tyre and road transport sector

Mitigation of microplastics generated during road transport activity offers several key interlinkages and synergies with climate, transport and air pollution policies. As outlined in Chapter 3, TRWP emissions may be reduced via ongoing efforts to reduce overall transport volumes and shift towards sustainable modes of passenger and goods transport. Policies supporting the wider uptake of eco-driving practices, generally aimed at improving safety, reducing GHG emissions and mitigating the impact of road transport on air quality, may also contribute to reducing the emission of TRWP into surface waters. Similarly, policies aimed at reversing trends towards heavier vehicles can reduce fuel consumption, mitigate the impact of road traffic on air quality, while contributing to TRWP mitigation. Despite the numerous co-benefits, as the example of the electrification of the vehicle fleet shows, climate and transport policies will not automatically translate into reductions in tyre wear, which suggests that specific policy action is required in order to adapt existing measures to ensure that these also address microplastics pollution.

In particular, the following strategic measures are proposed and detailed in Table 5.3:

- *Promoting cross-industry collaboration* and dialogue between the tyre manufacturing sector and other relevant stakeholders (e.g. road infrastructure developers, vehicle producers, water sector);
- Introducing *mandatory labelling schemes* for tyre tread abrasion, along with a number of other relevant environmental and safety parameters;
- Mandating *minimum performance standards* for tyre tread abrasion and road surfaces;
- *Promoting reductions in passenger vehicle use and shifts towards more sustainable transport modes* by guiding policy and infrastructure investment with a focus on accessibility, to reduce fuel consumption, mitigate the impact of road traffic on air quality and contribute to TRWP mitigation, in addition to other well-being goals;
- Seeking out and valuing co-benefits with *policy measures aimed at reducing exhaust and non-exhaust emissions and their toxicity*, for instance via vehicle light-weighting, regulations on tyre composition, measures aimed at managing traffic flows (e.g. speed limits) and the uptake of available mitigation technologies (e.g. advanced driver-assistance systems) (OECD, 2020[3]); and
- *Sharing responsibility for TRWP mitigation* across all relevant stakeholders and mitigation entry points, while prioritising intervention as close to the source as possible. Possible interventions include mandating the improved design and maintenance of road pavements, incentivising the production of lighter vehicles, or fostering research on the impact of road markings.

Table 5.3. Selected mitigation options for the reduction of microplastics pollution from tyres

	Relevant stakeholders	Mitigation measure [key co-benefits with other policy objectives]	Possible policy instruments
Cross-cutting	Governments, industry, research organisations	Strengthen knowledge of the factors which influence microplastics release, identify hotspots, identify and assess mitigation best practices and technologies	Necessary interventions for the introduction of subsequent policy measures
		Standardise and harmonise test methods for tyre tread abrasion and road surface abrasion	
		Promote international and interdisciplinary cooperation	
Design and manufacturing	Industry, government, municipalities	Eco-design of fibres and textiles • Research and innovation on tyre and road eco-design in line with lower wear rates, without compromising on other desirable characteristics • Avoidance of hazardous substances to reduce toxicity Eco-design of complementary products (roads, vehicles) • Research and innovation on roads and pavement surfaces to minimise emissions of microplastics, without compromising on other desirable characteristics • Reductions in vehicle weight [lower fuel consumption and GHG emissions, lower air pollution, lower noise pollution]	• Minimum standards, certification systems and labelling schemes (e.g. including tyre tread wear into existing labelling schemes) • Regulations on the content of tyres and other complementary products (e.g. road markings) • Disincentivising to car manufacturers (and consumers) the production (purchase) of heavier vehicles • Promotion and/or mandating of the implementation of tyre pressure monitoring systems in vehicles

	Relevant stakeholders	Mitigation measure [key co-benefits with other policy objectives]	Possible policy instruments
Use	Consumers, Industry, Government, Municipalities	• Reductions in transport volumes [lower fuel consumption and GHG emissions, lower air pollution, lower noise pollution] • Larger uptake of eco-driving practices [lower fuel consumption and GHG emissions, lower air pollution] • Larger uptake of regular maintenance of tyres and vehicles [higher safety, lower fuel consumption and GHG emissions, higher tyre durability] • Identification of hotspots for TRWP emissions • Adequate regular maintenance of roads	• Transport policies to reduce overall road transport km distance travelled and encourage shifts towards more sustainable transport modes • Promotion of policies to reduce speeds and congestion (e.g. implementing or lowering speed limits) • Consumer awareness campaigns • Provision of consumer-oriented information (e.g. speed, fuel consumption) via driver assistance systems • Restrictions on uses of tyres which lead to high unintentional releases (e.g. studded tyre restrictions) • Inclusion of wheel alignment checks in mandatory regular car inspections • Research initiatives to inform the assessment of different mitigation entry points for filtration devices (i.e. household vs commercial and industrial level).
End-of-life	Industry, municipalities, government, sport pitches operators	• Separate collection of waste tyres [opportunities for material recovery] • Identification of best practices for the mitigation of microplastics release from tyre material recovery applications (e.g. artificial sport turfs) • Further investigation and adoption into best practices for the reuse of tyre material without a higher burden on microplastics pollution	• Implementation of separate collection schemes for ELTs where these are not already present • Requiring industry to take responsibility for their products at end-of-life, e.g. via targets, taxes, or EPR schemes • Incentivising the larger adoption of best practices for the maintenance of sport pitches to prevent the leakage of rubber granulate

Note: Author's own elaboration

5.3.3. End-of-pipe capture

At the end-of-pipe stage, two main sets of mitigation measures exist: improvements in wastewater treatment to retain microfibres present in sewage and improvements in the management of stormwater runoff and road dust to treat diffuse microplastics. In both cases, identifying and valuing co-benefits with other pollutants will be key to improving the end-of-pipe capture of microplastics.

At the level of wastewater treatment, policy options may be limited as costly decisions on the design and operation of WWTPs will not be driven by microplastics pollution alone and sludge management remains an issue. Several policy options exist to finance WWTP upgrades and these are being considered notably to address pollutants of emerging concern (OECD, 2019[4]). Similarly, implementing measures to reduce diffuse water pollution, improving the management of road runoff and preventing the discharge of untreated stormwater into water streams may contribute to reducing the impact of several pollutants on freshwater quality, in addition to also preventing the direct discharge of microplastics (and larger plastic items) into water bodies.

Some key priorities for action are to:

- Further assess the *microplastics mitigation effectiveness* of available end-of-pipe technologies, differentiating by MP type and shape and including TRWP and smaller microplastics;
- *Standardise and harmonise analytical techniques* for microplastics in wastewater and stormwater;
- *Identify hotspots* for stormwater and road runoff (e.g. trafficked roads) and for sewage influents;
- Further evaluate the microplastics mitigation effectiveness of options to develop and/or improve existing *stormwater infrastructure* to address a range of diffuse water pollutants;
- Consider the implementation of *measures targeting road dust*, such as effective street sweeping and street washing, especially by prioritising hotspot areas; and

- Consider the implementation of *road-side capturing technologies for TRWP* (e.g. gully pots), *green infrastructure and nature-based solutions* (e.g. wetlands) which can also be effective at removing other diffuse pollutants (e.g. nutrients) and adequately maintain existing infrastructure.

References

OECD (2020), *Non-exhaust Particulate Emissions from Road Transport: An Ignored Environmental Policy Challenge*, OECD Publishing, Paris, https://dx.doi.org/10.1787/4a4dc6ca-en. [3]

OECD (2019), *Pharmaceutical Residues in Freshwater: Hazards and Policy Responses*, OECD Studies on Water, OECD Publishing, Paris, https://dx.doi.org/10.1787/c936f42d-en. [4]

OECD (2017), *Diffuse Pollution, Degraded Waters: Emerging Policy Solutions*, OECD Studies on Water, OECD Pubilishing, Paris, https://doi.org/10.1787/9789264269064-en. [1]

Sandin, G., S. Roos and M. Johansson (2019), *Environmental impact of textile fibers - what we know and what we don't know: Fiber Bible part 2*, Mistra Future Foundation, http://urn.kb.se/resolve?urn=urn:nbn:se:ri:diva-38198. [2]

UNEP (2019), *Addressing marine plastics: a systemic approach*, United Nations Environment Programme. Nairobi, Kenya, https://wedocs.unep.org/20.500.11822/31642. [5]

Glossary

Biodegradation	Biological process of organic matter, which is completely or partially converted to water, CO_2/methane, energy and new biomass by microorganisms (bacteria and fungi).
Degradation	The partial or complete breakdown of a polymer as a result of e.g. UV radiation, oxygen attack, biological attack. This implies alteration of the properties, such as discolouration, surface cracking, and fragmentation
End of Life Tyre (ELT):	A tyre that can no longer serve its original purpose (including on a passenger car, truck, two-wheel, airplanes, as well as off-road tires). This excludes used tyres that are retreaded, reused, or exported in used cars.
Microplastics	Solid synthetic polymer particulates with a size < 5 mm.
Nanoplastics	Solid synthetic polymer particulates with a size < 1 or < 100 μm
Non-exhaust emissions	Non-exhaust emissions are particle emissions from road traffic consist of airborne particulate matter (PM) generated by the wearing down of brakes, clutches, tyres and road surfaces, as well as by the suspension of road dust.
Primary/secondary microplastics	*Primary* microplastics are manufactured at the micro scale to be used in particular applications. *Secondary* microplastics stem from the fragmentation of larger plastics
River catchment area	A catchment area is any area of land from which precipitation waters flow into a river.
Road dust	Road dust is composed of all particles found on a road. It may consist of particles from road wear (road surfacing and markings), vehicle wear (e.g. brake pads, tyres, and studs), vehicle emissions, atmospheric deposition, and other particles, including organic materials from nearby vegetation that settle on the road.
Road runoff	The portion of precipitation which flows from road surfaces
Rubber granulate	Rubber particles generally manufactured from ELTs as well as from rubber derived from other sources (e.g. virgin elastomer alternatives such as EPDM rubber and TPE), intended to be used in a variety of industrial applications.
Stormwater runoff	Precipitation that flows over the ground, usually also transporting pollutants deposited on surfaces.
Toxicity	Inherent property of being poisonous or harmful to plant, animal or human life
Tyre and Road Wear Particles	Particles emitted due to the friction occurring between the vehicle tyres and the road surface, during normal use of tyres. These are composed of a mixture of tyre tread material (e.g. synthetic and natural rubber, silica, oil, carbon black, sulphur compounds, zinc oxide) and road pavement material. Other mineral particles originating from road surfaces or contained in road dust may be present in samples collected in the environment.
Tyre tread	The portion of the tyre that comes in contact with the road surface.
Value chain	A very large-scale business process that results in the delivery of a process or service to a customer.
Waste mismanagement	Waste that is either littered or inadequately disposed of.

www.ingramcontent.com/pod-product-compliance
Ingram Content Group UK Ltd.
Pitfield, Milton Keynes, MK11 3LW, UK
UKHW051505290926
15471UKWH00008B/1434

9 789264 961029